SHOW, DON'T TELL: LEGAL WRITING FOR THE REAL WORLD

SHOW, DON'T TELL: LEGAL WRITING FOR THE REAL WORLD

Adam Lamparello
Assistant Professor of Law
Indiana Tech Law School

Megan E. Boyd

 LexisNexis®

ISBN: 978-1-6304-4614-7 (print)
ISBN: 978-1-6304-4620-8 (eBook)

Library of Congress Cataloging-in-Publication Data

Lamparello, Adam, author.
Show, don't tell : legal writing for the real world / Adam Lamparello, Assistant Professor of Law, Indiana Tech Law School; Megan E. Boyd.
pages cm
Includes index.
ISBN 978-1-63044-614-7
1. Legal composition. 2. Law — United States. I. Boyd, Megan E., author. II. Title.
KF250.L36 2014
344.7301 — dc23   2014026740

This publication is designed to provide authoritative information in regard to the subject matter covered. It is sold with the understanding that the publisher is not engaged in rendering legal, accounting, or other professional services. If legal advice or other expert assistance is required, the services of a competent professional should be sought.

NOTE TO USERS
To ensure that you are using the latest materials available in this area, please be sure to periodically check the LexisNexis Law School web site for downloadable updates and supplements at www.lexisnexis.com/lawschool.

Editorial Offices
630 Central Ave., New Providence, NJ 07974 (908) 464-6800
201 Mission St., San Francisco, CA 94105-1831 (415) 908-3200
www.lexisnexis.com

MATTHEW◊BENDER

Introduction

Show, Don't Tell: Legal Writing for the Real World was written for law students, lawyers, law firms, law clerks, and judges who want to dramatically improve their legal writing skills in the "real world" of law practice.

As former law students, and now lawyers and law professors, the authors are keenly aware of the challenges law students face when entering the practice of law. A significant problem is that law schools do not spend enough time teaching students how to write well. The practice of law, however, is "a profession of words"[1] and requires law school graduates to be proficient writers.

Unfortunately, recent graduates often endure unnecessary stress, uncertainty, and panic because they are not equipped to perform even the most basic lawyering tasks. As others have observed:

> Ask judges and senior lawyers to identify the most disturbing aspect about younger lawyers, and they will reply in one voice, "They can't write."[2]

And it's not just that law students can't adequately draft legal documents — they often can't write well at all. Perhaps the most scathing indictment comes from United States Supreme Court Justice Antonin Scalia, who recently offered this opinion:

> [I]t became clear to me, as I think it must become clear to anyone who is burdened with the job of teaching legal writing, that what these students lacked was not the skill of legal writing, but the skill of writing at all * * * [T]he prerequisites for self-improvement in writing . . . are two things. Number one, the realization — and it occurred to my students as an astounding revelation — that there is an immense difference between writing and good writing. And two, that it takes time and sweat to convert the former into the latter."[3]

Show, Don't Tell addresses a pervasive and well-documented complaint about the quality of the writing of both recent graduates and seasoned lawyers. This book was written for law students throughout the country who want to know "how things work in the real world" and lawyers who want a straightforward, no-nonsense resource to improve their writing. We hope that everyone will benefit from the wealth of practical information in this book.

As the title suggests, *Show, Don't Tell* is designed to help all members of the legal profession learn to effectively draft the most common litigation documents. Far too many books offer tips and advice about good writing, but don't actually show the reader specific examples of good writing or show the reader why examples offered are effective. The authors have read many books on legal writing, but once we learned the basics of legal

---

[1] David Mellinkoff, The Language of the Law at vii (Boston, 1963).

[2] Sharon D. Nelson and John W. Simek, *"Why Can't Law Graduates Write?,"* 36 ABA J. 6, available at http://www.americanbar.org/publications/law_practice_magazine/2012/november-december/hot-buttons.html.

[3] *Scalia: Legal Writing Doesn't Exist.*ABA JOURNAL NEWS (Aug. 9, 2008), available at: http://abajournal.com/news/srticle/scalia_legal_writing_doesn't_exist/

Introduction

writing, we didn't learn anything in those books. We were exposed to the best theories, but never given practical, how-to tips to turn book knowledge into real-world skills. Most people can relate — you read a legal writing book or leave a lecture thinking you now know how to write. Then, when you sit down to write, you find yourself staring at a blank computer screen, feeling lost. We wrote *Show, Don't Tell* so that you can see real progress in your writing and feel confident in your ability to draft documents you will most frequently draft in litigation. After all, you can learn everything about how to fly a plane, but until you get into the cockpit, you're not a pilot. Learning is good, but doing is essential.

Show, Don't Tell will not only benefit law students, but will assist law schools that are transitioning to an experiential-based learning model and law firms that seek a concise, economic, and comprehensive guide to teach young lawyers litigation drafting.

Our book has a unique structure. Beginning with Chapter 1, *Show, Don't Tell* immerses the reader in an interesting, hotly contested hypothetical lawsuit. The following chapters take the reader through each step of the litigation process, from the initial memorandum to the appellate brief. Each chapter focuses on a specific legal document — such as a complaint or motion for summary judgment — and includes examples drafted and edited by each of the authors, who act as opposing counsel. For example, Chapter 2 discusses the purpose and scope of a legal memorandum, including the particular writing skills that ensure a high-quality memorandum. That chapter includes two full length memorandums by the authors and concludes by discussing the reasons these example memos are effective.

The authors hope that *Show, Don't Tell* reduces the fear that many new attorneys experience, aids the legal academy in improving the quality of legal writing instruction, and helps seasoned members of the profession improve their legal writing skills.

Adam Lamparello and *Megan E. Boyd*

Acknowledgments

We would like to thank our former student, Pamela "Krisi" Hartig, a graduate of Mercer University's Walter F. George School of Law, who suggested to us that we author a legal writing textbook showing students how to draft the most common litigation documents. Thanks to Krisi for her vision and support. Adam would also like to thank Kenneth Heifner, a second-year law student at Indiana Tech Law School, who reviewed an earlier draft of *Show, Don't Tell* and made very helpful suggestions. And Megan would like to thank Professors Linda H. Edwards and Jennifer Sheppard, who inspired her love of legal writing and understanding of its importance, and her husband, Jeremy P. Sale, who has provided unwavering love, support, and encouragement.

Table of Contents

Table of Contents

Table of Contents

Table of Contents

Table of Contents

Chapter 1

WATERS v. HARRISON

You're sitting behind a desk on your first day as a practicing lawyer, filled with excitement and anticipation. Seasoned lawyers in fancy suits scurry through the hallways, talking to clients on their cell phones and discussing upcoming trials at the nearby federal courthouse. You're eager to get involved and make a difference.

A few months ago, you graduated law school and, after a long and anxiety-filled summer, you took the bar examination. Now, it's time to apply what you've learned in class to the real world, where clients are depending on your expertise, and the stakes are high.

As you're getting settled into your new law office, a partner in the litigation department knocks on your door. "Welcome to the firm," he says. "We've got something for you and it's really important."

This is your chance to make an unforgettable first impression. You smile, but inside feel the jitters forming.

"This is an interesting, high-profile case," the partner says. "Our client is Kirsten Waters, a former senatorial candidate, and she's extremely upset. Here's the situation:"

*   *   *   *   *

Kirsten received her undergraduate degree from Stanford University in Palo Alto, California, and graduated at the top of her class from the University of California, Berkeley School of Law. Prior to entering political life, Kirsten was an attorney with the law firm of Jones, Davis, Bartlett and Strom, LLP, where she worked her way from junior associate to managing partner in the firm's litigation department. She decided to challenge then-incumbent Robert Larson for one of California's senate seats.

With the election only five days away, Kirsten was in a tight race with Larson, who was seeking re-election for the first time. By all accounts, the race was a statistical dead heat, and with one debate remaining, political commentators believed that the candidates' performances might decide the election.

While Kirsten's political views gained her substantial popularity among likely voters, many referred to her personal story as a source of inspiration and hope. Prior to the first debate, Kirsten acknowledged that, while in college, she struggled with alcohol and prescription drug abuse. Kirsten was very forthright about her past, and openly discussed the consequences substance abuse had on her personal and professional life. Kirsten's honesty during the campaign, coupled with her inspiring story of recovery, garnered support among voters across the political spectrum. During her campaign, Kirsten vowed to increase funding for addiction recovery programs and champion drug education in California's public schools.

The final debate between Kirsten and Larson was held at the Shrine Auditorium in Los Angeles. Before a sold-out crowd and nationally televised audience, the moderator, former governor Patricia Brown, began with the following question:

> Ms. Waters, can you talk about your personal struggles, how they have changed your life, and what impact, if any, they may have on you as a United States Senator?

Kirsten responded as follows:

> Thank you, Governor Brown. I appreciate the opportunity to be here tonight with the voters of California and, of course, Senator Larson. As you know, I've been very forthcoming about my struggle — many years ago — with alcohol and prescription medication. It was the darkest period of my life. Perhaps the worst moment came on August 2, 1994, the summer of my junior year at Stanford when, due to a regrettable mistake in judgment, I was responsible for driving under the influence of alcohol and possessing an unauthorized controlled substance. For me, this was rock bottom and a wake-up call that I had to make immediate changes in my life. My first step was to accept responsibility for my actions, which I did. After being ordered to serve 30 days in the Palo Alto County Jail, followed by a 90-day stay at a residential treatment facility, I continued the life-changing process of taking my life back. Looking back, I don't know if I would be here tonight without having faced the consequences of my actions. From this experience, I learned what it means to truly struggle in life. I learned how to cope with adversity and life's difficult challenges. I came to know the value of accountability, hard work, and perseverance. These are values, in my opinion, to which all of California's voters, regardless of background or political party, can relate. If elected, I will be a compassionate senator who understands the struggles of all Californians and who believes in the value of honesty. Thank you.

Governor Brown then asked Senator Larson if he would like to respond. Senator Larson stated as follows:

> First, I would like to thank you, Governor Brown, the voters of California, and Kirsten for giving me the opportunity to participate in tonight's debate. I think we should all applaud Kirsten for her inspiring story and the courage she has displayed. I'm really looking forward to a lively debate on the important issues facing California.

After a spirited debate, commentators were sharply divided concerning how Kirsten's eleventh-hour admission would affect her chances for election. Preliminary fact-checking confirmed that, on August 2, 1994, Kirsten was arrested and charged with driving under the influence of alcohol, and possession of a controlled substance.

Five days later, in one of the closest elections in California history, Kirsten defeated Senator Larson by 314 votes.

*   *   *   *   *

Simon Harrison, originally from San Jose, California, is now a resident of Erie, Pennsylvania, more than 2,400 miles away. Simon, a computer programmer, operates a well-known blog, www.justtellthetruth.com. Simon describes his blog as "telling the whole truth and nothing but the truth." He seeks to expose corruption in all areas of public life. Simon has been credited with, among other things, uncovering a bribery scandal involving Philadelphia's mayor, and exposing the use of performance-enhancing substances by several high-profile athletes.

Simon also attended Stanford University, and he met Kirsten during their freshman year. Although they were friends throughout college, they eventually went their separate ways and no longer remain in contact. Simon was, however, closely watching Kirsten's final debate.

After Kirsten answered Governor Brown's first question, Simon was flabbergasted. Simon was shocked to hear Kirsten discuss her past, particularly because Simon was very close to Kirsten during college and knew the events in question very well.

After the debate, Simon posted an urgent message on www.justtellthetruth.com. The headline read, "Kirsten Waters blatantly lied at the final debate . . . details coming shortly." Approximately thirty minutes later, Simon posted the following statement on his blog:

> Sadly, I have uncovered yet another politician who cannot tell the truth. Kirsten Waters intentionally lied during her debate with Senator Larson. Kirsten's statements about her past struggle with substance abuse — obviously designed to sway California voters — are fabrications. I was Kirsten's friend during college, and I unconditionally supported Kirsten while she struggled to overcome addiction. I am shocked that Kirsten would exploit her past for political gain. More specifically, while Kirsten was arrested for driving under the influence of alcohol and possession of a controlled substance, **she was neither incarcerated nor ordered to spend even a single day in a residential treatment program. After pleading guilty, Kirsten was sentenced to 90 days probation and 100 hours of community service. Additionally, as part of the plea deal, the controlled substance charge was dropped. Kirsten only sought residential treatment because her parents threatened to stop paying her tuition at Stanford. Kirsten's lies show that she is not fit for public office**.
>
> In addition, because I am committed to telling the whole truth, I must disclose that, while at Stanford, Kirsten engaged in highly questionable conduct. During our last two years at Stanford, Kirsten was engaged to a mutual friend (who I will not reveal at this time). Kirsten suddenly broke off the engagement and admitted to having a lengthy affair with another man throughout the duration of the relationship. I will soon release a letter Kirsten wrote to our friend admitting the affair.
>
> The whole truth is that Kirsten reluctantly sought treatment — only to save herself — while repeatedly lying to and eventually betraying a very decent man.

[handwritten margin notes: "elaim", "claim"]

I would like to add one final comment. While at Stanford, Kirsten performed poorly in her studies. Kirsten was not a good student, and I doubt she has the ability to effectively serve in any elected capacity. I don't know how she was accepted by the University of California-Berkeley School of Law. I do know this: her dad is one of Berkeley's most generous donors. Kirsten's *Claim* admission to Berkeley wasn't about merit. It was about favoritism and money. *Claim* I also question how Kirsten ever graduated from Berkeley. I can't imagine her passing all of those difficult law school classes without receiving significant help from her family. *Claim*

Despite Simon's best efforts, this information was not revealed publicly prior to the election. Everything changed, however, when Simon posted a letter Kirsten received from her probation officer, dated November 10, 1994. Among other things, the letter stated:

Dear Kirsten:

As you know, the court sentenced you to a probation term of 90 days, and 100 hours of community service. Having complied fully with these responsibilities, your sentence is hereby complete and this matter now concluded.

*   *   *   *   *

One week after the election, Simon's story became national news. Under extraordinary pressure from her party, coupled with damaging public opinion polls, Kirsten released the following statement:

I made certain inaccurate statements at my final debate with Senator Larson. Some of the details regarding my past were inconsistent with the facts. At no time, however, did I intentionally lie or mislead the voters of California. The additional statements made on Mr. Harrison's website are intentionally and maliciously false. In the interest of sparing California any further attention from this matter, I will resign as your Senator, yet continue to fight for the vital issues affecting all citizens of this state. I do intend to pursue all available legal remedies against Mr. Harrison for what is nothing more than a callous attack on my character.

In response to Kirsten's statement, Simon posted the following:

Kirsten still can't tell the truth. Should Kirsten file a baseless lawsuit against me, I will have an airtight defense: it's the whole truth and nothing but the truth.

Two days later, Kirsten filed a complaint against Simon in the United States District *Issue* Court for the Northern District of California. Kirsten is suing Simon for defamation and invasion of privacy under California law. She is seeking $5 million in damages.

*   *   *   *   *

"Wow, now I can understand why she's upset," you say.

"You have no idea," the partner says. "She wants him to pay for this."

You nod and muster a forced smile, trying to exude confidence. Inside, though, you're not sure if you have the experience to handle such a high-profile case.

"I need you to get started right away," the partner says. "Get us a victory — we're counting on you."

The partner gets up and walks toward the door, stopping to offer encouraging words.

"Remember — we wouldn't have hired you unless we believed that you had the talent to litigate this case to a successful conclusion."

Fear grips the pit of your stomach. A few moments later, the phone rings.

"How's the big-shot lawyer doing?" your best friend asks.

"I'm having a panic attack," you say. "I just got my first case, and have no idea what I'm doing."

"Just apply what you learned in law school," your best friend says. "And please try to relax."

"You don't understand. In law school, I wrote, like, one or two memos and an appellate brief, and I did those two years ago. They don't teach this stuff in school. During my final semester I took two seminars — European Union Law and American Legal History."

"You'll figure it out," your best friend says.

After the call ends, you sit in your chair, unsure where to begin.

You think, "I'm going to screw this case up. They're going to fire me. What should I do?"

*   *   *   *   *

New lawyers should not be placed in a situation where they are unprepared to handle the tasks they are assigned. After spending three years in law school, you should be confident that, from day one, you'll be able to write and effectively advocate on behalf of your clients. Read on the as the authors litigate *Waters v. Harrison* and show you how to practice law — in the real world.

- Defamation
  - perse
  - per qua
- Invasion of Privacy Tortious
- Invasion of Privacy State Statute

= Punitive Damages

Complaint:
. no civil cover letter
. follow local rules provided
. length is in local rules

NDCA: case law

Chapter 2

TIPS FOR WRITING IN THE REAL WORLD

Once you learn the basic forms of predictive and persuasive writing, you've got a good foundation to start learning the more advanced techniques of legal writing — techniques that can really make your writing stand out in the real world. The tips we offer in this chapter are invaluable no matter what type of legal document you're drafting. We'll discuss tips specific to the types of litigation document addressed in this text in their respective chapters.

I. THE WRITING PROCESS

The writing process is the same whether you're drafting a memo, legal brief, or a children's book. Even after learning to draft memos and appellate briefs, most legal writers don't know or understand the writing process. That's unfortunate because in law practice, the writing process is critical to creating clear, concise documents.

The writing process occurs in three stages: (1) writing (the first draft); (2) re-writing (the macro or developmental edit); and (3) revising (the micro or copy edit). The practice of law requires you both to see the big picture and explain that picture to others through meticulous attention to detail. The best lawyers — and legal writers — are both big picture and small picture people. Embracing all three stages of the writing process will help you become the best legal writer possible.

A. The Writing Stage

The first stage of writing is, unsurprisingly, to write, and keep writing until you have a draft. Remember — you can't re-write or revise a blank sheet of paper. Don't worry too much about things like grammar and sentence structure at this stage — just get down the things you need to say. And don't think about length too much either. You can always cut-down your document later.

Resist the urge to try to collapse the re-writing and revision stages into the writing stage. If you try to combine the writing stage with the other two stages, you'll spend a week trying to make the first three pages a masterpiece when you could have had the whole document written and be well on your way toward the final product. This is difficult to do sometimes — we know. But trust us on this one — follow the process. Write. Re-write. Revise.

B. The Re-Writing Stage

After you have a solid first draft, the re-writing stage begins. At this point, you're looking for macro-level problems. That is, large-scale or big-picture problems including, but not limited to, organization, flow, clarity, repetition, and irrelevancies. You also need to examine whether your legal discussion and factual analysis are accurate and comprehensive. Simply put, the re-writing stage is where you identify and fix major issues with the content and structure of your document.

During the re-writing stage, you should be checking to ensure your document is not disjointed, that your paragraphs and sentences make sense, that legal principles are not discussed multiple times in different sections of your document, and that the sections of your document are distinct and don't bleed into each other. If you inadvertently failed to discuss an obvious counter-argument or didn't adequately explain the factual background, the re-writing process is the time to add the counter-argument or additional facts to your document. During the re-writing stage you should be sure that you've explained even those things you think are obvious. For example, if you haven't included a discussion of a claim element because there is no dispute that the element is satisfied, say so.

We know how it feels to think you've finished a document, only to realize you failed to address issues that need to be considered and know you'll need substantial time to adequately complete the document. It stinks. But avoid the temptation during the re-writing phase to think, "What I've got is good enough."

To get the most out of the re-writing stage, print out your draft and read it on paper. Numerous studies have shown that reviewers catch more errors when they review hard copies versus electronic ones. Reviewing your draft on the computer does not allow you to look at the entire document simultaneously, which is necessary to assess flow, organization, and redundancy and to compare different sections. Reading on paper is also easier on the eyes — staring at a computer screen for hours can cause you to miss mistakes.

During the re-writing phase, don't get "cold feet" when it comes to deleting unnecessary, confusing, or repetitive writing. We know it's hard to erase entire paragraphs (or pages), but sometimes doing so is necessary to improve your document. If you're writing about defamation, for example, and you find you've meandered into a discussion of invasion of privacy, you need to delete to avoid creating a jumbled, confusing mess. Likewise, if you went on for seven pages about the "horrific damages that defendant's comments caused," you'll need to make cuts. Yes, it hurts to delete writing that you worked on for a long time, but it hurts more if your writing causes the reader to wonder, "Why can't this writer just get to the point?" If that happens, the reader might stop reading, and never get to your brilliant legal analysis.

Ultimately, re-writing is what elevates your documents — and writing skills — to superstar status. After all, "if it sounds like writing . . . rewrite it."[4] Refining your skills, dealing with imperfections in your writing, and making the commitment to

---

[4] Elmore Leonard, *Elmore Leonard's Ten Rules of Writing* (William Morrow, 2007).

become a better re-writer is what separates mediocre legal writers from great ones. Don't make the mistake of thinking that the best legal writers are "better" than you. They may not be — they just work harder. As legendary basketball player Michael Jordan once said, "Everybody has talent, but ability takes hard work."[5]

This doesn't mean, of course, that you must always re-write substantial parts of your document. You will find there are some occasions where the first draft requires only modest changes — but those are pretty rare. Don't avoid the re-writing process, however, because it's difficult. Find the problems and fix them. You — and your client — will be happy that you spent the time to produce the best document possible.

Also, resist the temptation to collapse the revising stage (which we sometimes refer to as the editing stage) into the re-writing stage. If you combine these stages, your memorandum may be completed sooner, but the quality will be lacking. It's difficult, if not impossible, to review for content and detail simultaneously. If you try, you'll inevitably overlook various problems with both. Of course, if you find obvious grammatical or other "micro" mistakes during the re-writing process, you should go ahead and fix them. Micro-editing just shouldn't be your focus in the re-writing stage.

C. The Revising Stage

The revising stage is where you perform micro or copy edits. This is where the small details — grammar, syntax, and sentence structure — take center stage. The nitty-gritty details are extremely important to discerning readers, and what might seem unworthy of your attention could mean everything to your reader. While it's very difficult to produce an error-free document, don't be willing to settle for "good enough."

Sloppy documents make the reader question whether the writer's substantive points are sloppy, too. It's difficult to trust the research and arguments presented by a writer who produces a document replete with grammatical errors and misspelled words. As in the re-writing stage, editing your documents via hard copy (rather than on a computer screen) will help you catch more errors. We'll discuss more about the types of problems you should look for later in the chapter. Just remember — as with almost everything — practice makes perfect. Your revision and editing skills will evolve throughout your career, but no matter how good you are, you can always get better. Commit to the revision process; it will serve you well.

II. TIPS FOR THE WRITING AND RE-WRITING STAGES

A. Don't Talk So Much

If the authors could give law students and lawyers only one piece of advice about legal writing, it would be this: be concise. Concise writing requires attention to technique and detail as well as good editing skills. This famous quote says it all: "I didn't have time to write a short letter, so I wrote a long one instead." Consider how

---

[5] http://quotecorner.com/Michael-Jordan-quotes.html.

these tips can enable you to say what you need to say concisely.

B. Exposition and Legal History

Law review articles, treatises, and the like often provide an exposition on the history and purposes behind laws. These types of discussion are unnecessary in most litigation documents as they generally add no value and bog down the reader. If you are analyzing whether Kirsten Waters can successfully bring a defamation claim against Simon Harrison, there is generally no reason to write something like:

> **Defamation is an important part of our jurisprudence and a limitation on the First Amendment right to freedom of speech.**

That's a lovely sentence, but who cares? The sentence does nothing to answer the question you're addressing: Will Waters be able to prove Harrison defamed her?

Discussing legal background and history can be important, however, if you are arguing for a change in the law or a particular interpretation of the law that is consistent with the reason the law was enacted or the public policy behind the law. In those cases, legal history likely forms the basis of your best argument. Otherwise, don't waste valuable time and space discussing legal history.

C. Don't Be Unnecessarily Repetitive

We know you've heard it before, but (ironically) it bears repeating — avoid unnecessary repetition. Don't repeat the same thing seventeen times. The reader gets it. Worse, don't repeat the same thing in consecutive sentences (or paragraphs). For example, don't say,

> **The plaintiff was improperly fired from her job because plaintiff's supervisor did not like her political views. Plaintiff's supervisor is a member of the egalitarian party and fired plaintiff because she is of a different political persuasion.**

Why write the second sentence? Does it really serve any purpose that wasn't served by the first sentence?

Unnecessary repetition does not make your point stronger. It annoys the reader and suggests that the writer is an amateur. Needless repetition also raises questions concerning your credibility. This type of repetition suggests that the writer is merely seeking to instill a Pavlovian response in the reader — "If I say it enough times, the reader will believe it is true" — but doesn't actually have any evidence to support the position.

To be clear, there are instances when repetition can be effective, such as when you're reiterating a critical fact or statement of the law that supports your case. Even then, though, you should be careful. You can have too much of a good thing. The same principle applies within individual sentences. Don't repeat the same word three times in a sentence. The overused word will steal attention from the point you're trying to make.

D.   Omit Unnecessary, Lengthy Words and Phrases

Every word should serve a purpose. Certain phrases and words common in law can be shortened without changing the meaning. Consider the phrase "cease and desist." What does the addition of "and desist" add to a request that someone cease doing something? Nothing.

The same is often true for nominalizations, which add bulk and reduce clarity. Nominalizations occur when the writer takes a verb and makes it into a noun. Nominalizations take many forms, but keep a sharp eye out for words that end in –ion, –ment, and –ence. There's a good chance those words are nominalizations. Consider the clarity and conciseness of these two sentences:

The detective made an investigation into the victim's claims.

The detective investigated the victim's claims.

In the first sentence, "investigation" is a nominalization. The second sentence is clearer and 1/3 shorter than the first sentence. Don't use more words when fewer words are more effective.

E.   Don't Write Like a Lawyer — Write Like a Writer and Remember the Reader

Many law students think their writing should sound like the written opinions they've read in law school. And many lawyers think they must write a certain way because their clients won't see value in the lawyer's services unless the lawyer "sounds like a lawyer." Both of these beliefs are completely untrue. You should strive to write clearly and in a way that can be understood by an intelligent person untrained in the law. These tips will improve the clarity of your writing.

1.   Don't Use Legalese

We've all read opinions replete with legalese — hereinafter, heretofore, herein-under, etc. Legalese muddles writing, slows the reader, and decreases the reader's understanding of the writer's substantive points. Consider this sentence:

Plaintiff, a party of the first part, signed said contract based on the misrepresentations contained herein, and proffered herewith.

What does that mean? It means:

Defendant misrepresented the contract's terms.

If you take a simple fact and say it in a complex way, the reader likely will not understand — or worse — will stop reading.

If you're arguing that a statute banning the sale of video games to minors violates the Equal Protection Clause of the United States Constitution, say something like:

Laws prohibiting minors from purchasing "The Call of Duty" discriminate against an entire class of citizens and have no reasonable justification.

Avoid a sentence like:

> **The state statute banning video game sales to minors constitutes an invidious classification that *de facto* discriminates against minors without the requisite and concomitant rational basis.**

What?! Don't torture your reader — make reading easy. Big words don't make you look smart. They annoy the reader.

The use of Latin produces the same effect. Supreme Court opinions from 1871 may show an affinity for Latin phrases like *post hoc ergo propter hoc, nunc pro tunc,* and *ipso facto,* but you should generally avoid them like the plague. Run. Hide. Do whatever you can to get away from them. See if you can figure out what this sentence means:

> **The facts delineated *supra* are, *ipso facto* proof of *animus nocendi*, that is *contra legem* and thus *ex turpi causa non oritur actio*.**

The authors can't. We think we're pretty intelligent people, but we don't know what this sentence means, and we don't think we're the only ones. If there's a simple way to say something, say it that way. Excessive use of Latin will make you the *persona non grata* at your firm and in the courtroom.

If you're not sure whether your writing is clear, check out examples of good legal documents and good literary works. For example, briefs written by John Roberts prior to taking the bench and opinions drafted by Justice Kagan are excellent examples of good, clear legal writing. Good legal writing — like good writing generally — should make the reader smile, not shudder.

2. Check Pronouns

Avoid cloudy pronoun usage. Consider these short, yet confusing sentences:

> **Smith struck Jones, injuring his hand.**

Did Smith injure Jones's hand, or did Smith injure his own hand?

> **The defendant told the judge he was sorry. He then sat down.**

Did the defendant say "I'm sorry," or did the defendant tell the judge, "You're sorry." Who sat down? The judge? The defendant? Make sure your sentences are precise and your use of pronouns doesn't confuse, even if that means making your sentences a little longer.

3. Avoid SAT Words

In legal writing, think twice before you use fancy or esoteric words. Good legal writing isn't about displaying your knowledge of SAT words or writing an inspirational narrative that leaves the reader in tears. Words like "lugubrious" and "obstreperous" generally should be avoided. If you force your reader to consult a dictionary, you've distracted the reader from the substance of your argument. Don't make your reader work too hard to figure out what you are trying to say. Consider these sentences, from a brief in opposition to a motion to dismiss:

The *mise en scene* of these proceedings emanates from a background of Machiavellian intrigue, cunning deception, and sensational double *entendre*. Essentially, it is a text book example of myopic greed and clandestine chicanery designed and intended to conceal from respondents' knowledge a pre-existing business relationship between the movant and others. . . .[6]

What? Even sentences that aren't that over-the-top can be clearer. For example,

The defendant's conduct had a nocuous effect on and rendered nugatory plaintiff's faith in the legal system.

That sentence isn't awful, but it could be better:

Plaintiff lost faith in the legal system because of Defendant's conduct.

The first sentence has 17 words. The second has 12 and is much easier to read and understand.

Verbose language distracts from the substance of your writing. It shows that the writer doesn't know how to write — or communicate. There's a time and place for these types of words, but your legal document is not one of those places.

4. Tense and Tone

Maintain consistency in verb tense — avoid writing interchangeably between the past and present tenses when discussing the law or performing your legal analysis. For example, don't say this:

After hearing the not guilty verdict, the defendant ran jubilantly out of the courtroom and shakes the reporters' hands.

That is grammatically incorrect and will jump out at the discerning reader.

There are, however, limited situations when the past and present tense can be used in the same sentence. Consider the following example:

Since the defendant intentionally stabbed and killed, this jury should find the defendant guilty.

Thus, when you are relying upon past conduct to support your present claim for relief, the tenses can change.

In most circumstances, though, pick a tense and stick to it. Documents are usually referred to in the present tense, such as:

The contract provides . . .

The statute reads . . .

The settlement agreement calls for . . .

---

[6] *Kochisarli v. Tenoso*, . . . [2006 U.S. Dist. LEXIS 95862, at *16–*17] (E.D.N.Y. Mar. 21, 2006).

If referring to documents in the present tense feels awkward, you can refer to them in the past tense. Just be sure you're consistent.

5. Terms

Once you have defined a term in your writing, use that term consistently. For example, if you have defined a document as the "security deed," refer to it as the "security deed" throughout — do no refer to it as the "security deed" in some sentences, the "agreement" in others, and the "contract" in others. Doing so doesn't add variety to your writing. It just confuses the reader. Stick to a single term.

Similarly, be careful with the use of acronyms and initialisms (collectively "acronyms"). Obviously, you should have no qualms about using commonly understood acronyms, such as FBI, NLRB, and NASA. But you will usually simplify your writing by avoiding acronyms, especially if you employ them heavily throughout your document. Consider this sentence, from an opinion concerning air pollution control, an area of law notorious for confusing acronyms:

> **In their request, the legislators cited "serious concerns" regarding whether the AQCC's and the PUC's analysis and approval of the SIP amendments were conducted in accordance with the agencies' duties under the APA.[7]**

As one court has noted, "the use of acronyms tends to obscure, certainly in the reader's mind and sometimes even in the writer's, the underlying reality of a case, and the legal issues on which it must turn."[8] Try to avoid acronyms except the most easily understood.

You should also be sure to avoid similar acronyms for business entities with similar names. For example, assume you are involved in litigation with three defendants, America's United Bank, America's United Bank Holding Company, and America's United Bank Mortgage Corporation. Consider how much confusion you would create by calling them AUB, AUBHC, and AUBMC:

> **AUB was incorporated in 1990 and AUBMC was incorporated the following year. In 2001, AUBHC was formed to serve as a holding company for both AUB and AUBMC.**

That's confusing. Consider the improvement in clarity:

> **The Bank was incorporated in 1990 and the Mortgage Corporation was incorporated the following year. In 2001, the Holding Company was formed to serve as a holding company for both the Bank and the Mortgage Corporation.**

Much better.

---

[7] *Colorado Mining Ass'n v. Urbina*, . . ., 318 P.3d 562, 565 . . . (Colo. Ct. App. 2013). In fairness, this opinion includes a specific list of acronyms in an appendix to assist the reader.

[8] *Nat'l Paint & Coatings Ass'n, Inc. v. South Coast Air Quality Mgmt. Dist.*, 100 Cal. Rptr. 3d 35, 37 n.1 (Cal. Ct. App. 2009).

6.   Adjectives

Many writers love — and we mean *really* love — adjectives. They think adjectives paint a more persuasive picture of the information they're trying to convey. But the excessive use of adjectives comes across as "over the top" and can make the reader question the writer's credibility. Don't say:

> **The defendant's shocking behavior shows a horrendous disregard for plaintiff's revered status as an incredible and beloved lawyer.**

The adjectives in that sentence add no value to your argument. Don't use adjectives to *tell* the reader what you think — *show* the reader what happened and allow the reader to draw the conclusion for himself or herself. Consider writing something like this instead:

> **Despite knowing his allegations were untrue, Defendant sent an email to more than 3,000 defense lawyers claiming Plaintiff was "crazy," "mentally unstable," and "a danger to his clients." Plaintiff, an old-school lawyer who has practiced law for more than 40 years, has never been the subject of a bar complaint, has been awarded the state bar's "Lawyer of the Year Award" on three separate occasions, and has been recognized as a *Super Lawyer* by his peers every year since 1995.**

The second set of sentences takes more space, but they *show* the reader why the defendant's conduct was so egregious. Don't ask the reader to take your word for it — use facts, rather than adjectives, to show the reader that your position is the better one.

7.   Don't Be Artificial

Be wary (not *weary*) of over-emphasizing words, sentences, or paragraphs through use of artificial emphasis. Exclamation points, boldface, italics, and capital letters are often overused. It's fine to emphasize, for example, a contractual provision that supports your cause of action. You certainly can say, "The contract unambiguously stated that plaintiff would not divulge our company's trade secrets *during or six months after employment*." It is not fine to say **"THE CONTRACT STATED THAT PLAINTIFF WOULD NOT . . . ."** A sentence composed of all capital letters is not only difficult to read, it suggests to the reader that you are yelling. Don't be one of those people.

And don't use exclamation points unless they are already part of the case citation or trial record from which you are quoting. The strength of an attorney's legal analysis is based on the attorney's reasoning, not artificial gimmicks. Exclamation points don't add any value and often detract from the substance of your writing. Think about it this way: if you are using artificial methods to persuade the reader, it might mean that your argument is not really persuasive.

8. Don't Be Rhetorical

Generally, rhetorical questions are not effective, so do not pose questions in your litigation documents. Partners, clients, and courts don't want pop quizzes, even if they're rhetorical. Consider whether this sentence could add anything to a memo or brief: "Based on the preceding cases, can anyone question whether Waters has a viable cause of action?" That sentence serves no purpose. Spend your time showing the reader why Waters has a viable cause of action.

Think twice about posing hypothetical situations as well. Unless those hypotheticals are dead-on, they generally do nothing more than detract from the case at hand. Remember, courts decide actual controversies, not potential future ones. Don't waste precious space on hypotheticals — use the pages you have to address the pending case.

9. Watch Sentence and Paragraph Length and Structure

As you craft your documents, make a promise to yourself that overly long sentences — and paragraphs — are unwelcome guests. Readers can't pay attention to sentences that keep going, and going, and going, and going . . . . If your sentence goes beyond three-and-a-half lines, you might have a problem and should consider revising or rewriting that sentence. Just because a sentence isn't a run-on sentence doesn't mean it can't be improved.

Don't make the mistake, like one attorney did, of assaulting the court with a 345-word sentence.[9] If you're trying to get the reader's attention, a sentence like that will do the trick, but it's not the right kind of attention ("any press is good press" doesn't apply here — sorry). "But my underlying point was one-hundred percent true!" you say. What point? Nobody knows the point you were trying to make — it's lost in the verbose maze of that 345-word sentence. And if you can't figure out how to punctuate a sentence, it's too long.

The same holds true for long paragraphs. Never write a single paragraph that occupies an entire page; in fact, if a paragraph is more than half a page, break it up. Try to limit paragraphs to 3 to 5 sentences.

And don't be afraid of short paragraphs. In most cases, only one aspect of the law, e.g., one element or factor, should be discussed in each paragraph. The same holds true for legal arguments. As a general rule: one paragraph equals one argument, even if you only need a sentence or two to make that argument.

10. Passively Yours

Of course, you've heard for years that the passive voice is evil, and the active voice is good. Generally, passive voice leads to longer sentences and cloudy writing and, for those reasons, you should avoid it — even in short sentences.

A fine will be levied.

But who is to levy the fine?

---

[9] *See* Stanard v. Nygren, 658 F.3d 792, 798 (7th Cir. 2011).

The Department will levy a fine.

Consider the readability of these two sentences:

The plaintiff slipped on the water.

The water was slipped on by the plaintiff.

Passive voice isn't always bad, though. If you want to de-emphasize a particular fact, for example, use the passive voice. Saying,

The agreement, while ambiguous, was signed by my client.

is much more effective than

My client signed an ambiguous agreement.

Passive voice is also appropriate when the writer does not know the actor or wants to de-emphasize the actor's role. For example, consider these sentences:

The documents were destroyed.

Plaintiff destroyed the documents.

If you represent the Plaintiff, which would you rather use to tell the court that documents your client should have retained were destroyed? Learn the difference between active and passive voice and use passive voice selectively and sparingly to achieve maximum effectiveness.

III. TIPS FOR THE REVISION PHASE

A. Editing for Grammar, Spelling, and the Like

Take the time to meticulously check for spelling and grammatical errors, overused words, unnecessary words, and commonly confused words (e.g., "than" versus "then"). Don't solely rely on spell check to catch spelling errors (consider the word "tortious" — if you follow spell check, you'll end up with "tortuous"), and don't think that an online grammar checker, such as Grammarly, will find every improperly used semicolon, dangling modifier, or faulty parallelism. Do the editing yourself, not only to make the product better but to master the rules of writing and hone your revision skills. Good writing requires you to be an excellent editor.

Double-check small and similar words, such as "is," "it," "if," "in," "too," "to," "two," "of," "or," and "on." And know the difference between "its" and "it's"; "their," "there," and "they're"; and words like "affect" and "effect." Spell check won't catch these errors. Active proofreading will go a long way toward helping you ensure (not insure) you've used words correctly.

And while we're talking about words, don't make up words that aren't in the dictionary, like *irregardless* and *supposably*. There are about 250,000 words in the English language. Don't use non-existent words when you have such a large selection from which to choose. We know you have high standards. We promise there's a word in the dictionary that's just the right fit for you.

If you find yourself frequently making the same types of errors in legal documents, develop a checklist to consult during the revision stage. Eventually, you'll be able to revise and edit documents without it, but while you're learning to be a thorough editor, use the checklist.

B. Footnotes versus In-text Citations

Legal writers are split on whether citations should be made in-text or placed in footnotes. There are arguments for both positions. The authors generally prefer in-text citations, and the sample memos and briefs in this book follow that format. However, some writers (and judges) prefer footnotes. Decide which method you prefer, and be consistent throughout your document.

What about substantive footnotes? You can use them, but you should do so sparingly. Don't draft a brief with 100 substantive footnotes. Doing so will disrupt the flow of your brief and make following the brief more difficult. Footnotes should be used sparingly and never for legal arguments or information because many courts (especially appellate courts) will not consider arguments made in footnotes.

Chapter 3

TIPS FOR PERSUASIVE WRITING IN THE REAL WORLD

Let's review some important persuasive writing techniques. In the persuasive writing context, think of yourself as a master story teller — not, as some lawyers say, an architect or madman. Architects create blueprints for various structures that *others* build. Forget blueprints — they are impersonal, too technical, often based on rigid formulas, and incomplete. While you need to create a solid structure, e.g., an outline, it's how you build upon the foundation, i.e., *tell the story*, that determines the persuasiveness of your argument. In so doing, know that you play every part in how the story is told. You write the screenplay, direct the actors (the parties are the stars), and produce the final product. You must be creative and tell such a persuasive tale that the judge has no choice but to grant your motion.

Of course, you should always adhere to the earlier principles we discussed in Chapter 2. Many legal writing principles are applicable to both predictive and persuasive writing. But there are several skills that apply with particular force to persuasive writing. Follow them, practice them, and master them. These are the tools of persuasion.

I. GOOD WRITERS ARE GREAT NARRATORS

A. Choosing a Theme

Before you start writing any persuasive brief, you've got to know why your client should prevail and be able to articulate the answer in a sentence or two. Think of great taglines from movies, such as the *Shawshank Redemption*: "Fear can hold you prisoner. Hope can set you free." The tagline, or hook, excites readers and sparks interest in your story. First impressions are critically important, and the first paragraph of your brief is where you win at the beginning by hooking the reader into a story that ends in victory for your client.

Before you start writing any brief — whether it's a brief in support of a motion to dismiss or an appellate brief — you should develop a theme. Based on the relevant facts and law, why should your client prevail? The answer helps you to develop your theme, where you weave the facts and law into a unified and compelling argument. Your theme is an important step toward developing a credible, compelling storyline that has: (1) believable characters (the parties); (2) a persuasive plot (the facts and law); (3) a logical story arc (a beginning, middle, and end); and (4) a powerful ending (why your client must prevail). Think, for example, about great movies or literary novels. What made these artistic works so powerful that they made a lasting impression on you?

Great movies have captivating opening scenes that set the theme, just like great literary works have memorable opening lines ("It was the best of times, it was the worst of times."[10] Your theme should be interesting, persuasive, easily understood, and supported by the facts and the law.

Assume you represent Simon Harrison, who believes the California courts cannot exercise personal jurisdiction over him for statements he made about Kirsten Waters. What could your theme be?

> **The California courts lack personal jurisdiction over Simon Harrison because he lives in Pennsylvania, not California, and his statements were posted to a website from his home in Pennsylvania.**

That's not a good theme — while it's easily understood, it's not interesting. Nor is it persuasive. Instead, consider a theme like:

> **Forcing a litigant to travel more than 2,500 miles to defend a lawsuit — based solely on two online blog posts — is unreasonable, unfair, and unconstitutional.**

This theme is much better because it concisely sets forth Harrison's two strongest arguments: He does not live in and has few contacts with California, and the burden of having to defend the lawsuit in California would be substantial. And consider the inclusion of the distance. The reader implicitly knows that Pennsylvania is a long way from California, but detailing exactly how far — more than 2,500 miles — is much more persuasive.

Depending on the type of case you're handling, your theme may invoke emotion, such as sympathy or outrage, logic, equitable principles, public policies, or some combination.

Consider, for example, insurance coverage cases, where an insurer seeks to avoid coverage, often under the language of an obscure provision in the policy that the insured likely did not know about. If you are representing an injured insured, your theme might involve equitable principles and emotion:

> **Stacey has timely paid insurance premiums to American Insurance every three months for the last 10 years. She had no idea the policy might not provide coverage if no third-party witness was present to corroborate her testimony that a John Doe driver caused the accident. Stacey was hospitalized for four days after the accident, suffered facial injuries for which she has needed plastic surgery, and was unable to work for more than three months after the accident. If American Insurance is able to escape liability under the policy on a technicality, Stacey will have no source of recovery and will have to bear more than $35,000 in uncovered medical expenses and lost wages, which she paid premiums to cover and**

---

[10] CHARLES DICKENS, A TALE OF TWO CITIES (Chapman and Hall, 1859).

believed would be covered if she suffered an accident like the one that occurred.

B.   Introduction

Unless the relevant rules prohibit them, you should use introductions. Your strategy is to win at the beginning and throughout your brief. That means using every opportunity to persuade and not waiting until the middle of your brief to start making your argument.

Your introduction should get the court's attention, succinctly state why your motion should be granted, and make the court want to rule in your favor. Think of your strongest legal argument or a powerful fact that supports your claim and craft an introduction that immediately tilts the scales in your client's favor.

Your introductory paragraph should also tell the court precisely what relief you are seeking. Don't hide the ball or ask for remedies that are unlikely to be granted. Tell the court what you want — money, an injunction, a restraining order — and make sure there is no room for misinterpretation. The goal of an introduction is to set forth your argument and provide an effective roadmap.

The introduction is just the beginning of the story, though. It sets the tone for what follows. Don't try to say everything in your introduction. If you try to do too much too soon, you'll jumble the message and lose your audience.

The first sentence, of course, is the start of your opening scene, not a show unto itself. If you were drafting Harrison's motion to dismiss, discussed above, your introduction would, ideally, explain *why* it is unreasonable to make Harrison travel more than 2,500 miles to California, particularly after he made such inflammatory blog posts. That may be a long distance, but if you do some bad things — like target a forum resident with piercing and potentially career-ending invective — you might find yourself on a plane to the West Coast.

Judges are busy and want to know what remedy you are seeking and why the facts and law support a result in your favor. Use your introduction to lay out your case.

C.   Don't Wait to Persuade

Many lawyers wait . . . and keep waiting . . . to set forth their best arguments. Some lawyers, for example, wait until the Legal Argument section of a brief to begin persuasively arguing their case. Don't do that. Begin to persuade the court as soon as possible.

For example, the Table of Contents gives you the opportunity to showcase persuasive point headings, while the Table of Authorities allows you to demonstrate the depth and quality of your research. Your Question Presented should be drafted in a manner that makes the court want to rule in your favor. But how do you do that? Let's look at Harrison's motion to dismiss. Don't say:

> **The question presented before this Court is whether it is constitutional to exercise personal jurisdiction over Simon Harrison.**

Instead, say this:

> **Does the United States Constitution allow a court to exercise personal jurisdiction over an out-of-state resident who resides more than 2,500 miles from the forum based solely on two blog posts that were drafted and posted from the defendant's residence?**

The obvious answer — the one you seek — is "no."

Likewise, in your Procedural History (for appellate briefs), don't just blandly recite the history of your case. Sprinkle in a few sentences suggesting the reasons the lower court properly dismissed the other party's claims, or the reasons the trial court was wrong to dismiss your client's claim via summary judgment. Don't overdo it, though — you're writing a Procedural History, not manufacturing a second Legal Argument section. Consider the following example:

> **On January 15, 2004, Plaintiff filed a complaint in the United States District Court for the Eastern District of Tennessee, arguing that Boost Your Bank Account, LLC committed fraud by promising Plaintiff he would make $5,000 in extra income per year by following the *Keep Your Two Cents* Program. In its Answer, Boost claims the contract contains a disclaimer indicating that the average earnings are slightly above $3,000.00, and that Plaintiff in fact profited from the program. During discovery, Plaintiff acknowledged that he made $4,048.00 in extra income and that he read the disclaimer prior to beginning the program.**

> **At the conclusion of discovery, the lower court granted Defendant's motion for summary judgment, holding that "Boost Your Bank Account made clear, repeated, and unambiguous representations that the average income was approximately $3,000.00. Plaintiff's profit was substantially higher, approximately 80% of the $5,000.00 figure." Despite this finding, Plaintiff now appeals, claiming that the trial court did not properly apply the elements of fraud.**

D.   Language Choice

We've all heard the phrase, "It's not what you say—it's how you say it." The words you use directly impact the persuasive value of your brief and your credibility as an advocate. In fact, words can win—or lose—the case. Thus, be sure to write with a respectful, balanced, and professional tone.

For example, avoid over-the-top language. Think twice before using words such as "clearly," "indisputably" and "unmistakably" in persuasive writing. They add no value. Don't waste precious brief space telling the court something is clear. Show the court why instead.

Err on the side of formality with word choice and avoid colloquialisms. For example, choose "child" over "kid" (unless you are talking about a baby goat), "elderly" over "old," and "overweight" over "fat."

Even though the authors consider ourselves progressive when it comes to legal writing, we're still traditionalists about the use of contractions in formal legal writing. In our opinion, you shouldn't use them. We know some legal writing professors and judges disagree.

E. Sentence Length

We've talked before about avoiding long, confusing sentences. But in persuasive writing, short, powerful sentences can be used to punch holes in your adversary's arguments. Consider these examples from John Roberts in what has been called the "best brief" the Supreme Court has ever seen. Roberts, then a partner at Hogan & Hartson, represented Alaska in a case that pitted the EPA against the state over Alaska's control decisions with respect to emissions from the state's Red Dog Mine:[11]

> The EPA, however, "disagree[d]" with the State's decision to select Low NOx, rather than SCR, as BACT for the new generator . . . .Rather than challenge the State's decision through the available state review process, the EPA issued a series of orders prohibiting the construction of the generator. The EPA, however, had no authority to do so.[12]

> * * * * *

> The court also cast aside ADEC's utility cost analysis, noting that "Cominco does not, in fact, buy power from an electric utility." . . . Of course, that is just the point.[13]

> * * * * *

> Determining the "best" control technology is like asking different people to pick the "best" car. Mario Andretti may select a Ferrari; a college student may choose a Volkswagen Beetle; a family of six a mini-van. A Minnesotan's choice will doubtless have four-wheel drive; a Floridian's might well be a convertible. The choices would turn on how the decisionmaker weighed competing priorities such as cost, mileage, safety, cargo space, speed, handling, and so on. Substituting one decision-maker for another may yield a different result, but not in any sense a more "correct" one. So too here.[14]

The short sentences add interest and effectively contrast to the longer sentences that surround them. You can do great damage by doing so little. Remember, less *is* more.

---

[11] The authors learned of these examples from an article written by Ross Guberman titled "Five Ways to Write Like John Roberts," available at: www.legalwritingpro.com/articles.

[12] Brief for Petitioner at 4, *Alaska Dept. of Envt'l Conservation v. United States Envt'l Protection Agency*, 540 U.S. 461 (2004) (no. 02–658).

[13] *Id.* at *80.

[14] *Id.* at *44.

F. Metaphor

The use of metaphors in legal writing is an issue about which many legal writing professors disagree. Some believe metaphors are helpful and add interest and value to legal writing. Others argue that metaphors often have a different meaning to the writer than they do to the reader and, therefore, lack the clarity required of legal writing. The authors see both sides of the discussion and feel compelled to discuss metaphors — at least briefly — because they are so prevalent.

A well-placed, well-thought-out metaphor can be priceless. Consider a metaphor from *Alaska v. EPA*, discussed above. Remember, the litigation was over Alaska's decisions about emissions from the Red Dog Mine. What type of metaphor did Roberts choose? A really good one:

> **The awkwardness of considering whether the EPA was arbitrary or capricious in deciding that the State was arbitrary or capricious should be the canary in the mine shaft, signaling that something is very much amiss.**[15]

On the other hand, a poor or overused metaphor may actually harm the client's case. Clichéd legal metaphors such as "slippery slope" and "second bite at the apple" are grossly overused. Any value the "slippery slope" metaphor ever had has long since dissipated.

Thus, if you choose to use metaphors, ensure they are specific, apropos, and cannot be misunderstood or misinterpreted. Use metaphors sparingly and only when they truly add value to your writing.

G. Emotion

Emotion can be a very powerful tool in the legal writer's arsenal. And a powerful, emotional story can certainly impact the outcome of a case.

But avoid over-using emotion. Use the appropriate amount of emotion for the circumstances. Consider, for example, you represent a client who suffered a broken leg in an automobile accident. Writing something like "Plaintiff suffered debilitating injuries that effectively ruined her chance at a happy life" is unquestionably too over-the-top. Plaintiff suffered a broken leg — and that's unfortunate — but no judge or jury is going to believe that the Plaintiff's life has been completely ruined by a broken leg. Instead, you and your client will lose credibility by attempting to over-use emotion in your favor.

Relying too heavily on sympathy can cost your client for another reason as well. The appropriate use of emotion is fine, but you need to ensure your client's position is also supported by law. A injured plaintiff who failed to perfect service on the defendant — no matter how sympathetic that plaintiff may be — won't be able to survive a motion to dismiss for lack of service of process. Don't overload your writing

---

[15] *Id.* at 19.

with emotion and fail to make the legal arguments you must make for your client to prevail.

H. Personalize your Client

If you represent an entity or corporation — particularly an unsympathetic one — you must do what you can to personalize your client. Instead of referring to actions taken by the corporation, describe actions taken by the corporation's employees:

Bank of America denied Plaintiff's request to modify the loan.

Loan servicer Beverly Smith denied Plaintiff's request to modify the loan.

We discussed the use of acronyms in Chapter 2. We think you should generally avoid them. Acronyms are substantially less personal than other names you could select and are a particularly poor choice if you represent an unsympathetic client. Imagine you represent the three defendants named in Chapter 2, America's United Bank, America's United Bank Holding Company, and America's United Bank Mortgage Corporation, which foreclosed on a home owned by an elderly woman whose husband died the previous year. While the law might be on your clients' side, sympathy is not. You're not going to help the situation by referring to the entities by impersonal acronyms — AUB, AUBHC, and AUBMC. Instead, you could collectively refer to the defendants as the "Mortgagor" and refer to the elderly woman as the "Mortgagee," serving to put the big, bad corporations on the same field as the sweet, elderly woman.

I. Alternative Arguments

In many cases, alternative arguments are not only appropriate, but necessary. For example, assume you represent a client who claims to have a contract with a distribution company, but there are questions about whether the contract is complete and enforceable. The distribution company took money from your client, but failed to honor its end of the bargain. You'd be remiss if you only argued breach of contract — what if a judge were to rule that there was no meeting of the minds or that the contract was unenforceable for some other reason? You'd also want to argue that the distribution company is liable to your client under the theory of promissory estoppel.

Of course, make your strongest argument first, then move on to the alternative argument. If, under the scenario above, the contract argument is the better one, make it first and make it persuasively. Then argue that even if the parties don't have a contract or the contract is unenforceable, the distribution company is still liable under the theory of promissory estoppel. If you are crunched for space, be sure to say all you need to say about your most compelling argument — if you have to choose between making the best case for your strongest argument or including multiple secondary arguments, choose the former.

And remember — don't allow yourself to make outlandish alternative arguments. As we've said before, bad arguments detract from good ones.

J. Never Attack a Lawyer or a Court

Watch the words you use. We talked earlier about choosing strong, precise words. However, when describing the conduct of opposing counsel or any judge, avoid inflammatory language.

Alleging the opposing party's arguments are "ridiculous," "absurd," or the like is generally a poor idea. Courts frequently chastise attorneys for using those types of words — even though they may be true. Consider the difference between these two sentences:

> **The plaintiff's argument is unsupported by the law or the facts.**

> **The plaintiff's argument is absurd and is supported by nothing more than her lies to this court.**

Remember, your goal is not to tell the court something is ridiculous or absurd — you must show the court why that is so and allow the court to draw the conclusion you seek.

And never verbally attack any member of the judiciary. This frequently happens in cases on appeal, where the appellant alleges the trial court's ruling was erroneous. If you are the appellant, you should argue the trial court's *ruling* was erroneous (after all, that's why you appealed), but you shouldn't attack the trial *judge*. And you shouldn't use words like "crazy," "stupid," "moronic," and "ridiculous." There are ways to show that a court's ruling was out in left field without saying the judge is an "uninformed moron."

II. THE FACTS OF LIFE

If you're still clinging to the "I'm a big picture person" mantra, maybe this will help untangle you from that perception. Cases are won on the facts — the nitty-gritty details that the parties cull from each other during discovery. You're not going to win any cases by writing a Pulitzer-Prize-worthy brief expounding beautifully upon the notions of justice and liberty. Get in the trenches. Show why the relevant facts support your position and warrant a ruling for your client.

Like we said above, a brief is all about persuasion, and cases are won or lost on the facts. The law is certainly important — and you cannot skimp on the legal analysis — but the facts often make the difference between a favorable outcome and an unfavorable one. Think about it: every case has different facts and therefore calls for a case-specific application of the relevant law. Some factual scenarios even present novel legal questions. Thus, you will rarely find a prior case that is identical to your case and definitively controls the outcome. You likely would not be litigating on behalf of your client, or ever get your client's case to trial, if such a case existed. In other words, the facts *distinguish* your case from those that have come before you, and courts may use your facts to apply precedent in different ways. Even a single fact can lead to a different interpretation of the law or a result that the judge believes is more equitable and just. After all, a judge is a human being with a conscience. Judges don't want to make decisions that are unfair or that lead to a reversal on appeal. Tell a story that shows why the outcome you seek is the "right" one.

To do that, you have to craft a compelling Statement of Facts. Make sure, even if you have to re-write it twenty times, that your Statement of Facts tells a memorable — and compelling — narrative. The Statement of Facts is where the plot thickens and the action increases. Devices such as pace, voice, tone, flow, and clarity are important here. If, for example, you tell a boring story that drags on forever, your reader will fall asleep. And if you go too fast, fail to break-down a complex factual history, or tell a disjointed narrative that doesn't flow, the reader will not follow your client's story.

But you should avoid recounting the factual history like a disinterested historian. You're allowed to put your own slant on the facts and tell your client's version of the story. Just make sure you're honest and retain a balanced perspective. Think about the difference between the *New York Times* and the *National Inquirer*. Don't make the court think you write for the *National Inquirer*.

"How should I arrange the facts," you ask? Well, how you choose to present the facts depends on their strength, relevance, and perceived persuasive value. Often, facts presented chronologically are easiest to understand. Sometimes, however, a topical approach is best. At other times, a combination of the two approaches provides the best result. No matter which method you choose, ensure that your Statement of Facts flows, contains all material facts and information, and does not overwhelm the reader with irrelevant facts.

What about "bad" facts you have to address — how should you include those in your Statement of Facts? You should attempt to weave "bad facts" into your Statement of Facts in a logical way based on the method you've chosen to present the facts. If you're offering the facts in chronological order, for example, place the bad facts in chronological order as well so you don't draw attention to them and so the reader just perceives them as another part of the story. Let's think about how we might do this in *Waters v. Harrison*. Waters' admission that she did misrepresent her punishment for DUI is harmful to her case against Harrison — it's a "bad fact" for Waters. How might she minimize its impact?

> **At the final debate, Waters told voters about her history of alcohol and prescription drug abuse, detailing a 1994 arrest for DUI and possession of a controlled substance. Waters, who stated that she served jail time and spent 3 months in a rehabilitation facility, explained that the incident was "rock-bottom" and a "wake-up call."**

> **Waters' personal story made her popular with voters, many of whom could relate to her past struggles and efforts to overcome them. Waters' statements about the exact nature of her criminal punishment were slightly inaccurate, in that she did not serve any jail time following the 1994 incident. However, Waters was put on probation and ordered to complete community service as a result of her arrest and completed her criminal sentence.**

> **After the debate, Harrison, who has had no relationship with Waters for nearly 20 years, posted highly inflammatory statements about Waters on Harrison's website. Many of the statements were wildly inaccurate.**

*   *   *   *   *

These paragraphs do a good job of telling the court that Waters' statements during the debate were inaccurate in a way that doesn't draw attention to that "bad" fact.

You can also de-emphasize the importance of bad facts by placing them in the middle of a paragraph, in a subordinate clause, or at the beginning of a sentence.

Consider the difference in these two sentences:

> **Even though Waters did not actually serve any jail time, she was punished criminally for driving under the influence and possessing a controlled substance.**

In the first sentence, the emphasis is Waters' punishment for her criminal conduct.

> **Waters was punished criminally for driving under the influence and possessing a controlled substance, but did not serve any jail time.**

In the second sentence, the emphasis is on Waters' lack of jail time. The first sentence does the better job of informing the reader of a bad fact while de-emphasizing it both by putting it at the beginning of the sentence and putting it in a subordinate clause.

You must also remember that the Statement of Facts should not rival the Warren Commission Report in either length or complexity. Irrelevant or trivial facts add unnecessary length to your brief and distract the reader from your substantive arguments. For example, if you're drafting a motion to suppress drugs found on your professional-baseball-player client, there is no reason to mention that your client has a 95 mph fastball and two World Series rings. That's wonderful, but what does it have to do with your case?

On the other hand, if you represent that same client in a negligence case where the client broke his elbow and lost his baseball career, you'd be quite smart to remind the court that the client's elbow helped him throw a 95 mph fastball and win those two Word Series rings. Now that career is gone because of the defendant's negligence.

The Statement of Facts should, however, include every relevant fact you plan to reference in the Legal Argument section of your brief. As a reader, it can be confusing to discover additional, undisclosed facts later in the brief. Shock and awe might be effective devices in novels (think of *The Firm*) and movies (good horror flicks), but they have no place in your brief. The reader will pause and wonder, "Wait, how does this fact I just discovered fit into the case?"

Whatever you do, don't "fudge" or exaggerate the facts. Telling a great story requires honesty and hard work. Your adversary, and the judge, will uncover any misrepresentations or untruths, and you might find yourself defending against a malpractice lawsuit. For example, don't say, "The defendant failed to repair the broken sidewalk despite four warnings over the course of ten months," if there were only two warnings in the last nine months.

And remember, don't omit unfavorable material facts. Instead, show why those facts don't affect the outcome of your case. If your client was struck by a negligent driver while crossing the street, don't omit that your client had just spent twelve hours at the Broken Heart Saloon and had a blood alcohol level of .22. Explain to the court why your client's inebriation did not contribute to the accident or mitigate the driver's culpability. In other words, strike the proper balance between advocacy and forthrightness. Doing that enhances your credibility and maximizes the persuasive value of your arguments.

III. THE STORY OF THE LAW

The Legal Argument section should include two sub-sections: (1) presentation of the law; and (2) application of the law to the facts (the Analysis subsection). The Legal Argument section should seamlessly flow from your Statement of the Facts and reinforce your theme. When presenting the law, avoid a rote regurgitation of the relevant legal principles. Your brief will have little, if any, persuasive value, and you'll make it easy for the adversary to draft an effective response that picks apart your arguments. Remember that most sections of the brief give you an opportunity to persuade. This part is no exception. "But how do I do that?" you ask.

Let's think about the summary judgment standard for a minute. Under Rule 56 of the Federal Rules of Civil Procedure, "[t]he court shall grant summary judgment if the movant shows that there is no genuine dispute as to any material fact and the movant is entitled to judgment as a matter of law." This is high standard, but one that's achievable, as courts grant motions for summary judgment all the time.

Assume you represent the party seeking summary judgment. How might you word the summary judgment standard in a way that's accurate but persuasive? How about, "When the moving party shows there are no genuine issues of material fact and he is entitled to judgment as a matter of law, the court is obligated to grant a motion for summary judgment."

Now assume you represent the party opposing summary judgment. How would you word the summary judgment standard? What about, "The standard for granting summary judgment is high. Summary judgment may only be granted where the moving party shows there are absolutely no issues of material fact and the movant is entitled to judgment as a matter of law."

Do you see the difference in the persuasiveness of these sentences? They both outline the summary judgment standard accurately. But the first is drafted in a way that favors the grant of summary judgment, while the second is drafted in a way that cautions against the grant of summary judgment. Every section of your brief presents an opportunity to persuade.

In the Legal Argument section should begin by presenting the law that is most favorable to your position, from the general, e.g., the elements, to the specific, e.g., the standards you must satisfy for each element. In a motion to dismiss in *Waters v. Harrison*, for example, you would begin with the four elements necessary to state a successful claim for defamation. Then, using headings you should separate each element into its own subsection, provide the relevant law for that element, apply it to the facts, and say whether the element has been met. This is called a "mini-I/CRAC," and it is an effective way to organize your Legal Analysis into manageable, distinct sections.

In your Legal Analysis section, don't be afraid to acknowledge law that undermines your position. People aren't perfect, and neither are legal arguments. Once you've acknowledged the "bad" law, show the court why that "bad" law does not affect the strength of your arguments or support a ruling for the other party. You might argue, for example, that the facts of a prior case are distinguishable. Perhaps there are policy reasons counseling against the court's reliance on an unhelpful case. There may have been further developments in the law after the adverse precedent was issued that calls its validity into question. You'll gain credibility, and your client will benefit by facing the truth instead of trying to wiggle around it with disingenuous arguments.

How should you organize favorable and unfavorable law? Unlike "bad" facts, which you should weave into your Statement of Facts, you should begin with the most favorable law and discuss that law completely before confronting adverse precedent. Don't mix favorable and unfavorable law. Doing so dilutes the strength of favorable law and leads to a muddled legal presentation. Remember that you're in control of your brief. Don't let unfavorable law or facts get so much attention in your brief that you inadvertently undermine your position. Consider the following example:

> **When defendant struck plaintiff with a hammer, he did so in self-defense, believing that he was in danger of serious bodily harm. Defendant acknowledges that this belief must also be objectively reasonable. He also admits that plaintiff, the assailant, was hitting him with a fly swatter and that he suffered no injuries. Defendant also accepts that most decisions of this and other courts do not support defendant's argument. Significantly, however, defendant will demonstrate that, while she was hitting him with the fly swatter, plaintiff reached into her pocket, saying, "I've got something in here, and it's a bullet with your name on it."**

The worst thing you can do as an attorney is de-emphasize your strongest point. Why would you do that? "I was just trying to be honest with the court," you might say. We commend you — attorneys should always be honest. But there's a time and place for everything. Beginning a factual or legal argument with your weakest points increases — exponentially — the likelihood that you'll lose. Don't let "bad facts" overshadow good ones. Control the argument. You're the storyteller.

A. Don't Fudge the Law

As you did in the Statement of Facts with "bad facts," don't conceal or hide unfavorable law. For example, if you're defending a state statute that prohibits abortion, don't omit *Planned Parenthood of Southeastern Pennsylvania v. Casey*, which affirmed the central holding in *Roe v. Wade* regarding a woman's right to terminate a pregnancy.[16] The Court will find that law. If, for some reason, the court does not find the law you are hiding, your adversary will and then promptly alert the court to the unfavorable law you forgot to mention.

---

[16] 505 U.S. 833 (1992).

And don't try to use quotes from a case to suggest the case stands for a proposition it does not. For example, it is inappropriate to suggest to the court that, under Georgia law, "one not in privity of contract with another lacks standing to assert any claims arising from violations of the contract."[17] Although this statement is a direct quote from *Dominic*, it is not a complete representation of Georgia law, which also allows third party beneficiaries to sue for breach of contract.[18]

Under Rule 3.3 of the Model Rules of Professional Conduct, a lawyer has an ethical duty to disclose binding authority that is directly adverse to the lawyer's position if opposing counsel has not brought that authority to the court's attention. And what we're talking about above is *directly adverse* binding authority. You are *not* ethically required to disclose unhelpful authority that isn't binding or isn't directly adverse to the position you're taking. You may be wise to present that authority to gain credibility with the court and to take away the opposing party's thunder in presenting it to the court — but you don't have to.

B.   Holdings v. Dicta

In your Legal Argument, you should strive to cite holdings, not dicta. Dicta may add persuasive value to your argument, but it isn't binding. A dictum is "a remark, an aside, concerning some rule of law or legal proposition that is not necessarily essential to the decision and lacks the authority of adjudication."[19] Remember, too, that headnotes, recitations of the lower court's holding, and statements in case syllabi are not authority and should not be cited.

C.   Altering Quotes

Do not change or alter quotes from statutes, regulations, or cases unless you let the court know you have done so, the alteration does not change the meaning, and the alteration doesn't create the potential for misinterpretation, misapplication, or ambiguity. Use ellipses to show that you have removed a portion of the quote and use brackets to show that you have altered language. And if you rely on a case that has been reversed on other grounds, let the court know you're aware of that fact by, for example, using a parenthetical.

D.   Hard-to-Find Authorities

If you cite authority that may not be readily accessible to the court, attach a copy of the authority to your brief. For example, copies of information from websites (which frequently disappears), foreign cases, trial court opinions, or obscure treatises should be attached as an exhibit to your brief.

---

[17] *Dominic v. Eurocar Classics*, 310 Ga. App. 825, 828, 714 S.E.2d 388, 391 (2011).

[18] O.C.G.A. § 9-2-20(b).

[19] *U.S. v. Crawley*, 837 F.2d 291, 292 (7th Cir. 1998) (*quoting Local 8599, United Steelworkers of Am. v. Bd. of Educ.*, 209 Cal. Rptr. 16, 21 (Cal. Ct. App. 1984)).

E.   The Analysis

The Legal Analysis section of your brief is the place where you apply the relevant law to the facts of your case to explain to the court why your position is the correct one. It is where you explain why a particular case, statute, or regulation applies, why helpful precedent applies, why unhelpful precedent does not apply, and why policy arguments favor your client's position.

Your Analysis should not be a regurgitation of prior parts of the brief, and you should not simply cut and paste your Statement of Facts into the analysis section. That's not an Analysis. Neither is relying on circular reasoning — supporting a premise by repeating that premise. For example, "The plaintiff should prevail because the plaintiff's case is the better one." If you're not sure whether your reasoning is circular, employ the "why" test. If your explanation of "why" does not reference facts or law or both, you've engaged in circular reasoning.

Let's look at an example. Suppose you represent a church and are challenging a city ordinance banning statues more than 20 feet in height based on your belief that the city targeted the church in enacting the ordinance. How would you draft the analysis section?

> **This case is exactly like *Church of the Lukumi Babalu Any, Inc. v. City of Hialeah*, 508 U.S. 520 (1993), and the other cases cited above. Because those cases control, the City's ordinance is an impermissible restriction of religious practice and is void.**

The sentences above are grammatically correct. However, that paragraph is not an adequate analysis. In fact, it's not an analysis at all. The legal conclusions in the above paragraph are not supported by specific facts, rendering the argument shallow and unpersuasive. The Analysis below, however, strikes the proper balance: it supports the arguments with depth and specificity, is not overly lengthy, and maximizes the persuasive force of the reasoning.

> **This case is controlled by *Church of the Lukumi Babalu Any, Inc. v. City of Hialeah*, 508 U.S. 520 (1993), where the Supreme Court held that a law that is not neutral and does not have general applicability may be upheld only where it serves a compelling government interest and is narrowly tailored to advance that interest. The City's law that prevents the display of statues more than 20 feet in height ("Law") is neither neutral nor a law of general applicability. Furthermore, the Law serves no compelling interest and is not narrowly tailored. The Law, therefore, is void.**
>
> **The City Council passed the Law in response to the erection by the First Unitarian Universalist Church ("Church") of a 50 foot statue of Jesus Christ, known to many as "I-75 Jesus." During the emergency session in which the Law was passed, members of the City Council expressed their desire to require "them [the Church] to remove that monstrosity [referring to I-75 Jesus]," and their interest that the City "not be known as a town of religious freaks." In passing the Law, the City**

specifically targeted the Church and its religious freedom, as the City of Hialeah did in *Lukumi* by passing a law that prohibited sacrificing animals in an effort to prevent Santena practitioners from worshipping in the city. Furthermore, the Law has had no impact whatsoever on any organization other than the Church. Since the Law was passed, the Church is the only person or organization that has been forced to remove a statue pursuant to the Law.

The City has offered no compelling government interest that justifies the need for the Law, much less any evidence the Law is narrowly tailored to advance that interest. The City claims the Law is justified because it protects the public interest and lessens the likelihood that drivers will be distracted and cause auto accidents. The law, however, is underinclusive, like the Lukumi law which the city claimed was enacted to protect public health and prevent cruelty to animals but which permitted many types of animal killing, including fishing, extermination of rodents, euthanasia and did not address public health concerns with respect to those types of killings. Here, the City has done nothing to prevent other types of driver distractions — the City specifically permits the erection of billboards and allows drivers to operate cell phones while driving. This leads to the conclusion that the Law "cannot be regarded as protecting any interest of the highest order," because it "leaves appreciable damage to that supposedly vital interest [of public safety] unprohibited."[20] Thus, the Law is not neutral or generally applicable, the City cannot show the Law furthers any compelling government interest, and the Law is not narrowly tailored. Under *Lukumi*, the Law is void, and this court should grant the Church's motion for summary judgment.

The Analysis section should be about 15–20 percent of the length of your brief and integrate your theme and the story's elements (the facts, law, and policy) to create a memorable ending. You should use the Analysis to tie all the pieces together and show the court why a ruling for your client is right and just.

In some cases, as we've previously discussed, you will have more than one strong argument. Choose to explain your strongest argument first, followed by your second strongest argument, and so on. But don't waste the court's time by making frivolous arguments. Bad arguments detract from good ones and harm your credibility.

As you can see in the example above, the Legal Analysis section is also where you should address relevant counter-arguments your adversary has raised or is likely to raise and explain why they do not affect the outcome you are seeking. In the example above, the author outlines the reasons the Law is neutral and generally applicable and addresses a potential counter-argument the City might raise: even if the law is not neutral, it is justified by a compelling government interest and is narrowly tailored. If your jurisdiction allows reply briefs, you may choose to address anticipated counter-arguments in your initial brief — before the opposing party has the opportunity to make them — or wait until the reply brief.

---

[20] *Id.* at 547.

Remember that even the best counter-arguments do not warrant a multi-page response; while preemptive strikes can be effective, excessive emphasis on the adversary's arguments could end up detracting from your own. In other words, acknowledging the weaknesses in your argument(s) and concisely telling the court why it should nonetheless embrace your position is the hallmark of effective and honest advocacy.

F. Make Strategic Concessions

Do not be afraid to make strategic concessions or acknowledge and address weaknesses in your argument. But avoid arguing for the sake of arguing. By acknowledging weaknesses, you give yourself the opportunity to explain why unfavorable facts or law do not affect the outcome of the case. For example, unfavorable law may be factually distinguishable. Don't vehemently stick to an unreasonable or tenuous position just for the sake of arguing — this will seriously impact your credibility. Acknowledge weaknesses and address them forthrightly.

IV. THE CONCLUSION

As you complete the first draft of your brief (and before the re-writing and revising process), think about your ending, especially the last sentence. What type of lasting impression do you want to leave on the reader?

Although you're not writing a movie script, the same principles apply: good stories and memorable endings lead to positive results. Endings that leave the court unsatisfied, or lead to more questions, are ineffective. Just as someone says, "I can't imagine anyone giving this movie a bad review," you want the court to say, "I can't imagine what the adversary will say to counter these arguments." Of course, since most cases are hotly contested, and involve gray areas of the law, that's not going to be easy. No matter how unfavorable the facts or law, however, you can always present a well-written, persuasive, and honest argument for victory and sum that up with a strong conclusion.

V. FRIENDLY REMINDERS

A. Checklists

Checklists are wonderful tools for improving your legal writing. You should work to develop your own comprehensive checklist that includes both substantive and stylistic tips. A checklist can serve as an important reminder — while you write, re-write, and revise — of those things you may have overlooked. Some items you may want to include on your checklist are:

Writing/Re-Writing:

- Do I have a powerful "Introduction"?
- Does my Factual Background section tell the story of why my client should win?

- Did I accurately outline the facts in a way that isn't misleading?
- Have I presented the law accurately and persuasively?
  - Have I thoroughly explained the status of the law in a way that is understandable to someone who knows nothing about this particular area?
  - Did I ensure that my authority is still "good law"?
  - Have I discussed threshold issues?
- Did I include a thorough "Analysis" section?
  - Did I acknowledge weaknesses in my own argument and explain why those weaknesses do not affect the outcome of my case?
  - Did I effectively address relevant counter-arguments?
- Overall impression
  - Are my sentences too long and convoluted?
  - Does the order/organization make sense?
  - Does the brief "flow"? Is it easily readable?
  - Does my brief comply with the relevant court rules?
  - Did I accurately cite authority and include pinpoint cites?
  - Does my document say what I want it to say?
  - Have I made all the substantive points I want to make?

Revising:
- Did I spell-check my document?
- Did I proofread for spelling and grammatical errors?
  - Is there subject-verb agreement?
  - Do I have parallel tenses?
  - Is my comma usage correct?
  - Is my word usage proper?
- Did I avoid unnecessary words, "fancy" words, and legalese?
- Is the font consistent? (Don't laugh — MANY briefs contain multiple fonts.)

B. Comply with Deadlines and Local Court Rules

Courts are generally dead serious about deadlines, especially deadlines pertaining to the filing of motions and briefs. If you cannot meet the deadline set by the court or the local rules, request an extension, and do so early. Calendar your deadline as soon as you know it and give yourself plenty of time to write, re-write, and revise.

A word about page limitations: Think long and hard before asking for a page limit extension. Even if the court grants your request, it likely will do so begrudgingly. In his *The Winning Brief*, Brian Garner notes that Charles Alan Wright successfully opposed a petition for certiorari to the United States Supreme Court in a mere six pages.[21] Wright used only six pages of straightforward, to-the-point sentences to convince the highest court in this country that a circuit court's decision was correct and did not warrant review. If Wright could accomplish that in a mere six pages, the rest of us can learn to keep our briefs brief, too. Request a page extension only when absolutely necessary.

---

[21] BRYAN A. GARNER, THE WINNING BRIEF: 100 TIPS FOR PERSUASIVE BRIEFING IN TRIAL AND APPELLATE COURTS (Oxford Univ. Press 2d ed. 2004).

Chapter 4

THE LEGAL MEMORANDUM

The Legal Memorandum Checklist

√ Draft a single-sentence Question Presented that incorporates some factual background and lets the reader know the applicable law

√ Include a Brief Answer

 √ Answer the Question Presented with a complete sentence, avoiding a "maybe" answer

 √ Briefly outline the facts and relevant law

 √ Perform a short analysis

 √ Make a prediction about the likely outcome

√ Present the facts objectively, including all relevant facts — whether good or bad — that impact the analysis

 √ Include "missing" facts that could change your analysis

√ Present relevant law

 √ Include all relevant statutory language, if applicable

 √ Offer primary authority from your jurisdiction and rely on reported cases, if possible

 √ Present all law, not just the law that supports your conclusion

 √ Be mindful of trends in the direction of the law

 √ Shepardize

√ Organize the rule explanation from broad rules to specific elements

 √ Address threshold issues, such as whether certain elements are met

 √ Analyze all law, not just the law that supports your conclusion

 √ Generally avoid string cites

 √ Avoid over-quoting authority or misrepresenting the law when paraphrasing

√ Perform a strong analysis

 √ Apply the relevant law to the facts of your case and make a prediction about the likely outcome

 √ Explain why a particular case, statute, or regulation applies or doesn't apply

 √ Address why certain cases are analogous and why other cases are inapplicable or distinguishable

 √ Defend your prediction by explaining why you believe it is the likely outcome.

✓ Draft·a conclusion, giving a short summary of the law and facts and summarizing the reasons you believe a certain outcome is the likely one

    ✓ Consider offering a proposed course of action

In your three years of law school, you read more than most humans do in a lifetime. You endured the Socratic Method, and now you know how to think like a lawyer. That's good, but it's not good enough. A strong thinker does not a strong writer make. You've got to learn to write like a great lawyer, and that involves putting yourself in the reader's shoes. The best lawyers aren't just outstanding *legal* writers — they're excellent writers who understand how to see the world through other people's eyes.

If you cannot write well, your encyclopedic knowledge of the law will have no practical value. Writing, in various forms, is the primary vehicle by which lawyers fight for their clients' rights and present legal arguments to a judge. Whether through a legal memorandum, complaint, motion to dismiss, first set of interrogatories, or summary judgment or appellate brief, lawyers must know how to communicate effectively with words. If you aren't familiar with the types of documents you must draft in litigation practice and the specific writing techniques that apply to each one, you will not be an effective advocate for your client. We're going to tell you what you need to know, and show you how to do it.

In this chapter, we discuss the legal memorandum, a document most law students write during their first year of law school but don't always understand. Below are several writing principles that, while important to all litigation documents, apply with particular force to legal memorandums. Follow these guidelines. Great lawyers do, and so should you.

I. YOU'RE A DOCTOR — DON'T ARGUE. DIAGNOSE.

When writing a legal memorandum, you should remember that your job is *not* to be an advocate. The legal memorandum is where you engage in a balanced, objective analysis. It's not a forum for persuasive advocacy. You'll get the chance for that later.

For purposes of drafting the legal memorandum, think of yourself as a doctor. A legal memorandum writer must look at the symptoms; namely, the facts provided by the client. Once you have those facts, it's time to research and study the relevant law, like a physician searching medical materials to diagnose a strange disease. That process allows you to make an accurate, neutral, and detached diagnosis about whether your client is likely to succeed in a court of law. Although some partners may not request this, you can recommend a course of treatment through your memo, such as whether your client should file a complaint or motion for injunctive relief or not pursue the case at all.

Like a doctor, on whom patients rely to get the correct diagnosis, you've got to do everything in your power to arrive at the correct answer. You must work very hard to ensure that you get the law right and make as accurate a prediction about the likely outcome as possible. Your job is to analyze the client's case in light of favorable and unfavorable law and helpful and unhelpful facts.

II.   IRAC IS NOT A COUNTRY

We've introduced you to some of the skills necessary to craft an effective legal document. But we haven't talked about one of the most important aspects of litigation drafting — organization.

In law school, you probably learned some version of the IRAC or CRAC method, an organizational structure in which the writer organizes the law and facts in a manner that: (1) states the legal (I)ssue; (2) discusses the (R)ule; that is, the relevant law; (3) (A)pplies that law to the facts of your case; and (4) arrives at an informed (C)onclusion. With respect to CRAC, the (C) replaces the (I), and requires you to state the (C)onclusion both first and last.

While these methods are designed to teach unfamiliar law students how to organize legal arguments and help ensure proper flow and readability, you must keep in mind (they didn't tell you this in law school) that there is no "one size fits all" approach. You don't have to mercilessly cling to a single method or formula. In certain cases, other methods will result in a better structure. "Wait, what?" you say. "Throughout law school, I've been hit over the head with IRAC and CRAC. Now you're telling me to experiment with more creative approaches? That's crazy!" Relax, and keep reading.

An alternative organizational structure is necessary in some situations. The partner for whom you work may prefer a different structure. For example, the partner may call you into his office and say, "I need a memo on defamation in California. Just give me the law. Bullet points are fine. Forget the other stuff."

Sometimes the specific circumstances of your case are not amenable to the formal IRAC or CRAC structures mentioned above. For example, if you find a recent state supreme court case that is directly on point and wins the case for your client, don't wait to talk about that case — discuss it immediately.

Additionally, you may write your memo knowing that its content will later be used to draft a motion. Many jurisdictions and courts set specific rules about organization and structure of briefs, so you may want to mirror that structure in your memo for ease of use later.

We don't mean to suggest that the IRAC or CRAC methods should be disregarded. Most of the time, these methods will result in a well-organized memorandum. They especially shouldn't be disregarded simply because you think there's a "better" way to draft the document. The reader will see the light and thank you, right? No. As a young lawyer, your job is to do the things asked of you by older, more experienced lawyers. And as a lawyer of any age, you must follow the requirements of the courts in which you practice. If you try to buck that system, you'll be pegged as someone who doesn't listen well or can't follow instructions, even if your intentions were good.

All we're saying is that it's alright to be different when the situation calls for it.

III. ELEMENTS OF A LEGAL MEMORANDUM

A. The Question Presented

Ideally, your question presented should be a single sentence that incorporates some factual background and lets the reader know the applicable law — it's equivalent to the (I) in IRAC. Avoid generic questions presented, such as:

Whether Client will be able to prove Defendant was negligent?

What makes Client or the lawyer think Client might have a claim for negligence? And what law will determine whether Client does have a negligence claim? This example is much better:

Whether Norwood, the victim of a slip-and-fall, can prove Fresh Foods was negligent under Georgia law for failing to remove water that had puddled on its floor?

This example incorporates some factual background and lets the reader know that Georgia law applies to the analysis. "Why do I need a precise Question Presented?" you may ask. "The partner gave me the assignment — she knows what she asked me to do."

A precise Question Presented is important for a number of reasons. First, the partner for whom you work may have failed to adequately explain the issue or you may have misunderstood the issue you need to research. By drafting a specific Question Presented, there will be no confusion about the issue(s) the memo addresses.

Second, the partner may pass the memo on to the client. The client may have legal training or may not. By drafting a specific Question Presented, you enable the client to see the precise issue you researched. Third, lawyers often save memos for future reference, and you may need to look at a similar issue in the future. By drafting a precise Question Presented, you will ensure that if you look at the memo for reference in the future, you will easily be able to tell what issue(s) you've analyzed.

B. The Brief Answer

Your Brief Answer should be, as the name suggests, "brief." The Brief Answer should be "movie preview" length — generally no more than a page. In the first sentence, answer the Question Presented in a complete sentence. Don't simply say "Yes" or "No." And try to avoid answering the Question Presented with "Maybe," but you can (and probably should) hedge your answer some. Consider this first sentence of the Brief Answer to the Question Presented in the Norwood slip-and-fall case:

Norwood likely can prove Fresh Foods was negligent in failing to remove water it knew or should have known had puddled on its floor.

After you answer the Question Presented, give the reader a condensed version of the law, which should include the elements of a particular cause of action, and one (or two) legal principles that directly influence and support the answer you reach. Finish the Brief Answer with a brief application (in a new paragraph) of the law to the relevant facts of your client's case, demonstrating why your conclusion likely is the correct one. Don't, however, be conclusory. Avoid saying, for example, "The statements were defamatory because they injured plaintiff's reputation and were made with actual malice." Tell the reader why those statements were defamatory in light of the law. A good brief answer, like a movie preview, should tell the reader enough about the characters and the plot to make the reader want to continue reading to learn the complete story. Let's take a look at a good Brief Answer in the Norwood case:

> **Norwood likely can prove Fresh Foods was negligent in failing to remove water it knew or should have known had puddled on its floor. To recover from Fresh Foods for injuries she sustained when she slipped and fell near the flower section of its store, Norwood must prove that (1) Fresh Foods had actual or constructive knowledge of the water; and (2) Norwood, despite the exercise of ordinary care, lacked knowledge of the water on the floor. Norwood may prove Fresh Foods had constructive knowledge of the water by proving either that an employee of Fresh Foods was in the area near the water and could have seen it or that the water had been on the floor for a sufficient length of time that, had Fresh Foods been exercising ordinary diligence, it would have discovered the water.**

> **Norwood likely can prove that Fresh Foods had actual knowledge of the water on the floor and, if necessary, also likely can prove that Fresh Foods had constructive knowledge of the water. After Norwood slipped, a Fresh Foods employee told Norwood's daughter, Reagan, that the flowers had been watered earlier that day, that water had dripped onto the floor, and that the employee had alerted the manager to the problem, but the manager had done nothing to remove the water. This fact, if true, likely is sufficient to prove Fresh Foods had actual knowledge of the presence of water on the floor.**

> **If she cannot prove Fresh Foods had actual knowledge of the water, Norwood may be able to prove it had constructive knowledge of the presence of water on the floor. The Fresh Foods employee who assisted Norwood after she fell was just a few feet from the area where the water had puddled and likely could have seen it. Additionally, it appears the water had been on the floor for approximately two hours before Norwood fell. That two-hour period likely is a sufficient period of time for Fresh Foods to have discovered and removed the water, had it been exercising ordinary care.**

> **Additionally, there is nothing to suggest that Norwood was not exercising ordinary care for her own safety at the time she slipped and fell. Norwood and Reagan both indicated they did not see the water on the floor prior to Norwood's fall, and there do not appear to be any facts that suggest Norwood was distracted or otherwise was not acting reasonably to protect herself from injury. At this time, it is unclear whether Fresh Foods had placed a "Wet Floor" or similar sign near the flower section. If a sign was present, Fresh Foods might use that fact to argue Norwood knew or should have known of the presence of water on the floor. Absent**

information suggesting that such a sign was present, it appears Norwood can prove Fresh Foods was negligent in failing to remove water from its store floor.

This Brief Answer is excellent. It answers the Question Presented in a complete sentence, outlines the relevant Georgia slip-and-fall law, analyzes the facts in light of the law, lets the reader know a missing fact that could change the outcome — the presence or lack of a wet floor sign — and makes a prediction about the client's likelihood of success.

C. The Statement of Facts

Your Statement of Facts should tell the factual background of the case and include all facts that are essential to the legal analysis. And if there are missing facts that could change your analysis, summarize what you don't know as well. If the facts are lengthy or convoluted, use subheadings to organize and guide the reader's understanding of the factual background.

Do not forget that memo-writing is *objective* writing. In persuasive writing, you want to present the facts in the most persuasive way possible, while still being honest and forthright. In objective writing, however, your job is to predict the likely outcome of the scenario you're addressing and to let others know how and why you reach the conclusion you do. You can't do that if you've skewed the facts in a way that favors one outcome over another (or makes one outcome appear more likely). Your Statement of Facts should contain all relevant facts — whether good or bad — and you should present them in a straightforward matter.

So long as it includes all facts relevant to the analysis, your Statement of Facts need not be long. Sticking with the slip-and-fall case discussed above, let's look at a good Statement of Facts:

> **At about 1:30 p.m. on January 1, 2012, Norwood and her daughter, Reagan, traveled to the Fresh Foods store in Rome, Georgia to purchase groceries. Neither Norwood nor Reagan saw any water on the store floor, but as they approached the flower section, Norwood slipped on water, fell, and struck her head on the floor. After Norwood fell, a Fresh Foods employee who had been working approximately 10 feet away came to assist Norwood. The employee told Reagan that the flowers had been watered at approximately 11:30 a.m. that morning, that the employee had noticed water had dripped on the floor from the flowers, and that the employee had told her manager about the water, but the manager had done nothing to remove the water from the floor. It is unclear whether a "Wet Floor" or similar sign had been placed in the area near the flowers.**

This Statement of Facts is short — a single paragraph — but tells the reader all facts the reader needs to know (and a missing fact that could be important) to understand the legal analysis.

A comprehensive Statement of Facts is important for several reasons. The likely outcome of a case often hinges on the specific facts of that case, so ensure you state any facts on which you rely in the Statement of Facts. As with the Question Presented, there may be a miscommunication about the precise facts of the case between you and the partner who assigned the memo — facts that could change the analysis. By outlining the specific facts, you ensure everyone is on the same page.

D. The Legal Discussion

The Legal Discussion section of your memo is the place where you outline pertinent law (the "Rule" subsection) and then apply that law to the facts to predict the likely outcome (the "Analysis" subsection).

1. The Rule — Legal Research

This is a legal writing textbook, so we don't want to spend too much time talking about legal research. However, legal research is critical to developing a comprehensive "Rule" section that: (1) includes primary authority from your jurisdiction that is factually similar to your case; (2) contains a comprehensive discussion of the law upon which your client's case is based; (3) includes the language of all relevant statutes or regulations, if applicable; and (4) does not include cases that have been overruled or are no longer controlling or statutory language that has been repealed.

2. Knowing What Law to Look For

Before we go too far — a quick word about knowing what law applies. In the majority of cases, the law of a particular jurisdiction unquestionably applies. But sometimes — especially in contract cases — there may be questions about which jurisdiction's law applies. You should be prepared to take a position early about which jurisdiction's law applies, though you likely will need to research law from multiple jurisdictions in the event the court disagrees with your position. And remember — in cases brought in federal court, state substantive law will apply to state law claims.

What if you know what law applies, but can't find any relevant authority within your jurisdiction? Sometimes it will be necessary to look outside of your jurisdiction if there is no binding law directly on point. That's okay — oftentimes you can use cases from other jurisdictions to support your client's position. But make sure that you find all the controlling authority you can and don't inadvertently miss a relevant case in your jurisdiction.

Can you cite unreported cases? You should try to find reported cases — those that the courts have approved for publication — if possible. You'll find them in state reporters, such as the New Jersey Law Reports, and federal reporters, such as the Federal Supplement. Unreported or unpublished opinions can be used, however, if: (1) there are no or few reported cases on point; (2) the unreported case is very recent; (3) the case comes from the specific district or court where your case is being litigated; or (4) the law is new or evolving.

Remember, though, some jurisdictions do not allow litigants to cite unreported cases. This matters for your memo because you can't base your opinion on the likely outcome of litigation if you won't be able to cite the case or cases that form the basis of that opinion to a court.

Additionally, remember to stick to primary sources, if possible. Secondary sources, such as treatises, can be helpful if there is no binding authority or if the author is a well-known, respected authority in the particular area of law you are addressing. But try to avoid citing a secondary source itself. Instead, cite the primary authority cited in the secondary source.

When performing legal research and writing your Rule section, you also should be mindful of trends. More recent cases on a particular legal issue are likely to more accurately reflect the current status of the law, especially if older and newer authority appears contradictory. Of course, if a seminal case establishes the governing law, always include that case.

And please, please, please Shepardize all authority and save yourself the embarrassment of relying on a case that's been overruled or a statute that's been repealed.

3. Writing the Rule Section

Now that you've found relevant authority, it's time to start writing. But where do you start? And how much of the authority you've found should you cite?

Generally, you should start by broadly outlining the relevant law before digging down into a more detailed explanation of specific elements of the law. For example, assume you are writing a memo on whether a document constitutes an enforceable contract between two parties. Start with the general elements that must be satisfied:

> **An enforceable contract is formed when there is: (1) an offer; (2) an acceptance in compliance with the terms of the offer; (3) a meeting of the minds; (4) consent by each party to the terms of the contract; and (5) execution and delivery of the contract.** *Vermont Info. Processing, Inc. v. Montana Beverage Corp.*, 227 S.W.3d 846, 853 (Tex. App. 2007).

Then, break down the general elements (offer, acceptance, etc.) in the same order they were outlined:

> **An offer is an expression by the offeror to the offeree of the terms of the proposed contract.** *Smith v. Renz*, 840 S.W.2d 702, 704 (Tex. App. 1992). **The terms of the offer must be sufficiently clear and definite so as to be understood by the offeree.** *Copeland v. Alsobrook*, 3 S.W.3d 598, 605 (Tex. App. 1999). **The test for determining whether an offer has been made is an objective one; that is, would a reasonable person believe that an offer was made.** *Id.* at 604.
>
> **The offer also must contain the "essential terms" (also called material terms) of the proposed contract.** *Smith*, 840 S.W.2d at 704. **Essential terms are those terms necessary to permit a court to determine the respective rights and duties of the parties.** *Id.* **There is no single definition of the term "essential," and each purported contract must be examined on a case-by-case basis to determine which terms are "essential."** *G.D. Holdings, Inc. v. H.D.H. Land & Timber, L.P.*, 407 S.W.3d 856, 861 (Tex. App.**

2013). Generally, however, a provision detailing payment is an essential term of every contract. *Id.*

Acceptance of the offer is an expression of ascent by the offeree, in a manner permitted by the offeror, to the terms offered by the offeror. *Engelman Irrigation Dist. v. Shields Bros. Inc.*, 960 S.W.2d 343, 352 (Tex. App. 1997). If the offeror requires that acceptance be made within a specific time or in a specific manner, the offeree must comply with those requirements to create an enforceable contract. *Town of Lindsay v. Cooke County Elec. Co-Op Ass'n*, 502 S.W.2d 117, 118 (Tex. 1973). However, if the offeror does not specify a time period for acceptance, the offeree may accept within a reasonable time, unless the offeror has revoked the offer. *Embree, Inc. v. Southwestern Bell Media, Inc.*, 772 S.W.2d 209, 210 (Tex. App. 1989). And if the offeror does not specify how acceptance may be made, acceptance may be effectuated by any reasonable means. *Town of Lindsay*, 502 S.W.2d at 118.

*   *   *   *   *

If an element or sub-element is at issue, you will want to spend extra time discussing that element. For example, if the contention in the contract case above is that the writing between the parties does not contain all essential terms, you should spend much of your Rule section discussing what makes a term "essential" and discussing cases that address that particular issue. If an element or sub-element is not in dispute, you will still want to note that element, but you can explain in a sentence or two why the element is not in dispute, then move on. For example, if the dispute is only over whether the offeree accepted the offer, you don't need to spend an inordinate amount of space discussing the intricacies of offers. There's no dispute that the offer was made and that it contained all essential terms — note that the offer element is satisfied, and move on.

4. Citing Cases

Despite what you may have seen in law review articles, it is not necessary (or advisable) to cite every case in the universe that could possibly be relevant. For example, suppose your "law" is: "Courts in Montana often require specific performance of a contract." You do not need to cite forty-seven cases for that proposition. One or two cases are sufficient.

An exception may arise, however, if you're asking the court in your jurisdiction to follow the authority of a number of other jurisdictions. In that situation, it may be appropriate to cite a case in each of those other jurisdictions to show the court that your client's case is sound — after all, if 47 other jurisdictions follow the rule your client is asking the court to adopt, that must mean it's a pretty good rule, right?

5. Quoting versus Paraphrasing

Legal writers often ask whether they should quote cases and statutes directly or paraphrase. Either option is fine, with a few caveats.

While quoting cases or statutes is an excellent way to ensure you accurately state the law, make sure that your Rule section does not consist of quote, after quote, after quote . . . or rule, after rule, after rule. Generally, you should quote interesting, specific language from statutes and cases and paraphrase everything else. And use transition words like "furthermore," "moreover," and "additionally," to ensure flow and clarity. Consider using shorter transitions too, like "and" and "but." Do not, however, use transition words to begin every sentence — doing so will create artificial barriers to comprehension. Use your judgment, knowing that disjointed writing disrupts the logical flow of your analysis.

If you paraphrase, ensure you don't inadvertently misrepresent the law. For example, if the direct quote from a court is "Summary judgment requires that there exist no genuine issue of material fact between the parties," do not paraphrase by saying "Summary judgment is appropriate where there is no genuine factual dispute between the parties." You just misstated the law. Summary judgment is proper only where the *material* facts are not in dispute — there are factual disputes in almost every case, but that doesn't mean every factual dispute is material to the issues presented. Paraphrasing is a good way to ensure flow in a document, but be sure you paraphrase accurately.

Let's look at two examples. Consider the differences between these two passages, which discuss law relevant to the First Amendment rights of students.

> In *Tinker v. Des Moines Independent Community School District*, 393 U.S. 503, 506 (1969), the Supreme Court noted that the First Amendment to the United States Constitution gives citizens broad rights to freedom of speech. Those rights, "applied in light of the special characteristics of the school environment, are available to teachers and students." *Id.* Thus, "it can hardly be argued that either students or teachers shed their constitutional rights to freedom of speech or expression at the schoolhouse gate. This has been the unmistakable holding of this Court for almost 50 years." *Id.* However, the First Amendment rights of students "are not automatically coextensive with the rights of adults in other settings." *Bethel School Dist. No. 403 v. Fraser*, 478 U.S. 675, 682 (1986). Furthermore, students' First Amendment rights are "applied in light of the special characteristics of the school environment." *Hazelwood School Dist. v. Kuhlmeier*, 484 U.S. 260, 266 (1988). Additionally, a school may regulate speech that is "inconsistent with its 'basic educational mission,'" even if that same speech could not be regulated in a non-educational setting. *Id.* (quoting *Fraser*, 478 U.S. at 685).

This paragraph isn't awful, but the relevant authority is over-quoted, information that isn't really important to the analysis is included, and transitions are overused to the point that they become distracting. Consider the better paragraph below:

> The First Amendment to the United States Constitution gives citizens broad rights to freedom of speech. *Tinker v. Des Moines Indep. Community School Dist.*, 393 U.S. 503, 506 (1969). Those rights are available to both teachers and students, who "do not shed their constitutional rights to freedom of speech or expression at the schoolhouse gate." *Id.* The First

Amendment rights of students in school settings, however, are not necessarily the same as the rights of adults in non-school settings. *Bethel School Dist. No. 403 v. Fraser*, 478 U.S. 675, 682 (1986). Students' First Amendment rights much be considered in conjunction with the "special characteristics of the school environment." *Hazelwood School Dist. v. Kuhlmeier*, 484 U.S. 260, 266 (1988). Therefore, a school may regulate speech that is "inconsistent with its 'basic educational mission,'" even if that same speech could not be regulated in a non-educational setting. *Id.* (quoting *Fraser*, 478 U.S. at 685).

Here, the transitions aid, rather than hinder, readability and understanding. Only the interesting and most important language of the authority is cited, and the rest is paraphrased appropriately.

6. Comprehensiveness

Importantly, a "comprehensive" rule section does not mean that you should include every tangentially relevant legal rule that, only in those rarest of scenarios known as a law school hypothetical, might be relevant. For example, if you are writing a memo about whether the National Inquisitor newspaper's statements about your client were libelous, don't discuss slander, which applies only to verbal (or spoken) defamation.

In addition, don't think that comprehensiveness requires you to include every last legal detail lurking in the shadows of your law firm library. Remember, if the success of your client's claim turns on only one element of a five-element statute, don't spend too much time discussing the other elements. What's the point if those elements aren't in dispute? But be sure to let the reader know why you aren't explaining those elements. Mention to the reader that the parties agree the first four elements of the claim are met, so the only element at issue is element five.

7. The Legal Analysis

The Legal Analysis is a section of memos (and briefs) that law students and lawyers often struggle with. The problem is that most writers fail to actually analyze the issues by thoroughly and comprehensively applying the law to the facts and comparing concrete facts from precedent to concrete facts from the case at issue. After drafting a detailed Statement of Facts and thorough outline of the Rule, writers will simply use the Analysis section to summarize or present the facts in a conclusory manner. This is a mistake. You must use your Legal Analysis section to directly apply the relevant law to the facts of your case and make a prediction about the likely outcome. When drafting the Analysis section, you must explain: (1) why a particular case, statute or regulation applies or doesn't apply; (2) why certain cases are analogous; (3) why other cases are inapplicable or distinguishable; and (4) why you believe the prediction you make is the likely outcome. Consider the following:

This case is exactly like *Smith* and *Jones* and is distinguishable from *Rogers*. Because *Smith* and *Jones* control, Green is unlikely to be able to prove intentional infliction of emotional distress.

The sentences above are grammatically correct; however, that paragraph is not an adequate analysis. In fact, it's not an analysis at all. Something akin to that paragraph won't cut it. You must use your Analysis section to explain why *Smith* and *Jones* are analogous. Are the facts of your case more similar to those of *Smith* and *Jones* than they are to those of *Rogers*? Why do you think Green can't prove intentional infliction of emotional distress? Do *Smith* and *Jones* make you believe Green can't prove certain elements? What about those cases leads you to that conclusion? These are the types of questions you need to consider — and answer — when drafting the Legal Analysis section of your brief. It's difficult to offer a sample analysis in the abstract, so we'll discuss analyses later in this chapter's sample memos.

8.   Conclusion

Your conclusion should briefly summarize the law and facts — much like your brief answer — and again state the likely outcome. Don't simply say "for the reasons discussed above, the client likely can state a claim." Give a short summary of the law and facts again. Busy readers frequently will review only the Question Presented, Brief Answer, and Conclusion. Make sure your conclusion provides facts and law that support the likely outcome.

You may also choose to offer a proposed course of action in your conclusion. Your proposal will depend on the type of case and legal issue(s) you are analyzing, but a proposed course of action could include:

- Filing a complaint (or not filing a complaint if you don't believe your client will succeed in proving the client's claim);

- Filing a motion to dismiss (or not filing a motion if you've concluded that doing so would likely be fruitless);

- Requesting certain information in discovery (if there is unknown information that, if discovered, might enable you to later file a motion);

- Filing a motion for summary judgment (or not filing a motion if you've concluded that the motion likely won't be granted);

- Moving for a new trial; or

- Appealing, or not appealing a trial court's ruling or a jury's verdict.

*   *   *   *   *

Waters v. Harrison, Memorandums

All of this information doesn't help much, though, if you don't know how to use it. What does a good memorandum look like? Read on.

Below are two memorandums that analyze defamation and invasion of privacy under California law. After reading the memorandums, think about why they are effective, and consider ways in which they can be improved.

MEMORANDUM ANALYZING DEFAMATION UNDER CALIFORNIA LAW

To: Supervising Attorney
From: Associate Attorney
Re: *Waters v. Harrison*
Date: April 5, 2013

QUESTION PRESENTED

Under California law, were Simon Harrison's ("Simon") statements about Kirsten Waters' ("Kirsten") criminal, educational, and personal background on www.just-tellthetruth.com defamatory?

BRIEF ANSWER

Under California law, Kirsten has a viable cause of action for defamation. To state a prima facie case for defamation, a party must demonstrate the following: (1) publication; (2) of a false statement; (3) that is defamatory; (4) unprivileged; and (5) damages. *Ringler Associates Inc., v. Maryland Casualty Co.*, 96 Cal. Rptr. 2d 136, 148 (Cal. Ct. App. 2000). The level of fault required — negligence or actual malice — depends on whether the party alleging defamation is an all-public, limited-purpose public, or private figure. *McGarry v. University of San Diego*, 64 Cal. Rptr. 3d 479-480 (Cal. Ct. App. 2007).[22]

Harrison published statements on his blog based upon several provably false facts that, if untrue, may be defamatory. After these statements were published, however, Kirsten held a press conference where, after narrowly defeating incumbent senator Robert Larson, she resigned. At this press conference, Kirsten acknowledged that some of the statements she made during her final political debate with Larson were inaccurate. Thus, while Kirsten's allegations will be sufficient to survive motions to dismiss under California's anti-SLAPP statute (CAL. C.C.P. § 425.16) and FED. R. CIV. P. 12(b)(6), the discovery process will determine her likelihood of success at trial.

STATEMENT OF FACTS

A graduate of Stanford University, the University of California-Berkeley School of Law, and formerly a partner at Jones, Davis, Bartlett, and Strom, LLP, Kirsten entered public life by challenging incumbent Robert Larson for one of California's senate seats. Based on her political views and public acknowledgement of prior alcohol and substance abuse, Kirsten was popular with California's voters. Going into their final, nationally televised debate at the Shrine Auditorium in Los Angeles, the race was by all accounts a statistical dead heat. As the debate began, the moderator, former Governor Patricia Brown, asked Kirsten the following question: "Ms. Waters, can you talk about your personal struggles, how they have changed your life, and what impact,

---

[22] The standards governing public versus private figures are discussed in Section (E) below.

if any, they may have on you as a United States Senator?"

Kirsten surprised the audience by disclosing that, on August 2, 1994 she was arrested for Driving Under the Influence of Alcohol and possessing a controlled substance. She stated that her decision to "accept responsibility" resulted in a sentence of 30 days in the Palo Alto County Jail, followed by 90 days in a residential treatment facility. Kirsten claimed that this incident led to "the life-changing process of taking my life back," and caused her to appreciate the values of accountability, honesty, and perseverance. Five days later, Kirsten defeated then-incumbent Senator Larson by 314 votes, the closest margin in California's history.

Simon operates a well-known internet blog (www.justtellthetruth.com) dedicated to exposing corruption by public officials. He was friends with Kirsten while they attended Stanford. After watching the debate, Simon posted a scathing message attacking the accuracy of Kirsten's response. He claimed that Kirsten "intentionally lied" about her sentence "to exploit her past for political gain." Simon asserted that Kirsten was never incarcerated in the Palo Alto County Jail, instead receiving a more lenient sentence of 90 days probation and 100 hours of community service. Simon also alleged that Kirsten's residential treatment was in response to a threat by her parents to stop paying Kirsten's undergraduate tuition. Simon produced a letter, allegedly from Kirsten's probation officer, corroborating his statement.

Additionally, Simon asserted that Kirsten had a lengthy affair with another man while engaged to a mutual friend. He claims that Kirsten wrote a letter admitting to the affair. Finally, Simon attacked Kirsten's educational background, saying her admission to the University of California-Berkeley School of Law resulted from special treatment and favoritism. The statement alleges that Kirsten's acceptance was based on her father's status as one of the law school's most generous donors. Simon made additional statements attacking Kirsten's intellectual ability and fitness for public office. They include: "Kirsten was not a good student, and I doubt she has the abilities to effectively serve in any elected capacity," "I also question how Kirsten ever graduated from Berkeley," "Kirsten reluctantly sought treatment only to save herself," and "I can't imagine her passing all of those difficult law school classes without receiving significant help from her family."

Simon's statements were reported by national news media organizations and caused a sharp decline in Kirsten's popularity. One week after the statements were published, Kirsten held a press conference resigning from the United States Senate and acknowledging that some of her statements were inaccurate. Contrary to Simon's assertions, however, Kirsten claimed that she never "intentionally lied," or sought to "mislead the voters of California." Alleging that Simon's statements were "intentionally and maliciously false," Kirsten vowed to pursue all available legal remedies. She subsequently filed a two-count complaint in the United States District Court for the Northern District of California alleging defamation and invasion of privacy. Kirsten is seeking damages in the amount of five-million dollars.

LEGAL DISCUSSION

Defamation is "an invasion of the interest in reputation."[23] *Ringler*, 96 Cal. Rptr. 2d at 148. Under California law, defamation requires: (1) publication; (2) of a false statement; (3) that is defamatory; (4) unprivileged; and (5) has a natural tendency to injure or which causes special damages." *De La Rosa v. City of San Jose*, . . . [2010 Cal. App. Unpub. LEXIS 3504, at *34] (Cal. Ct. App. May 13, 2010) (*quoting* 5 Witkin, SUMMARY OF CAL. LAW. (10th ed. 2005), Torts, § 529, p. 782 (*citing* CAL. CIV. CODE §§ 45, 46)).[24]

A. Publication

There will be no dispute regarding publication.

"Publication, which may be written or oral, is defined as a communication to some third person who understands both the defamatory meaning of the statement and its application to the person to whom reference is made." *Ringler Assocs.*, 96 Cal. Rptr. 2d at 148. The publication "need not be made to a large group; communication to a single individual is sufficient." *Id.* Additionally, "reprinting or recirculating a libelous writing has the same effect as the original publication." *Id.*

On his well-known blog, www.tellthetruth.com, Simon posted a detailed message accusing Kirsten of, among other things, lying about her criminal history, being unfaithful to her fiancée, and lacking the intellectual ability to succeed at Stanford or gain admission to the University of California-Berkeley School of Law. Simon's message was intended to attract attention from a wide audience and undermine the statements Kirsten made during her final debate. The publication element is therefore

---

[23] Defamation is comprised of libel and slander. Under CAL. CIV. CODE § 45, libel is defined as follows:

> [A] false and unprivileged publication by writing, printing, picture, effigy, or other fixed representation to the eye, which exposes any person to hatred, contempt, ridicule, or obloquy, or which causes him to be shunned or avoided, or which has a tendency to injure him in his occupation.

CAL. CIV. CODE § 46 defines slander as follows:

> A false and unprivileged publication, orally uttered, and also communications by radio or any mechanical or other means which:
> 1. Charges any person with crime, or with having been indicted, convicted, or punished for crime;
> 2. Imputes in him the present existence of an infectious, contagious, or loathsome disease;
> 3. Tends directly to injure him in respect to his office, profession, trade or business, either by imputing to him general disqualification in those respects which the office or other occupation peculiarly requires, or by imputing something with reference to his office, profession, trade, or business that has a natural tendency to lessen its profits;
> 4. Imputes to him impotence or a want of chastity; or
> 5. Which, by natural consequence, causes actual damage.

Here, because the alleged defamatory statements were written on an Internet blog, they are governed by CAL. CIV. CODE § 45.

[24] CAL. CIV. CODE § 48a provides that "in any action for damages for the publication of a libel in a newspaper, or of a slander by radio broadcast, plaintiff shall recover no more than special damages unless a correction be demanded and be not published or broadcast." Here, the alleged defamatory statements were made on an Internet blog created by a private individual, thus rendering § 48a inapplicable.

satisfied.

B. A False Statement — The Fact versus Opinion Distinction

Many of the statements are provably false.

Statements can only be defamatory if they are "provably false," and a "statement of *fact* rather than opinion." *Ringler*, 96 Cal. Rptr. 2d at 149 (emphasis in original). Courts use a "totality of the circumstances" test when determining if a statement is actionable fact or non-actionable opinion. *McGarry v. Univ. of San Diego*, 64 Cal. Rptr. 3d at 479. Both the language and context within which the statement was made are relevant in determining whether "a reasonable fact finder could conclude that the published statements imply a provably false factual assertion." *Id.*; *see also Copp v. Paxton*, 52 Cal. Rptr. 2d 831, 838 (Cal. Ct. App. 1996). Importantly, "editorial context is regarded by the courts as a powerful element in construing as opinion what might otherwise be deemed fact." *Ferlauto v. Hamsher*, 88 Cal. Rptr. 2d 843, 849 (Cal. Ct. App. 1999) (*quoting Morningstar, Inc. v. Superior Court*, 29 Cal. Rptr. 2d 547, 556 (Cal. Ct. App. 1994)).

Comments that are "broad, unfocused, and wholly subjective" constitute non-actionable opinion. *Fletcher v. San Jose Mercury News*, 264 Cal. Rptr. 699, 709 (Cal. Ct. App. 1989). For example, "shady practitioner," "crook," "crooked politician," "creepazoid attorney" and "loser wannabe lawyer" are not actionable. *Copp*, 52 Cal. Rptr. 2d at 837 (*quoting Lewis v. Time, Inc.*, 710 F.2d 549, 554 (9th Cir. 1993)); *Lauderback v. American Broadcasting Companies*, 741 F.2d 193, 195-198 (8th Cir. 1984)).

Similarly, statements calling the plaintiff "the worst teacher at FHS" and a "babbler" are protected opinion because they can be "reasonably understood only 'as a form of exaggerated expression conveying the student-speaker's disapproval of plaintiff's teaching or speaking style.'" *Copp*, 52 Cal. Rptr. 2d at 837–838 (*quoting Moyer v. Amador Valley Joint Union High School Dist.*, 275 Cal. Rptr. 494, 498 (Cal. Ct. App. 1990)). In other words, statements constituting "rhetorical hyperbole," "caricature," "vigorous epithet[s]," "lusty and imaginative expression[s] of . . . contempt," and language used "in a loose, figurative sense" are constitutionally protected. *Nygard, Inc. v. Uusi-Kerttula*, 72 Cal. Rptr. 3d 210, 226 (Cal. Ct. App. 2008) (citations omitted).

An opinion, however, can be actionable "if it implies the allegation of undisclosed defamatory facts as the basis for the opinion." *Id.* (*quoting Okun v. Superior Court*, 175 Cal. Rptr 157, 162 (1981)). The implied defamatory facts "must themselves be true." *Ringler*, 96 Cal. Rptr. 2d at 149; *see also Eisenberg v. Alameda Newspapers, Inc.*, 88 Cal. Rptr. 2d 802, 821 (Cal. Ct. App. 2000). Furthermore, "if those facts are either incorrect or incomplete, or if the person's assessment of them is erroneous, the statement may still imply a false assertion of fact." *Ringler*, 96 Cal. Rptr. 2d at 149. Thus, the dispositive question "is whether a reasonable factfinder could conclude that published statements *imply* an assertion of defamatory *fact*." *Id.* (emphasis in original); *see also Milkovich*, 497 U.S. at 18–20.

Additionally, "[w]here the words . . . are of ambiguous meaning, or innocent on their face and defamatory only in light of extrinsic circumstances, the plaintiff must plead and prove that as used, the words had a particular meaning, or 'innuendo' which makes them defamatory." *Smith*, 85 Cal. Rptr. 2d at 402. Also, "the plaintiff must also allege the extrinsic circumstances which show the third person reasonably understood it in its derogatory sense." *Id.* at 402–403.

Most, but not all, of Simon's statements constitute actionable facts, or opinions implying the assertion of underlying defamatory facts. For example, the statements about Kirsten's criminal history, including the sentence she received, are provably false. At this point, though, it is unclear whether Simon's statements are false. During her press conference, Kirsten acknowledged the she made "inaccurate" and "inconsistent" statements during the debate. She did not, however, discuss how, and to what extent, these statements were inaccurate. Additionally, Simon posted a letter on his blog from Kirsten's probation officer that allegedly corroborates some of the statements. Thus, discovery will determine the truthfulness of both parties' claims. If discovery reveals that Simon's statements are neither true nor substantially true, they will form a valid basis for defamation.

In addition, the statements relating to Kirsten's alleged acts of infidelity are also provably false. Discovery will likely reveal whether Kirsten: (1) was unfaithful while engaged; (2) admitted to having the affair; and (3) drafted a letter containing this admission. The individual with whom Kirsten was allegedly engaged can be identified and provide a first-hand account concerning the circumstances of their relationship. Should discovery reveal that these statements are neither true nor substantially true, they will also form a valid basis for defamation.

Simon's statements regarding Kirsten's intellectual abilities and educational history are only partially actionable. The statements concerning Kirsten's admission to the University of California-Berkeley School of Law are probably actionable because they imply the assertion of underlying, potentially defamatory facts. Simon's statements include "I don't know how she was accepted by the University of California-Berkeley School of Law," "I do know this: her dad is one of Berkeley's most generous donors," and "Kirsten's admission to Berkeley wasn't about merit. It was about favoritism and money." These statements are arguably opinion-based because they express a belief, based on Simon's personal interactions with Kirsten while they attended Stanford, that she possesses neither the qualifications nor skills to attend a law school of University of California-Berkeley's caliber.

Discovery, however, may show that Kirsten's credentials, e.g., undergraduate GPA and Law School Admission test score, justified her admission to Berkeley, and uncover whether, and to what extent, Kirsten's father was a "generous" donor. The University of California-Berkeley may also provide evidence demonstrating that Kirsten's admission was consistent with the qualifications of other admitted students or justified by the totality of her application. Simon may argue, however, that given the complexity of the admissions process — which often extends beyond objective criteria — it is not possible to ascertain whether Kirsten's admission was merit-based. While that may be true, Berkeley's objective criteria — if they show that Kirsten's qualifications were similar to other admitted applications — are likely to support an inference that Simon's assertions were false.

The remaining statements Simon posted include:

- "Kirsten was not a good student, and I doubt she has the abilities to effectively serve in any elected capacity";
- "I also question how Kirsten ever graduated from Berkeley";
- "I am shocked that Kirsten would exploit her past for political gain"; and
- "Kirsten reluctantly sought treatment only to save herself."

These statements are probably not actionable. Although demeaning, the statements are more akin to the types of epithets and exaggerated expressions of contempt, e.g., "crooked politician," "loser wannabe lawyer" that courts have protected. *See Copp*, 52 Cal. Rptr.2d at 837. They reflect personal beliefs based largely upon perception and viewpoint rather than verifiable or provably false facts.

C. Defamatory Statements

A few of Simon's statements may be defamatory *per se*, and several may be defamatory *per quod*.

"Whether a statement is reasonably susceptible to a defamatory interpretation is a question of law for the trial court." *Smith*, 85 Cal. Rptr. 2d at 403. When making this determination, "courts look 'not so much [to the allegedly libelous statement's] effect when subject to the critical analysis of a mind trained in law, but [to] the natural and probable effect upon the mind of the average reader.' " *Ferlauto*, 88 Cal. Rptr. 2d at 849 (*quoting Morningstar*, 29 Cal. Rptr. 2d at 553) (brackets in original).

As a general matter, defamatory statements include those exposing a person "to hatred, contempt, ridicule, or obloquy, or which causes him to be shunned or avoided, or which has a tendency to injure him in his occupation." *McGarry*, 64 Cal. Rptr. 3d at 478 (*quoting* CAL. CIV. CODE § 45).

1. Libel *Per Se*

A statement can also be libelous *per se* "if it contains a charge by implication from the language employed by the speaker and a listener could understand the defamatory meaning without the necessity of knowing extrinsic explanatory matter." *McGarry*, 64 Cal. Rptr. 3d at 478 (*citing MacLeod v. Tribune Publishing Co.*, 52 Cal. 2d 536, 548–550 (1959)). Libel *per se* is present where the statements tend "directly to injure [a person] in respect to his office, profession, trade or business, either by imputing to him general disqualification in those respects which the office or other occupation peculiarly requires, or by imputing something with reference to his office, profession, trade, or business that has a natural tendency to lessen its profit." *McGarry*, 64 Cal. Rptr. 3d at 478 (*quoting* CAL. CIV. CODE § 46).[25] If the statements contain "such a charge directly . . . without the need for explanatory matter, [they] are libelous per se." *McGarry*, 64

---

[25] Although § 46 addresses slander, identical statements made through libelous means are also defamatory as a matter of law. *See Peterson v. Rasmussen*, 47 Cal. App. 694 (1920) (statements imputing that the plaintiff was unchaste are libelous as a matter of law).

Cal. Rptr. 3d at 478 (*citing* CAL. CIV. CODE § 45a).[26] Where a statement is libelous *per se*, general damages are presumed. *See Clark v. McClury*, 215 Cal. 279 (Cal. 1932).

2. Libel *Per Quod*

If the listener "would not recognize the defamatory meaning without 'knowledge of specific facts and circumstances, extrinsic to the publication, [and] which are not matters of common knowledge rationally attributable to all reasonable persons,' the matter is deemed defamatory per *quod*." *McGarry*, 64 Cal. Rptr. 3d at 478–479 (*quoting Barnes-Hind v. Superior Court*, 226 Cal. Rptr. 354 (1986)). Statements that are defamatory *per quod* "require pleading and proof of special damages."

3. Application to *Waters v. Harrison*

Simon's statements about Kirsten's criminal history and alleged infidelity may qualify as libel *per se*. These statements will likely cause injuries relating directly to Kirsten's "office, profession, trade or business" because they can be understood to imply dishonesty, deceit, and deliberate betrayal of the public trust. The statements suggest that Kirsten does not possess the high ethical standards, trustworthiness, and character expected from those who serve the public in a professional or elected capacity. As a result, Simon's statements have the tendency, without requiring extrinsic or explanatory evidence, to prevent or to disqualify Kirsten from pursuing future political opportunities, public-office designations, or the practice of law. At the very least, these statements likely exposed Kirsten to "hatred, contempt, ridicule, or obloquy," thus establishing a cognizable claim for libel *per quod*.

The statements about Kirsten's educational history may qualify as libel *per se* if discovery reveals that Kirsten's credentials warranted her admission to the University of California at Berkeley. This would present a closer question, and will depend upon evidence adduced during discovery. If it is shown that Kirsten's qualifications warranted her admission to the University of California at Berkeley, then the statements that her "admission to Berkeley wasn't about merit," but "favoritism and money," may be libelous *per se*. Among other things, they suggest that Kirsten was given special treatment by admissions officials. Reasonable people could view such conduct as dishonest and unethical, therefore imputing "general disqualification in those respects which the office or other occupation peculiarly requires."[27]

D. The Plaintiff's Status as an All-Purpose Public, Limited-Purpose Public, or Private Figure

Here, Kirsten will be considered a public figure, and thus will be required to prove actual malice.

The level of fault required — negligence or actual malice — depends on the

---

[26] Section 45a provides as follows: "A libel which is defamatory of the plaintiff without the necessity of explanatory matter, such as an inducement, innuendo or other extrinsic fact, is said to be a libel on its face."

[27] CAL. CIV. CODE § 46.

plaintiff's status as an: (1) all-purpose public; (2) limited-purpose public; or (3) private figure. *See McGarry*, 64 Cal. Rptr. 3d at 479–480.

1. The All-Purpose Public Figure

An "all purpose" public figure is an individual "who has 'achiev[ed] such pervasive fame or notoriety that he becomes a public figure for all purposes and in all contexts.' " *Id.* at 479 (*quoting Gertz v. Robert Welch, Inc.*, 418 U.S. 323, 351 (1974)) (brackets in original).

A public figure must show that the alleged defamatory statement was made with actual malice, namely, "knowledge that it was false or with reckless disregard of whether it was false or not.' " *McGarry*, 64 Cal. Rptr. 3d at 480 (*quoting Reader's Digest Ass'n v. Superior Court*, 208 Cal. Rptr. 137, 149 (Cal. 1984)); *see also New York Times Co. v. Sullivan*, 376 U.S. 254, 296 (1964). Actual malice must be shown by clear and convincing evidence, and the evidence must "be of such a character 'as to command the unhesitating assent of every reasonable mind.'" *McGarry*, 64 Cal. Rptr. 3d at 480 (*quoting Rosenaur v. Scherer*, 105 Cal. Rptr. 2d 674, 684 (Cal Ct. App. 2001)).

The actual malice standard "is 'a subjective test, under which the defendant's actual belief concerning the truthfulness of the publication is the crucial issue.' " *Reader's Digest Ass'n*, 208 Cal. Rptr. at 145. That belief must go beyond mere negligence. Thus, having "serious doubts" about the truth of a publication is generally sufficient to establish actual malice. *Copp*, 52 Cal. Rptr. 2d at 844-845 (*quoting St. Amant v. Thompson*, 390 U.S. 727, 731 (1968)). Additionally, the "failure to investigate before publishing, even when a reasonably prudent person would have done so, is not sufficient." *McGarry*, 64 Cal. Rptr. 3d at 480.

Importantly, however, a plaintiff may "attempt to prove reckless disregard for truth by circumstantial evidence." *Copp*, 52 Cal. Rptr. 2d at 845 (*quoting St. Amant*, 390 U.S. at 731). For example, "anger and hostility toward the plaintiff, reliance upon sources known to be unreliable, or known to be biased against the plaintiff . . . may . . . indicate that the publisher himself had serious doubts regarding the truth of his publication." *Id.* In each case, "the evidence must 'permit the conclusion that the defendant actually had a high degree of awareness of . . . probable falsity.' " *McGarry*, 64 Cal. Rptr. 3d at 480 (*quoting Harte-Hanks Communications v. Connaughton*, 491 U.S. 657, 688 (1989)).

Ultimately, it "must fairly be characterized as demonstrating the speaker purpose-fully avoided the truth or deliberately decided not to acquire knowledge of facts that might confirm the probable falsity of charges." *McGarry*, 64 Cal. Rptr. 3d at 480 (*citing Antonovich v. Superior Court*, 285 Cal. Rptr. 863 (Cal. Ct. App. 1991)).

The court will likely determine that Kirsten is a public figure. Kirsten's senatorial campaign attracted national media attention in part because her personal story was viewed by many "as a source of inspiration and hope." Kirsten was a popular political candidate — her final debate with Senator Larson occurred before a sold-out crowd and nationally televised audience. Kirsten's victory over Senator Larson was also noteworthy because the margin of victory (314 votes) was the closest in California's history. Based upon these facts, Kirsten achieved the type of "pervasive fame and notoriety" to justify her status a public figure. *See McGarry*, 64 Cal. Rptr. 3d at 479.

2. The Limited-Purpose Public Figure

To be characterized as a limited-purpose or "vortex" public figure, "there must be a public controversy, which means the issue was debated publicly and had foreseeable and substantial ramifications for nonparticipants." *Gilbert v. Sykes*, 53 Cal. Rptr. 3d 752, 762 (Cal. Ct. App. 2007). An individual "must have undertaken some voluntary act through which he or she sought to influence resolution of the public issue." *Id.* This requirement is satisfied where the plaintiff "attempts to thrust him or herself in the public eye." *Id.* Professional and collegiate athletes, for example, are limited-purpose public figures. *See McGarry*, 64 Cal. Rptr. 3d at 481.

Furthermore, in the limited-purpose public figure context, the alleged defamation "must be germane to the plaintiff's participation in the controversy." *Gilbert*, 53 Cal. Rptr. 3d at 762 (*quoting Ampex Corp. v. Cargle*, 27 Cal. Rptr. 3d 863, 871 (Cal. Ct. App. 2005)). Unlike "the 'all-purpose' public figure, the 'limited purpose' public figure loses certain protection for his [or her] reputation only to the extent that the alleged defamatory communication relates to his role [or her] in a public controversy." *McGarry*, 64 Cal. Rptr. 3d at 480 (*quoting Reader's Digest Assn.*, 208 Cal. Rptr. at 142). A limited-purpose public figure is required, however, to show actual malice by clear and convincing evidence. *Gilbert*, 53 Cal. Rptr. 3d at 763.

At the very least, Kirsten is a limited-purpose public figure. By campaigning for elected office at the national level and sharing deeply personal details about her private life, Kirsten thrust herself into the public eye. The fact is underscored by the notoriety Kirsten and the campaign attracted. Ultimately, though, Kirsten's classification as an all-public or limited-purpose public figure is of limited significance because either designation requires a showing of actual malice.

3. Private Figures

Private figures need only show that a defendant was negligent when publishing the alleged defamatory statement. *Khawar v. Globe Intern, Inc.*, 79 Cal. Rptr. 2d 178, 190 (Cal. 1998). The standard is whether "a reasonably prudent person would have published, or would have investigated before publishing, the defamatory statement." *McGarry*, 64 Cal. Rptr. 3d at 480. A plaintiff cannot, however, recover presumed or punitive damages in a defamation action without proving actual malice. *See Wilbanks v. Wolk*, 17 Cal. Rptr. 3d 497, 512 (Cal. Ct. App. 2004).

Kirsten will not be considered a private figure.

E. Damages

If Simon's statements are proven false, Kirsten will be able to prove damages.

CAL. CIV. CODE § 48a establishes three categories of damages: (1) general; (2) special; and (3) exemplary. General damages are defined as "damages for loss of reputation, shame, mortification and hurt feelings." *Id.* Special damages are "all damages which plaintiff alleges and proves that he has suffered in respect to his property, business, trade, profession or occupation, including such amounts of money as the plaintiff alleges and proves he has expended as a result of the alleged libel, and no other." *Id.*

Exemplary damages are "damages which may in the discretion of the court or jury be recovered in addition to general and special damages for the sake of example and by way of punishing a defendant who has made the publication or broadcast with actual malice." *Id.* General damages, however, are presumed where a publication is deemed libelous *per se*. As such, proof of special damages is not required. *Clark v. McClurg*, 215 Cal. 279, 284 (Cal. 1932); *Di Giorgio Fruit Corp. v. American Federation of Labor and Congress of Indus. Organizations*, 30 Cal. Rptr. 350, 355 (Cal. Ct. App. 1963) (*citing* CAL. CIV. CODE § 45a).

If Simon's statements are deemed libelous *per se*, Kirsten will not have to prove special damages. Should a court construe the statements as libel *per quod*, Kirsten can produce credible extrinsic evidence demonstrating that the statements were injurious. For example, after Simon posted the comments, they became national news and ultimately forced Kirsten to resign only one week after winning the election. The public humiliation and reputational damage Kirsten suffered may permanently jeopardize her chances of becoming a viable candidate for public office. Additionally, if Kirsten returns to the legal profession, her ability to gain the trust of prospective employers or clients may be compromised. Exemplary damages may also be available if Kirsten can prove, through direct or circumstantial evidence, that Simon knew his statements were false or entertained sufficient doubts to support a finding of actual malice.

F. Defenses

1. Truth

If Simon can prove that his statements were true, it will be a complete defense to the defamation claim.

"In all cases of defamation, whether libel or slander, the truth of the offensive statements or communication is a complete defense against civil liability, regardless of bad faith or malicious purpose." *Ringler*, 96 Cal. Rptr. 2d at 149; *see also Campanelli v. Regents of University of California*, 51 Cal. Rptr. 2d 891, 897 (Cal. Ct. App. 1996). Furthermore, "if the statements are not defamatory on their face but are capable of a defamatory meaning imputed by innuendo,[28] the defendant must demonstrate the truth of the statements in that sense in which the plaintiff's innuendo explains them. *Id.* In either situation, the defendant bears the burden of pleading and proving the

---

[28] An innuendo is required "where the words used are susceptible of either a defamatory or an innocent interpretation." Additionally, "when the offending language is susceptible of an innocent interpretation, it is not actionable *per se*, but, in addition to an innuendo, it is necessary for the plaintiff to allege special damages by reason of the meaning gained from the publication." *Smith*, 85 Cal. Rptr.2d at 403, n.4.

truthfulness of a particular statement. *Smith*, 85 Cal. Rptr. 2d at 403.[29]

A defendant is not, however, required to prove the literal truth of every word contained in the allegedly defamatory statement. Id. It is sufficient for the defendant to prove, despite slight inaccuracies in the statement, that "the *substance* of the charge . . . so long as the imputation is substantially true so as to justify the 'gist or sting' of the remark." *Id. (quoting Campanelli*, 51 Cal. Rptr. 2d at 897).

If Simon establishes that the statements were true, Kirsten cannot prevail. While she has already acknowledged making inaccurate statements concerning her criminal history, Kirsten has not specified the nature of these inaccuracies. Thus, discovery will be needed to corroborate or disprove the truthfulness of Simon's claim.

2. Privilege

CAL. CIV. CODE § 47 sets forth several privileges protecting otherwise-defamatory statements: (1) made in the proper discharge of an official duty; (2) occurring in judicial, legislative, or other proceedings authorized by law (the "litigation" privilege);[30] (3) between individuals with a shared interest, provided the communications are made without malice (the "common interest" privilege);[31] (4) constituting fair and true reports to a public journal of matters discussed in judicial, legislative, or other public proceedings, including verifiable charges or complaints made against public officials (the "fair reporting" or "fair comment" privilege); and (5) concerning lawfully convened public meetings or matters beneficial to the public. *Id.* at § 47(a–e). California has not adopted the "neutral reportage" privilege, which protects the "accurate and disinterested reporting" of "serious charges made against public officials by a respectable, prominent organization." *Khawar v. Globe Intern, Inc.*, 79 Cal. Rptr. 2d 178, 186 (Cal. 1998) (*quoting Edwards v. National Audubon Society, Inc.*, 556 F.2d 113, 120 (2d Cir. 1977), *cert. denied* 434 U.S. 1002 (1977)).

Although the "common interest" privilege protects "communications made in good faith on a subject in which the speaker and hearer shared an interest or duty," it does not create "any broad news media privilege." *Lundquist v. Reusser*, 31 Cal. Rptr. 2d 776, 783–784 (Cal. Ct. App. 1994); *see also Brown v. Kelly Broadcasting Co.*, 257 Cal. Rptr.708, 752 (Cal. 1989) (refusing to expand the common interest privilege into a "public interest" privilege because it would, as a practical matter, "mean that everything they [the news media] publish would be a matter of "public interest" and therefore privileged.") (brackets in original). For purposes of this privilege, the parties must have "a contractual, business or similar relationship, such as 'between partners, corporate officers and members of incorporated associations,' or between 'union members [and] union officers.' " *Kashian v. Harriman*, 120 Cal. Rptr. 2d 576, 593 (Cal.

---

[29] In actions by private individuals concerning matters of public concern the plaintiff bears the burden of proving falsity. *Lipman v. Brisbane Elementary School Dist.*, 11 Cal. Rptr. 97 (1961).

[30] This privilege is absolute, providing protection even if the statements were made with actual malice. *See Beroiz v. Wahl*, 100 Cal. Rptr. 2d 905, 909 (Cal. Ct. App 2000).

[31] The common interest privilege is usually described as qualified or conditional, meaning it can be overcome by a showing of actual malice. *See Kashian v. Harriman*, 120 Cal. Rptr. 2d 576, 594 (Cal. Ct. App. 2002).

Ct. App. 2002) (*quoting Rancho La Costa, Inc. v. Superior Court*, 165 Cal. Rptr. 347, 347-348 (Cal. Ct. App. 1980)).

Simon's statements are not privileged. The statements were made on his personal blog and not in the performance of any official duty. They did not occur in a judicial or legislative proceeding, between any individual with a shared interest, and were never communicated to a public journal. Finally, the debate was not a "lawfully convened" public meeting, and no cases exist holding that political debates involve matters beneficial to the public. Simon will base his defense on truth, as evidenced by the statement on his blog: "I will have an airtight defense: it's the whole truth and nothing but the truth."

3. The Anti-SLAPP Statute (Strategic Lawsuits Against Public Participation)

Kirsten will survive a motion to dismiss based on California's anti-SLAPP statute.

Under California's anti-SLAPP law, "[a] cause of action against a person arising from any act of that person in furtherance of the person's right of petition or free speech under the United States or California Constitution in connection with a public issue shall be subject to a special motion to strike, unless the court determines that the plaintiff has established that there is a probability that the plaintiff will prevail on the claim." *McGarry*, 64 Cal. Rptr. 3d at 475 (*quoting* CAL. C.C.P. § 425.16 (b)(1)) (brackets in original). The anti-SLAPP statute is intended to "encourage participation in matters of public significance by allowing a court to promptly dismiss unmeritorious actions or claims brought to chill another's valid exercise of the constitutional rights of freedom of speech and petition for the redress of grievances." *McGarry*, 64 Cal. Rptr. 3d at 475 (*quoting* CAL. C.C.P. § 425.16(a)).

A two-step process is used to determine whether a claim is subject to the anti-SLAPP statute. First, "the defendant bringing an anti-SLAPP motion must make a prima facie showing that the plaintiff's suit is subject to section 425.16 by showing the defendant's challenged acts were taken in furtherance of his or her constitutional rights of petition or free speech in connection with a public issue, as defined by the statute." *McGarry*, 64 Cal. Rptr. 3d at 475. If a defendant satisfies this standard, "the burden shifts to the plaintiff to demonstrate there is a reasonable probability he or she will prevail on the merits at trial." *Id.* The plaintiff must show "both that the claim is legally sufficient and there is admissible evidence that, if credited, would be sufficient to sustain a favorable judgment." *Id.*

Courts analyze "the legal sufficiency of and evidentiary support for the pleaded claims, and . . . whether there are any constitutional or nonconstitutional defenses to the pleaded claims and, if so, whether there is evidence to negate any such defenses." *Id.* at 476. A court, however, "cannot weigh the evidence," but must "simply determine whether the plaintiff's evidence would, if credited, be sufficient to meet the burden of proof." *Id.* As such, an "anti-SLAPP-suit motion is not a vehicle for testing the strength of a plaintiff's case, or the ability of a plaintiff, so early in the proceedings, to produce evidence supporting each theory of damages asserted in connection with the plaintiff's claims." *Wilbanks*, 17 Cal. Rptr. 3d at 513. It merely determines whether a plaintiff, "through a showing of minimal merit, has stated and substantiated a legally sufficient claim." *Id.*

Simon will not prevail on an anti-SLAPP motion. He published various comments that are provably false, unprivileged and, if untrue, may constitute libel *per se*. Credible arguments can be made regarding special and even exemplary damages, and circumstantial evidence likely exists to support a showing of actual malice. In other words, Kirsten's claim has "minimal merit" and will survive an anti-SLAPP motion.

CONCLUSION

Under California law, the statements Simon posted on www.justtellthetruth.com are provably false and may support a finding of libel *per se*. Kirsten's defamation claim will survive motions under the anti-SLAPP statute and Fed. R. Civ. P. 12(b)(6). Evidence adduced during discovery may reveal the statements to be false, defamatory, injurious, and the product of actual malice.

*   *   *   *   *

MEMORANDUM REGARDING INVASION OF PRIVACY UNDER CALIFORNIA LAW

MEMORANDUM

TO:	Partner
FROM:	Associate
RE:	California invasion of privacy for disclosure of criminal history
FILE:	*Waters*

QUESTIONS PRESENTED

Whether Waters can maintain an action for invasion of privacy against Harrison under either California tort law or the California constitution for Harrison's disclosure of Waters' criminal history?

BRIEF ANSWER

Waters is unlikely to succeed on her claims for invasion of privacy. In order to maintain a tort action for invasion of privacy under California law, a plaintiff must prove: (1) the defendant made a public disclosure; (2) of a private fact; (3) the disclosure would be objectionable to a reasonable person; and (4) the fact disclosed is not of legitimate public concern (i.e., is not newsworthy).

Harrison's disclosure was undoubtedly public and likely would be objectionable to a reasonable person. However, information contained in criminal records generally is not considered private because the information is available to the public. Furthermore, most any information that bears on a political candidate's credibility or fitness for office is considered newsworthy and of public concern. Several California courts have addressed this very issue and concluded that a political candidate's criminal history is newsworthy. Therefore, Waters likely cannot maintain an action against Harrison for invasion of privacy under California tort law.

The California constitution also protects individuals' privacy. A plaintiff may maintain a cause of action for invasion of privacy under the California constitution if: (1) the plaintiff had a legally protected interest in the information disclosed; (2) the plaintiff had a reasonable expectation of privacy in the information disclosed; and (3) the defendant's conduct constituted a serious invasion of privacy. As outlined above, Waters likely did not have a reasonable expectation of privacy in the information contained in her criminal history records because those records are available to the public. Likewise, Harrison's disclosure likely did not constitute a serious invasion of privacy because a person who runs for public office opens herself up to scrutiny, and information that bears on the candidate's fitness for office is considered valuable to the public. Thus, Waters likely cannot maintain a cause of action against Harrison for invasion of privacy under the California constitution.

FACTUAL BACKGROUND

Waters, a Stanford University and Berkeley Law graduate and lawyer, decided to run against incumbent Senator Ted Larson for one of California's two United States senate seats. Waters' personal story about overcoming drug and alcohol addiction, along with her promises to represent the interests of all Californians, made her a popular candidate. Waters and Larson were in a statistical dead heat when the two participated in a final debate.

During that debate, Waters talked about her past struggles with alcohol and prescription drug abuse. Waters detailed her arrest in 1994 for DUI and possession of a controlled substance. She described the incident as a "wake-up call." Waters told voters that as a result of her arrest, she was ordered to serve 30 days in jail and 90 days at a residential treatment facility. She explained that her arrest changed her life, and she learned accountability, hard work, and perseverance as a result.

After the debate, Simon Harrison, who attended Stanford with Waters, made a post on his blog, www.justtellthetruth.com, in which he claimed that Waters was:

> [N]either incarcerated nor ordered to spend even a single day in a residential treatment program. After pleading guilty, Kirsten was sentenced to 90 days probation and 100 hours of community service. Additionally, as part of the plea deal, the controlled substance charge was dropped. Kirsten only sought residential treatment because her parents threatened to stop paying her tuition at Stanford.

Harrison also made other statements about Waters' educational background and her relationship with a former fiancé. Those statements are not relevant to Waters' claim for invasion of privacy and, therefore, are not discussed in detail here.

Several days after the debate, Harrison posted a letter Waters received from her probation officer, dated November 10, 1994. The letter stated, in part:

Dear Kirsten:

As you know, the court sentenced you to a probation term of 90 days, and 100 hours of community service. Having complied fully with these responsibilities, your sentence is hereby complete and this matter now concluded.

*   *   *   *   *

One week after the election, Waters admitted that the information contained in the November 10, 1994 letter was accurate and that some of her statements about her 1994 arrest and prosecution were "inconsistent with the facts." Waters further claimed that she never intentionally lied or misled California voters, but she resigned from her Senate seat under mounting pressure from voters and her political party.

LEGAL DISCUSSION

A. Tortious Invasion of Privacy

The first issue in this matter is whether Waters can state a claim against Harrison for tortious invasion of privacy under California law. A plaintiff states a cause of action for wrongful disclosure of private information, a tort of invasion of privacy, when the plaintiff alleges: (1) public disclosure; (2) of a private fact; (3) the disclosure of which would be offensive and objectionable to a reasonable person; and (4) the fact is not newsworthy or of legitimate public concern. *Shulman v. Group W Productions, Inc.*, 18 Cal. 4th 200, 214 (1998) (citation omitted).

The first and third elements do not appear to be in dispute here. A public disclosure is one that is made to the public generally or to a large group of people. *Kinsey v. Macur*, 107 Cal. App. 3d 265, 270 (1980). Harrison's disclosure about Waters' criminal history was made on a website available to anyone with an Internet connection and apparently was viewed by many people. Thus, it appears the first element of public disclosure is met.

Additionally, the third element is satisfied where the disclosure is one that would be objectionable to a reasonable person of ordinary sensibilities. *Gill v. Hearst Pub. Co.*, 40 Cal. 2d 224, 229 (1953). Such a disclosure is one that goes beyond the normal limits of decency so that the defendant should have known that the disclosure would be offensive to the plaintiff. *Id.* There does not appear to be a dispute that Harrison's disclosure of Waters' criminal history likely would be objectionable to a reasonable person in Waters' shoes and, therefore, the third element is satisfied. Thus, the dispositive questions are whether the information disclosed was private and whether the information disclosed was newsworthy.

1. Private Fact

In order to state a claim for tortious invasion of privacy, the fact disclosed must have been a private one. There can be no wrongful disclosure where the fact is known or the information is available to the public. *Sipple v. Chronicle Publishing Co.*, 154 Cal. App. 3d 1040, 1046 (1984). Facts that are a matter of public record or available to the public are not private. *Green v. Uccelli*, 207 Cal. App. 3d 1112, 1120 (1990) (information contained in documents filed in divorce action were not private); *Bradshaw v. City of Los Angeles*, 221 Cal. App. 3d 908, 922 (1990) (information disclosed at public hearing was not private) (overruled on other grounds).

No cause of action will lie where the disclosure merely increases the degree of publicity of a previously public fact. *Sipple*, 154 Cal. App. 3d at 1047 (disclosure of plaintiff's homosexuality to general public was not actionable where plaintiff was well-known member of San Francisco gay community). And information on criminal charges and judicial proceedings is not private. *Wasser v. San Diego Union*, 191 Cal. App. 3d 1455, 1462 (1987) (information about teacher's prior arrest, trial, and acquittal for murder were public).

The information about Waters' criminal history disclosed by Harrison likely was not private. Under *Wasser* and *Green*, information available in public records, such as information contained in arrest and police records, is not private. Whether the information Harrison disclosed about Waters' criminal history was public record is unclear; however, Waters' criminal records likely are part of the public record. She incurred charges as an adult, and there is nothing to suggest that her record was sealed or otherwise withheld from the public. Thus, so long as the information about Waters' criminal charges and sentence was available in public records, that information was not private, and Waters likely cannot maintain a cause of action against Harrison for invasion of privacy.

2. Not of Legitimate Public Concern

If the information disclosed by the defendant is truthful and newsworthy, the plaintiff's claim for invasion of privacy is also barred. *Shulman*, 18 Cal. 4th at 215; *Wasser v. San Diego Union*, 191 Cal. App. 3d 1455, 1460 (1987). The newsworthiness analysis involves a balancing of First Amendment interests and each individual's interest in personal privacy. *Id.* Where the disclosure is logically related to a newsworthy subject and is not disproportionately intrusive, the information disclosed will be deemed to be of a legitimate public concern. *Id.* Conversely, where the disclosure is nothing more than a "morbid and sensational prying into private lives" (*quoting Virgil v. Time, Inc.*, 527 F.2d 1122, 1129 (9th Cir. 1975)) and serves no legitimate public interest, a cause of action will lie. *Id.* at 1462.

a. Newsworthiness

Stories about criminal charges and criminal and civil judicial proceedings are generally considered newsworthy, even when disclosed years after the charges were filed or the proceedings occurred. *Wasser*, 191 Cal. App. 3d at 1462. "The revival of past events that once were news, can properly be a matter of present public interest." *Id.* "Publishers are permitted to satisfy the curiosity of the public as to its heroes, leaders, villains and victims, and those who are closely associated with them." *Id.*

In determining whether a fact is newsworthy, the courts consider numerous factors including the social value of the facts disclosed, the depth of intrusion into the private affairs of another, and the extent to which the plaintiff's own conduct put the plaintiff in a position of public notoriety. *Kapellas v. Kofman*, 1 Cal. 3d 20, 30–36 (1969). When a person becomes involuntarily involved in a newsworthy event, not all aspects of the person's life are newsworthy; only those facts that bear some relationship to the event that made the plaintiff newsworthy are of legitimate public concern. *Id.* at 223–24. A line must be drawn "when the publicity ceases to be the giving of information to which the public is entitled, and becomes a morbid and sensational prying into private lives for its own sake, with which a reasonable member of the public, with decent standards, would say that he had no concern." *Sipple*, 154 Cal. App. 3d at 1049 (citation omitted).

When analyzing newsworthiness, the courts employ a type of sliding scale, balancing the impact of the intrusion with the value of the information disclosed. Where the social value of the disclosure is minimal but the intrusion is only slight, no cause of action will generally stand. Conversely, where the value of the disclosed information is substantial, the courts will tolerate a greater intrusion, particularly where the plaintiff became a public figure voluntarily. *Kapellas*, 1 Cal. 3d at 37. If the fact disclosed concerns an event that occurred in the past, the court must consider whether there is continued public interest in the fact disclosed. *Id.* at 38; *Forsher v. Bugliosi*, 26 Cal. 3d 792, 812 (1980). The plaintiff has the burden of proving a disclosure was not newsworthy. *Diaz v. Oakland Tribune, Inc.*, 139 Cal. App. 3d 118, 128 (1983).

b. The Plaintiff's Status

When a voluntary public figure, such as a political candidate, is the topic of a publication, "the authorized publicity is not limited to the event that itself arouses public interest, and to some reasonable extent includes publicity given to facts about the individual that would otherwise be purely private." *Id.* at 1463. The California courts have suggested that in some cases, a person may attain a position "of such persuasive power and influence" that the person will be considered a public figure "for all purposes." *Kinsey v. Macur*, 107 Cal. App. 3d 265, 273. (1980).

Public officials and those running for public office "have almost always been considered the paradigm case of public figures who should be subjected to the most thorough scrutiny." *Kapellas*, 1 Cal. 3d at 36. Because of the responsibilities of elected officials, "the public must, of course, be afforded the opportunity of learning about any facet of a candidate's life that may relate to his fitness for office." *Id.* at 36–37. As a result, the press may publish "all information that may cast light on a candidate's qualifications," and the public is "permitted to determine importance or relevance of the reported facts for itself." *Id.* at 37.

For example, in *Kapellas*, a newspaper urged the public not to cast votes for the plaintiff, a candidate for city council, suggesting she was a bad mother because her children had several run-ins with local police. *Id.* at 27. The plaintiff brought suit, alleging the newspaper invaded her privacy by publicly disclosing private facts about her family. *Id.* at 26.

The California Court of Appeals held the plaintiff could not maintain an action against the newspaper for invasion of privacy. *Id.* at 34. The court first addressed the newsworthiness prong, concluding that the information reported by the paper was newsworthy because "the candidacy of the children's mother . . . rendered [the children's] past behavior significant and newsworthy." *Id.* at 39. Furthermore, the court held that the disclosed information was not private because the newspaper only disclosed incidents which had been recorded on the police blotter and were, therefore, already public. *Id.* at 38. Thus, the plaintiff had no claim for invasion of privacy against the newspaper. *Id.* at 39; *see also Matson v. Dvorak*, 40 Cal. App. 4th 539 (1995) (information about political candidate's outstanding parking fines was of legitimate public concern); *Beruan v. French*, 56 Cal. App. 3d 825 (1976) (candidate's prior criminal convictions newsworthy); *Alim v. Superior Court*, 185 Cal. App. 3d 144 (1986) (public official's receipt of improper VA benefits was matter of public concern); *but see Diaz v. Oakland Tribune, Inc.*, 139 Cal. App. 3d 118 (1993) (student council member's status as transsexual not newsworthy because it bore no relevance to her fitness for office).

The information about Waters' criminal history that Harrison disclosed almost certainly was newsworthy. As a candidate for political office, Waters voluntarily subjected herself to public scrutiny. Because Waters was a political candidate, any information that might cast light on her qualifications for political office would be newsworthy under *Matson, Beruan*, and *Kapellas*, where the California Supreme Court held that even the criminal history of a political candidate's children was newsworthy. This case is distinguishable from *Diaz*. Unlike *Diaz*, where the disclosure of the plaintiff's status as a transsexual bore no relevance to her fitness for office, information about Waters' criminal history and information that suggests Waters might be untruthful is relevant to her qualifications for office. Thus, the information disclosed by Harrison is almost certainly newsworthy.

Additionally, this not a case where Harrison was the first person to disclose to the public that Waters previously had brushes with the law. Waters herself made her past criminal history an issue in her campaign. She represented to her potential constituents that she had been ordered to serve time in jail and in a treatment facility as a result of the criminal charges filed against her. In fact, she had not been ordered to serve jail time or time in a residential treatment facility. The true facts about Waters' criminal history, which contradicted her representations about that history, were newsworthy as they bore on her honesty, credibility, and fitness for office. Therefore, Waters likely cannot prove Harrison disclosed non-newsworthy facts. Thus, Waters likely cannot maintain a cause of action against Harrison for tortious invasion of privacy under California law.

B. Invasion of Privacy under the California Constitution

The second issue in this case is whether Waters can state a claim against Harrison for invasion of privacy under the California Constitution. The California Constitution guarantees individuals a right to privacy. California Constitution, article I, § I. A private cause of action exists for a violation of an individual's constitutionally protected privacy interest. *Heller v. Norcal Mut. Ins. Co.*, 8 Cal. 4th 30, 43 (1994). The right to privacy under the California Constitution protects "the individual's *reasonable* expectation of privacy against a serious violation." *Sheehan v. San Francisco 49ers, Ltd.*, 45

Cal. 4th 992, 998 (2009) (emphasis in original). The right to privacy under the California Constitution "has repeatedly been construed to provide California citizens with privacy protections broader than those recognized by the federal Constitution." *Jeffrey H. v. Imai, Tadlock & Keeney*, 85 Cal. App. 4th 345, 353 (2000).

In order to state a cause of action for invasion of privacy under the California constitution, the plaintiff must prove: (1) the plaintiff had a legally protected interest in the information disclosed; (2) the plaintiff had a reasonable expectation of privacy with respect to the information disclosed; and (3) the defendant's conduct constituted a serious invasion of privacy. *Id.* The courts must weigh the defendant's justification for the disclosure with the seriousness of the invasion of privacy. *Loder v. City of Glendale*, 14 Cal. 4th 846, 893 (1997). No cause of action will stand if a defendant negates any of the three elements or proves the invasion was "justified because it substantively furthers one or more countervailing interests." *Sheehan*, 45 Cal. 4th at 998.

1. Legally Protected Interest

The right to be "let alone" must be balanced against the disclosure of information "consistent with the democratic processes under the constitutional guarantees of freedom of speech and of the press." *Gill*, 40 Cal. 2d at 228. Whether the plaintiff has a protected interest in the information disclosed is a question of law. *Life Tech. Corp. v. Superior Court*, 197 Cal. App. 4th 640, 651 (2011).

2. Reasonable Expectation of Privacy

In determining whether the plaintiff had a reasonable expectation of privacy in the information disclosed, courts must consider "the actual circumstances of disclosure." *Jeffrey H.*, 85 Cal. App. 4th at 354. Where a person's life has "ceased to be private," no cause of action for invasion of privacy will stand. *Gill*, 40 Cal. 2d at 229. Whether a plaintiff had a reasonable expectation of privacy in the information disclosed is an objective standard based on widely accepted community norms. *Sheehan v. San Francisco 49ers, Ltd.*, 45 Cal. 4th at 1000. The expectation of privacy "must be objectively reasonable under the circumstances, especially in light of the competing social interests involved." *Id.* Courts properly consider "customs, practices, and physical settings surrounding particular activities" to determine whether the plaintiff had a reasonable expectation of privacy in the information disclosed. *Jeffrey H.*, 85 Cal. App. 4th at 354. The issue of whether the plaintiff had a reasonable expectation of privacy in the information disclosed is a mixed question of law and fact. *Life Tech.*, 197 Cal. App. 4th at 651.

3. Serious Invasion of Privacy

To be actionable under the California constitution, the invasion of privacy must be serious in nature, scope, and actual or potential impact to "constitute an egregious breach of the social norms underlying the privacy right." *Jeffrey H.*, 85 Cal. App. 4th at 355. The question of whether the invasion was serious is a mixed question of law and fact. *Life Tech.*, 197 Cal. App. 4th at 651.

The analysis of Waters' constitutional invasion of privacy claim is similar to that of her claim for tortious invasion of privacy. As was the case with her claim sounding in tort, Waters also likely cannot maintain a cause of action against Harrison for invasion of privacy under the California constitution. As outlined above, Waters likely did not have either a legally protected interest or a reasonable expectation of privacy in the information about her criminal history. The criminal charges filed against Waters and the adjudication of those charges almost certainly was a matter of public record.

Further, Harrison's disclosure likely did not constitute a serious invasion of Waters' privacy. When Waters decided to run for public office, her life "ceased to be private" and she subjected herself to scrutiny — including scrutiny about her credibility. Waters herself disclosed to the public that she had a criminal history but apparently misrepresented the punishment she received, perhaps in an attempt to garner public support and sympathy. It appears Waters was not completely truthful about her past, and Harrison's disclosure of the truth of Waters' criminal history likely did not constitute a serious invasion of Waters' privacy, particularly in light of her status as a candidate for political office. Thus, Waters likely cannot maintain a cause of action against Harrison for invasion of privacy under the California constitution.

CONCLUSION

Waters is unlikely to be able to prove invasion of privacy under either California tort law or the California Constitution. To maintain a tort claim for invasion of privacy under California law, Waters must prove that Harrison made a public disclosure of a private fact, that the disclosure would be objectionable to a reasonable person, and that the fact disclosed is not newsworthy.

It appears undisputed that Harrison's disclosure of information about Waters' criminal history was public and likely would be objectionable to a reasonable person. Waters, however, cannot satisfy the other elements of a claim for tortious invasion of privacy because information contained in criminal records, which are generally available to the public, is not private. Further, information that bears on a political candidate's fitness for office, including information about a candidate's criminal history, is newsworthy. Waters, therefore, likely cannot maintain an action against Harrison for invasion of privacy under California tort law.

Waters also likely cannot prove invasion of privacy under the California Constitution. To maintain such a claim, she would need to prove that she had a legally protected interest in the information Harrison disclosed, that she had a reasonable expectation of privacy with respect to that information, and that Harrison's disclosure constituted a serious invasion of her privacy. Waters likely cannot have had a reasonable expectation of privacy in the information contained in her criminal history records both because those records are available to the public and because Waters herself disclosed her criminal history to voters and should have expected that someone might attempt to verify her representations. Additionally, Harrison's disclosure likely did not constitute a serious invasion of Waters' privacy. A person who runs for public office is subject to public scrutiny, and information that bears on the candidate's fitness for office is considered valuable to the public. Therefore, Waters likely cannot maintain a cause of action against Harrison for invasion of privacy under the California constitution. Thus, it appears both of Waters' causes of action for invasion of privacy will fail.

* * * * *

Why is the invasion of privacy memo effective?

▶ *The Question Presented.* In the Question Presented, the author sets forth the relevant legal issues (invasion of privacy under California tort law and the California Constitution) and previews the relevant facts (disclosure of information about Waters' criminal history). The Question Presented is specific enough to let the reader know the basic issues without being overly wordy, ambiguous, or confusing.

▶ *The Brief Answer.* The author answers the Question Presented in a complete sentence: Waters is unlikely to succeed on her claims for invasion of privacy. The author then lists the four elements of the claim under California tort law, notes that two of the elements are not in dispute, outlines the law with respect to the two elements that are in dispute, and explains why Waters can't satisfy the two disputed elements. The author then outlines the elements of Waters' claim under the California constitution and explains why Waters cannot satisfy at least two of those elements either. After reviewing the Brief Answer, the reader knows: (1) the applicable law; (2) the operative facts; and (3) whether the claim likely will succeed.

▶ *The Statement of Facts.* The facts are outlined objectively. The author does not wax poetic about the amazing campaign Waters mounted against the popular incumbent Larson or detail Harrison's David-versus-Goliath fight against the evils of political corruption. The author avoids using adjectives or adverbs to describe the actors or their conduct and instead sticks to a more journalistic approach — answering the five Ws (who, what, where, when, and why). Note, too, that the author doesn't spend time delving into the motives of the actors — the author simply reports what they did. Why? Because the actors' motives are irrelevant for purposes of the invasion of privacy analyses. Harrison made statements that Waters claims invaded her privacy — Harrison's motive for making those statements is irrelevant, so the author has no reason to include that information in the Statement of Facts.

Additionally, the facts are generally presented in chronological order — the author starts with who Waters is and the statements she made at the debate, then outlines who Harrison is and the content of his statements about Waters made after the debate. Then, the author discusses Waters' admission, several days later, that her statements at the debate were inaccurate and concludes by noting that Waters resigned her Senate seat. An alternative construction — such as one in which the author discussed how Waters and Harrison knew each other before describing Waters' political campaign and statements at the debate — likely would have confused the reader.

Note that the memo does contain a few sentences that set the context of the litigation. The author outlines Waters' decision to run for office to explain why she attended a debate with Larson and states that Waters' personal story and background made her popular with voters. If the author jumped right in to a discussion of Waters' statements at the debate, the reader might be left wondering why Waters was attending a debate and why the statements she made about her criminal background matter at all.

You may also have noted that the Statement of Facts in this memo is substantially shorter than the Statement of Facts in the defamation memo, only contains Harrison's statements about Waters' criminal history, and does not include Harrison's statements about Waters' educational background or past relationship with her former fiancé. Why? Because the statements about Waters' criminal history are the only statements relevant to the claims for invasion of privacy. The other statements only are important for purposes of the defamation claim. The author isn't addressing Waters' defamation claim, so the author has no need to include those extraneous facts.

► **The Rule subsection of the Legal Discussion.** The author does a good job of outlining the law in a way that is straightforward and easy to understand. Take the tortious invasion of privacy section, for example. In that section, the author:

  • States the general rule: the four elements of a tortious invasion of privacy claim;

  • Addresses the two threshold elements that do not appear to be in dispute; and

  • Further breaks down the two elements at issue: whether the information disclosed was private and newsworthy. Notice that the author's outline of the law on what makes facts "private" is pretty short. Why? Because the law is well-settled that information contained in criminal records isn't private. The author need not cite or analyze numerous cases for this proposition, so the author does not. And there does not appear to be any contrary case law, so there is no potentially adverse authority for the author to outline. Sometimes that happens. There is no need to cite numerous cases or engage in an in-depth discussion of law when the law is clear. The author appropriately cites the clear law and moves on.

► **The Analysis subsection of the Legal Discussion.** The author performs a strong legal analysis by explaining why Waters is unlikely to be able to prove either tortious or constitutional invasion of privacy given the law and cases cited in the Rule sections. The Analysis sections in this memo are pretty short, but that's okay, given that the law is well-settled and several cases cited appear to be directly on point. The author still performs a short analysis, though. Even if a case appears directly on point or the law appears one-sided, you still must explain why that is true, which the author does. But note that the author does not unnecessarily belabor the analysis, given that one outcome appears highly likely. If the facts presented a closer question, the author would need to spend a great deal more time and space performing the analysis. Since they don't, the author doesn't.

► **IRAC:** Notice that the author uses IRAC structure throughout the memo. In the discussion of tortious invasion of privacy, for example, the author states the (I)ssue again; outlines the (R)ule, performs the legal (A)nalysis, and reaches a (C)onclusion. Each IRAC element is distinct from the others and there is no blending of, for example, the rule explanation and the legal analysis. If you were to cut this subsection into pieces, you'd easily be able to identify the distinct (I), (R), (A), and (C) and be able to put the memo back together in the correct order.

▶ ***The Conclusion:*** The conclusion, like the Brief Answer, is a short summary of the memo. If you look closely, you'll notice that the conclusion, like other parts of the memo, also follows an IRAC/CRAC structure. In the Conclusion, the author:

    ○ States the (C)onclusion the author has reached: That Waters won't succeed in proving her claims for invasion of privacy under either California tort law or the California constitution;

    ○ Reminds the reader of the basic (R)ules of law: the elements of tortious and constitutional invasion of privacy claims;

    ○ Outlines a summary of the legal (A)nalysis: That Waters likely will not be able to prove (1) tortious invasion of privacy because she cannot prove the facts disclosed were private and cannot prove the facts were not newsworthy; or (2) constitutional invasion of privacy because she cannot prove she had a protected interest in the facts disclosed and cannot prove the disclosure constituted a serious invasion of privacy; and

    ○ Restates the (C)onclusion.

▶ ***Headings and subheadings.*** The author uses general headings (Question Presented, Brief Answer, etc.) and subheadings (Tortious Invasion of Privacy, Constitutional Invasion of Privacy) to provide an easy-to-follow roadmap that guides the reader through the law on each element of Waters' claims for invasion of privacy.

▶ ***Sentence and paragraph length.*** The author adds interest by mixing in shorter sentences (She described the incident as a "wake-up call.") with longer ones (She explained that her arrest changed her life, and she learned accountability, hard work, and perseverance as a result). The author's paragraphs are generally five sentences long, but the author uses shorter paragraphs of one or two sentences to make a point or address an undisputed issue succinctly.

▶ ***Active voice.*** The author generally writes sentences in active voice rather than passive voice. For example, this sentence is written in active voice: When analyzing newsworthiness, the courts employ a type of sliding scale, balancing the impact of the intrusion with the value of the information disclosed. The passive alternative is much clunkier and difficult to understand: A sliding scale approach balancing the impact of the intrusion with the value of the information disclosed is employed by courts when they analyze newsworthiness.

▶ ***Quoting and paraphrasing.*** The author's rule explanation is a nice mix of direct quotes and paraphrased material. The author paraphrases much of the explanation of the relevant rules but sprinkles in quotes that are interesting and won't have the same effect if paraphrased ("Publishers are permitted to satisfy the curiosity of the public as to its heroes, leaders, villains and victims, and those who are closely associated with them.").

► *Word choice.* You do not see any fancy or esoteric words or Latin in the invasion of privacy memo, and the memo does not contain any pronouns that could cause confusion.

Analyze the defamation memorandum. What made it effective? Is there is anything that you would change to improve it? If so, what — and why?

Consider the organization of the invasion of privacy memo. Do you think the memo is organized appropriately?

Chapter 5

CLIENT LETTERS

√ Know the client
   √ How much does the client want to know about the details of the litigation?
   √ How often does the client expect to hear from the lawyer?
   √ Is the client trained in the law and will the client understand legal terms?
√ Keep client letters as short as possible while providing all necessary information
√ Consider writing an initial client letter
√ Explain legal concepts and litigation in terms the client can understand
√ Include a "Next Steps" or a "Future Handling" section that details what likely will happen in the near future in the litigation
   √ If you recommend a future course of action, outline your reasoning
√ Invite the client to contact you if the client doesn't understand the letter or has questions about the lawsuit

---

Drafting letters to clients is not the most glamorous aspect of being a lawyer (assuming there are any glamorous aspects). But it is essential. Client letters are important for a number of reasons. They inform clients of legal issues that may or will arise in litigation. They keep clients abreast of developments in their cases. They ensure clients know how long the case will take and the likely future outcome. And they update clients on potential weaknesses in their cases.

"Why even bother with letters? They take forever to write." you might ask. "I'll just call the client on the phone and tell them all this stuff." Sometimes it is easiest and best to contact clients by phone. And the client may prefer to be contacted by phone instead of email or letter. But letters serve a very important purpose for lawyers — they record what you've done and what you've told your client. It's commonly called "papering the file." And even if you do communicate with your client primarily by phone, send a short letter memorializing each conversation.

We don't want to scare you, but legal malpractice claims are filed against good lawyers every day. Litigation is often about strategy, and strategy can always be second-guessed if something goes wrong. Protect yourself by papering the file with letters summarizing what's happened in the litigation, what you expect will happen, and how you intend to handle the case. If you do, there's no way your client can ever say you didn't keep him updated on the status of the case or didn't communicate with him about your intended case strategy.

Learning to draft client letters isn't difficult, but you have to recognize that client letters are different from the other types of legal documents you draft. These tips will help you draft effective letters that clients can understand.

Know the Client

Client letters vary greatly in content and detail, depending on the purpose of the letter, the client's sophistication level, and a host of other variables. But before you sit down to write a client letter, you must know your client. Questions you should ask yourself include:

- Is the client trained in the law, will the client understand legal terms, and how much will the client understand about the course of the litigation?

- How often does the client anticipate receiving letters from me?

- How much detail does the client want to know about the course of litigation?

If your client contact is an in-house lawyer or a claims adjuster, the client will understand the litigation process and legal terms and concepts, like discovery and dispositive motions. That client likely will expect detailed analyses from you and may even expect references to cases, statutes, regulations, and the like.

An individual, on the other hand, may know little or nothing about the law. In that situation, you'll have to undertake the sometimes difficult task of explaining the law in plain and simple terms. That client may understand very little about the discovery process, wonder why he is being asked to answer seemingly irrelevant questions, and be unable to comprehend how a judge could grant a motion to dismiss and deny him his day in court.

Once you have an idea of what types of letters you'll need to write, you should think about how often your client expects to hear from you and how often you want to update your client on the status of the case. If you are working for a corporate client, that client's guidelines may require a status update letter every 60 or 90 days, even if nothing has happened in the litigation since the last letter. Some corporate clients want to be deeply involved in the minutia of the litigation, so you likely will have to reach out to them frequently. Other clients prefer to leave all strategic decisions up to the lawyer and don't want or expect frequent letters.

If you are representing an individual, that person may expect to hear from you on a monthly or bi-weekly basis, and if they don't hear from you, they may call or write your office asking for information. Other individual clients are uninterested in the litigation process and don't care what is happening. Whether you're representing a plaintiff or a defendant, and whether that party is a large corporation or an individual, you need to speak with your client at the beginning to ensure everyone is on the same page with respect to the type and frequency of communications from the lawyer.

Once you've decided how often you'll update your client, set a calendar reminder and try to stick to it. You likely will want to update your client when any major milestone occurs in the case, such as the end of the discovery period, even if that occurs between your scheduled updates.

Keep Client Letters as Short as Possible

A client doesn't want to have to read multiple pages of a letter to figure out what is going on in his case. This is true regardless of the client's level of sophistication or interest in the case. Be sure to provide the client with all necessary information, but keep your client letters as short as possible — generally, two pages or less.

Initial Client Letters

You should consider sending an initial client letter, apart from any retention letter.[32] In the initial client letter, you should again outline your understanding of why you've been retained — whether that's to write a demand letter or represent a client through trial. You should outline your understanding of the facts of the client's case and ask the client to let you know if something about that understanding is incorrect. For example:

> Based on our conversation last week, I understand that you were standing on the sidewalk at the corner of First and Broad Streets waiting to cross the road when Bernard Hollis lost control of his car, jumped the curb and struck you. I believe you said you saw Mr. Hollis's vehicle just seconds before you were hit but were unable to move in time. My notes indicate that after the accident, you heard Mr. Hollis speaking on the phone with his mother and you heard him tell his mother that he was attempting to send a text message at the time he lost control of the car.
>
> If you can remember any additional facts about the accident or if my understanding of what occurred is incorrect, please let me know as soon as possible.

Misunderstandings regarding the facts are common between lawyers and their clients, and it's better to learn there's a misunderstanding before you hang the case on your mistaken version of the facts. By outlining the facts of the client's case as you understand them, the client will have the opportunity to either confirm that you understand the facts or correct any misunderstandings.

In the initial letter, you'll also want to broadly explain what the client should expect and provide an anticipated timeline, if possible. If you've been retained to send a demand letter, that explanation might look like this:

> As we discussed, I will draft and send a cease and desist letter to Otter Books, demanding that it cease using Otter Clothing Company's Ollie Otter trademark. I will give Otter Books 45 days to comply with the request and will ask for written confirmation that it will cease using the trademark. If Otter Books does not respond or refuses to comply, we can then decide whether you want to incur the cost of filing suit to protect the trademark.

If you're representing a client in litigation or quasi-litigation (such as an administrative hearing), your explanation will be different:

---

[32] Retention letters are beyond the scope of this book. You should know, however, that attorneys often send retention letters as soon as they've been retained. These letters outline the parameters of the representation, including how the lawyer will be paid.

As you know, I'll be representing you in your attempt to obtain unemployment benefits form the Georgia Department of Labor. I will file your claim for unemployment benefits, and the Department will issue a letter indicating whether you qualify for unemployment benefits and the amount of benefits you will receive. This should occur within the next 30 to 60 days. If the Department determines you are not entitled to benefits, I will file a notice of appeal, and the Department will schedule a hearing, where we'll be able to present evidence supporting your claim for benefits.

Then explain what future action the client needs to take, if any, and notify the client about when the client can expect to hear from you again:

While I am preparing your personal injury suit, please review your records and provide me with a list of every doctor who treated you for injuries you sustained in the March 19, 2014 accident. I will need to contact those providers and obtain copies of your medical records and bills. Please attempt to get this information to my office by next week, if at all possible.

I expect to file your lawsuit within the next two weeks. Once the suit is filed, Oasis Properties, the owner of the parking lot where you fell, will have about 30 days to file a response, called an answer. Once I receive the answer, I'll contact you to discuss what likely will happen as the lawsuit progresses.

Conclude your initial letter the way you would any other — by inviting the client to contact you with questions.

Outline What's Happened

So, you've drafted your initial client letter and it's time for you to write to your client again. Ideally, you should start each client letter by updating the client on what has occurred since the last letter:

Since I last wrote you, I filed your complaint and served the defendant.

Or

I received a letter today from the Social Security Administration denying your claim for SSI benefits.

Or

The trial judge has ordered the parties to come to court on August 31 for a pre-trial hearing.

Your update needn't be lengthy if not much has happened. Or, if much has happened, the update may be longer. Don't forget, though, that client letters should be short. So keep your update short while providing necessary information.

Explain in Terms the Client Can Understand

Client letters shouldn't sound like pleadings. You can't copy and paste information you've put in a pleading into a client letter and expect the client to understand what's going on. You need to tailor the amount and detail of information to each client; as we discussed above, some will understand legal terms and want great detail while others won't.

If you have an unsophisticated client, don't say, "In order to prevail in the litigation, we'll have to prove the elements of tort: duty, breach, causation, and damages." That client will not understand what you mean.

Instead, write something like:

> **To recover from Mr. Smith, we'll have to prove that Mr. Smith, as a driver, owed you a duty of care, that he breached that duty, that you were injured as a result of the accident, and that the accident caused those injuries. We can easily prove that Mr. Smith owed you a duty and that he breached that duty because Mr. Smith was driving a vehicle in a reckless manner when he hit the vehicle you were riding in. I also believe we can prove that you were injured in the accident because you were diagnosed with a fractured lumbar vertebra after the accident. And I believe we can prove that you sustained damages because you incurred more than $9,000 in medical bills as a result of your injuries.**

A sophisticated, law-savvy client, however, likely will understand torts and you won't need to break down the individual elements and what will need to be proven. Don't talk down to clients, but recognize that something that seems easy to understand to you may be like a foreign language to them.

Next Steps and Future Handling

Good lawyers not only update clients about what has happened in the litigation, they also provide them with information about what likely will happen in the future or recommend a future course of conduct in the litigation. The client will then know what to expect and the lawyer will lessen the likelihood that the client is surprised about a future occurrence. It also notifies the client about the lawyer's litigation strategy and protects the lawyer from a future claim that the client didn't know how the lawyer was handling the case and didn't authorize the lawyer to take certain steps.

For example, your "future handling" section might look something like this:

> **The defendant has asked to take Dr. Tucker's deposition. As you may recall, Dr. Tucker was the orthopedist who treated you in the emergency room at Northside Hospital immediately after the accident. I am working with Dr. Tucker's office to find a good time for her deposition, which you are welcome to attend. I expect the plaintiff's lawyer will ask Dr. Tucker about your condition when you arrived at the hospital, x-rays that were taken at the hospital, and Dr. Tucker's treatment of you after you were admitted to the hospital. After the defendant takes Dr. Tucker's deposition, discovery will be complete.**

I know that you would like to put the accident behind you and avoid trial, if possible. You may recall that we discussed mediation at our first meeting and you told me you would be interested in settling the case through mediation if you could obtain a settlement of at least $100,000.

As I told you at our first meeting, I cannot guarantee that you will be able to recover any particular amount of money for the injuries you sustained in the accident. However, based on everything I have learned throughout the discovery process, I expect the defendant will be willing to settle the case for at least $100,000. Any mediation is non-binding, so if we attend mediation and you are unsatisfied with the amount the defendant offers, you can always walk away from the mediation.

Unless you object, once discovery is complete, I will approach the defendant's counsel and ask if the defendant would like to mediate the case. I will work with the defendant's counsel to select a mediator and then work with you to choose a date and time for mediation that works with your schedule. Once we get closer to mediation, we can plan a time to meet and discuss exactly what you can expect during the mediation process.

If you're recommending a future course of action that you previously haven't discussed with your client, outline the reasons you think that course of action is prudent. Assume you represent a defendant who claims he did not sign a personal guaranty on a business loan but that his signature was forged:

In reviewing the bank's discovery responses, we learned of another person, Lisa Browner, who claims to have witnessed you execute the guaranty. As you may recall, we had initially planned to take only the depositions of Mr. Lang and Ms. Foreman because it was our belief that they were the only two people who claimed to have seen you execute the guaranty. However, now that we have learned that Ms. Browner also claims to have witnessed that event, we believe it is necessary to take Ms. Browner's deposition as well.

As with the rest of a client letter, the tone and detail of your future handling section will vary depending on the client.

Invite Questions

Always close a client letter by inviting the client to contact you if the client has questions or concerns about the contents of the letter or the litigation itself. Don't make clients feel like communication is a one-way street from the lawyer to the client. Inviting clients to contact you helps prevent client confusion and decreases the likelihood of future legal malpractice claims, many of which arise when lawyers fail to properly communicate with their clients. Also, use the final paragraph to tell the client when the client can expect to hear from you again.

In the above example with Dr. Tucker, the closing paragraph might look like this:

We likely will schedule Dr. Tucker's deposition in May, and I will call you with that date once it is finalized. As always, if you do not understand

something in this letter or have any questions for me about your case, please feel free to call me.

Waters v. Harrison

Below is a client letter to Harrison from his counsel:

Dear Simon:

I have reviewed Ms. Waters's complaint against you and provide a summary of her claims and the relevant law below.

Defamation

To prove you defamed her, Ms. Waters must prove: (1) publication; (2) of a false statement; (3) the statement is defamatory; (4) the statement is unprivileged; and (5) the plaintiff is damaged as a result of the publication. However, if your statements were opinions, rather than assertions of fact, Ms. Waters will be unable to recover.

Ms. Waters has alleged that you published the following false statements about her on your blog:

- Statements alleging Ms. Waters lied about her criminal background and history;
- Statements alleging infidelity by Ms. Waters;
- Statements that Ms. Waters lacks the intelligence to serve as an elected official; and
- Statements that Ms. Waters's admission to Berkeley Law School was based on favoritism and money.

Ms. Waters alleges that the statements were defamatory and not protected by any privilege and that she was forced to resign from her Senate seat as a result of the statements. There can be little dispute that the statements you made about Ms. Waters on your blog were "published." We will argue, on your behalf, however, that the statements were opinions, rather than allegations of fact, that the statements weren't false or defamatory, and that Ms. Waters wasn't damaged as a result of your statements — she was damaged because she was untruthful to the public about her past criminal history.

Once we begin discovery and obtain documents and information from Ms. Waters, I'll be in a better position to evaluate the likelihood Ms. Waters will be able to prove you defamed her by making the above statements.

Invasion of Privacy

In order to maintain a tort action for invasion of privacy under California law, Ms. Waters must prove that you publicly disclosed a private fact, that the disclosure would be objectionable to a reasonable person, and that the fact disclosed was not newsworthy.

Ms. Waters claims that you invaded her privacy by disclosing information about her criminal history because that information was private, the disclosure was objectionable, and the disclosure wasn't newsworthy.

Based on my preliminary research, I do not believe Ms. Waters can succeed on an invasion of privacy claim. Generally, information in criminal records, which are available to the public, is not private. Additionally, according to the California courts, information that bears on a political candidate's credibility or fitness for office, including a candidate's criminal history, is considered newsworthy and of public concern.

If Ms. Waters does not agree to voluntarily dismiss this claim, I believe we should file a motion for summary judgment as to the invasion of privacy claim. Through that motion, we will be asking the court to issue an order that Ms. Waters may not recover for invasion of privacy.

Future Handling

As we discussed yesterday during our phone conference, I believe Judge Montana may find that she cannot exercise jurisdiction over you in this matter because you do not have sufficient connections with California. Thus, I believe we should go ahead and file a motion to dismiss for lack of personal jurisdiction. If that motion is granted, Ms. Waters will have to file the lawsuit in an appropriate jurisdiction if she wants to pursue her claims against you. If the motion is denied, I will file an answer on your behalf and we will proceed with discovery.

Please let me know as soon as possible if you approve of this course of action. And, of course, please let me know if you have any questions or concerns about this case.

*　　*　　*　　*　　*

Why is the client letter effective?

- ▶ *Organization:* This client letter is organized for ease of reading. The lawyer uses headings to ensure the client understands that defamation and invasion of privacy claims are separate claims with separate elements. The lawyer then separates the future handling section for ease of reference. The sentences and paragraphs are generally short and to the point.

- ▶ *Tone and style:* The client letter is appropriate in tone and style. Simon Harrison is educated, but not familiar with the law. The lawyer explains the law in a straightforward, to-the-point manner. He doesn't include case cites because Harrison is unlikely to care about where the lawyer's summary on the law comes from — Harrison only cares what the law is.

- ▶ *Future Handling:* Under the future handling section, the lawyer outlines his prior discussion with Harrison about personal jurisdiction and explains why he believes a motion to dismiss is appropriate. The lawyer also explains what Harrison can expect, depending on whether the motion to dismiss is granted or denied.

► *The lawyer invites questions:* At the conclusion of the letter, the lawyer reminds Harrison to contact the lawyer with questions. This ensures the client feels like the attorney-client relationship is a two-way street.

Of course, no document is perfect. Is there is anything that you would change to improve this letter? If so, what — and why?

Chapter 6

THE COMPLAINT

The Complaint Checklist

√ Check local rules for form and other requirements.

√ Research to know what claims you can make and what you must allege for each claim.

√ Allege subject matter jurisdiction, personal jurisdiction, and venue, citing specific statutes and cases.

√ Draft a short and plain statement of the factual allegations.

    √ If facts are lengthy or complex, use subheadings to guide the reader.

    √ Allege facts sufficient to support each cause of action to avoid a motion to dismiss for failure to state a claim.

    √ Allege all necessary facts without being overly specific.

    √ Attach and incorporate documents into the complaint, if appropriate.

√ Draft separate counts for each claim.

    √ Consider pleading alternative claims, if appropriate.

√ Plead facts with particularity, where required.

√ Offer expert support for claims, where required.

√ Allege facts sufficient to support claims for punitive damages and attorney fees.

√ Request the relief you are seeking (monetary damages, an injunction, a declaratory judgment etc.) and a jury trial, if you want one.

Even though the name suggests otherwise, a complaint isn't a license to hurl invectives at your adversary or passionately argue your client's case. The complaint is not a place to showcase your literary skills or the depth and breadth of your knowledge of the law. What is the purpose of a complaint, then?

As Judge Gerald Lebovits has noted, a complaint introduces your client to the court and tells the court what your client wants and why your client is entitled to it.[33] The tone of your complaint should be professional and matter-of-fact — as we'll discuss below, almost journalistic. And your complaint is not a place to telegraph your trial strategy or highlight the law most favorable to you. As we'll discuss below, "the law" is implicitly a part of your complaint, but is rarely explicitly outlined. Drafting

---

[33] Gerald Lebovits, *Drafting New York Civil Litigation Documents: Part II — The Complaint*, 82-OCT N.Y. St. B.J. 64 (Oct. 2010).

complaints isn't difficult, . . . once you get the hang of it.

I. DO YOUR HOMEWORK

A. Those Local Rules — Again

We know you're probably sick and tired of hearing about the local rules by now. We hope, however, that by the time you finish this book, the necessity of following them will be so ingrained in your head, you'll never forget to look at them. The local rules are just as important for complaints as they are for other types of pleadings.

The local rules — whether you realize it or not — may govern nearly every aspect of your complaint. In addition to the local rules for the specific court in which you'll be filing your complaint, e.g., the Northern District of California, you may find that your individual judge has local rules as well. You have to follow those, too.

For example, in *Waters v. Harrison*, the complaint will be filed in the Northern District of California. That district is divided into four divisions — San Francisco, San Jose, Oakland, and Eureka. There are local rules for the Northern District generally, within each Division, and for each judge. Yes, we know it can be tedious, but adhering to the rules is a vital part of being a professional, ethical, and zealous advocate. Check the local rules before you even start drafting your complaint.

B. Do Your Research

Before you draft a complaint, you must also research to know what you need to allege in order to state a claim against the defendant. If you don't, the defendant may file a motion to dismiss for failure to state a claim. Even if you are permitted to amend your complaint, you'll have gone through a lot of trouble and expense that could have been avoided if you had just done your homework beforehand.

For example, assume you want to file a claim against a debt collector for violation of the Fair Debt Collection Practices Act. First, you should research the Act to ensure that the debt collector you want to sue actually meets the definition of a "debt collector" under the Act. Then, you should research to determine which provisions of the Act you believe the debt collector violated. When you draft the complaint, you'll want to allege that the defendant is a "debt collector" under the Act, outline provisions of the Act the debt collector violated, and explain how the debtor collector violated those provisions.

We know this seems like a no-brainer — "This is common sense," you might say. Well, common sense isn't always so common, and you'd be surprised how many attorneys draft complaints without having any idea what they will ultimately need to prove, much less what they need to allege to survive a motion to dismiss. Don't make this mistake.

Another important point about doing your research first — you might discover additional causes of action that you can allege or you might discover that you can't state a claim at all. Unless strategic considerations apply, you should always allege all causes of action you have grounds to believe might succeed. And you should never allege causes of action you know with certainty you cannot prove—this violates the rules of professional conduct and could get both you and your client sanctioned. Doing your research beforehand will go a long way toward ensuring a strong complaint.

II.   WRITING A COMPLAINT THAT DOES ENOUGH, BUT NOT TOO MUCH

A.   Short and Plain Statements

Except for certain claims, which we'll discuss below, your complaint generally need only contain a "short and plain statement" of the grounds for jurisdiction and the claims. Fed. R. Civ. P. 8(a). This is the standard in cases filed in federal courts and in many other jurisdictions.

In most jurisdictions, for most causes of action, all that is required is "notice pleading," meaning that the complaint need not provide every relevant fact or detail. The complaint must, however, give fair notice of the claim or claims asserted against the defendant and should include at least minimal allegations of the underlying events and circumstances that give rise to the claim or claims.

"What is a short and plain statement," you ask? Just what it sounds like. A straightforward statement about the facts of the case or the applicable legal standards. Each allegation in the complaint should be made in a separate paragraph, and each paragraph should generally include only a single sentence or idea. The complaint is not the place to try to win the case by making your strongest arguments or showing all your cards. The rules do not require that, courts do not expect that, and it's just bad strategy to do that.

In many jurisdictions, complaints are drafted in this order:

• Allegations about the defendant and where the defendant may be served;

• Allegations that the court may exercise jurisdiction and that venue is proper;

• Factual allegations;

• Causes of action (with a separate heading for each cause of action); and

• Prayer for relief.

Complaints — no matter the cause of action — follow this general form, so once you learn it, you should be able to draft most any type of complaint. Of course, if the local rules require additional information or a different structure, you must follow those rules. If you discover in your own practice that some other structure works better for you, then use that structure. For now, though, while you're learning, follow this general outline.

B.   Factual Allegations about the Defendant

Your complaint should first contain general allegations about the defendant. By allegations about the defendant, we simply mean: whether the defendant is an individual, corporation, limited liability company, partnership etc., and where and through whom the defendant may be served. These may be encompassed in a single allegation, such as:

1.

Defendant Wal-Mart Stores, Inc. is a foreign corporation incorporated in the state of Delaware with its principal place of business in Benton-ville, Arkansas. Wal-Mart may be served with process through service on its registered agent, The Corporation Trust Company of Nevada, at 311 South Division Street, Carson City, Nevada 89703.

*   *   *   *   *

Obviously, if you are suing multiple defendants, you will need to include separate allegations for each defendant.

Drafting these general allegations isn't hard, but it does require some background work. If the defendant is an individual, you need to know where that person resides and where you might be able to perfect service. If the defendant is a business, you need to know the defendant's corporate status, the name of the defendant's registered agent, and where that registered agent is located.

A word of practical advice: figuring out the correct defendant to sue is not always easy. If you were to go the website for the secretary of state in your jurisdiction and search "Wal-Mart," you'd find many corporations that contain that name. First, you'd want to look for corporations with an active status (as opposed to inactive or dissolved). Another hint might be the corporation's principal place of business. Most people know, for example, that Wal-Mart is headquartered in Arkansas, so look for an entity with its principal place of business in Arkansas. You might also look at the defendant's website, which likely contains the entity's correct legal name. The bottom of the main page of Wal-Mart's website, www.walmart.com, shows that Wal-Mart's legal name is Wal-Mart Stores, Inc. Suing the wrong entity isn't necessarily fatal, but you'll save yourself time, money, and energy by doing just a little research about the defendant before drafting the complaint.

An additional note — some jurisdictions may require that you include information about the plaintiff before making allegations about the defendant. Generally, an allegation that the plaintiff is a resident of the state in which the court lies or some other allegation about why the plaintiff is bringing suit in the jurisdiction will suffice.

C.   Allegations About Jurisdiction and Venue

Next, you should include allegations that the court has jurisdiction and that venue is proper. Preferably, you should cite specific statutes rather than make blanket allegations. For example,

2.

This Court has jurisdiction over this matter pursuant to 28 U.S.C. § 1332(a) because Plaintiff and Wal-Mart are citizens of different states and the amount in controversy exceeds $75,000, exclusive of interest and costs.

3.

Venue is proper in this Court under 28 U.S.C. § 1391(b)(1) because Wal-Mart does business in Nevada and its registered agent for service is located in Carson City, Nevada.

*   *   *   *   *

These allegations are straightforward, but very important. You need to show the court why it can hear the case.

D.   Factual Allegations

After making the general allegations, you'll next want to outline the factual contentions that give rise to the claim you're asserting. As we've discussed with respect to other pleadings, facts should generally be presented: (1) in chronological order; (2) topically; or (3) in groups based on events or transactions. If you aren't sure how to group your facts, stick with chronological order.

Under the notice pleading standard, you do not need to include every relevant fact or detail. You only need to include enough facts to give the defendant some idea of the basis for the claims you are asserting. What facts to include will depend largely on the type of case and the number and causes of action you intend to assert. The allegations in a personal injury action arising from a two-car auto accident will obviously differ substantially from the allegations in an action challenging the constitutionality of a state statute. A good rule of thumb for the factual allegations is to include at least 3 of the 5 Ws — the Who, When, and What of the claim. That is, who was involved, what happened, and when did it happen.

Let's look at an easy example — a car accident. How would you draft a short and plain statement of the facts? How about this:

4.

On December 21, 2013, Plaintiff Marshall Turner was driving southbound on Highway 41A in Winchester, Tennessee.

5.

At the same time and place, Defendant Jason Bean was driving southbound on Highway 41A behind the vehicle driven by Turner.

6.

As Turner approached a traffic light at the intersection between Highway 41A and the Highway 41A Bypass Road, he slowed his vehicle because the traffic light was red.

7.

Bean, who was still travelling directly behind Turner, failed to slow or stop his vehicle and struck the rear-end of Turner's vehicle.

8.

Turner sustained injuries as a result of the accident.

*   *   *   *   *

These plain, straightforward allegations answer the Who (Turner and Bean), the When (December 21, 2013), and the What (an auto accident). As you can see, these allegations are simple, but they provide all necessary information.

For strategic or other reasons, you may decide to include only a minimum amount of information in your complaint. That's fine, so long as you satisfy the Rule 8 requirements (or similar state-specific requirements) and provide enough information for the defendant to understand the basis of the claim or claims.

For example, assume Mr. Turner, in the auto accident suit above, comes to you on the morning the statute of limitations expires and wants to file suit. He doesn't have the accident report and only knows that the accident happened on December 21, 2013, on Highway 41A. He doesn't know which direction he was traveling or the name of the intersection where the accident occurred. You don't have time to get the police report to figure out this information since you must draft and file the suit that day, so your complaint would necessarily be somewhat vague. You'd still, however, include the information you have, which is enough to fairly inform Bean that he's being sued for personal injuries Turner sustained in an auto accident that occurred on December 21, 2013. You'll still answer the Who (Turner and Bean), the When (December 21, 2013), and the What (an auto accident), even if the allegations aren't as detailed as those above.

Students (and lawyers) often try to make complaint drafting much harder than it actually is. As long as you remember you just need to include short and plain statements that sound like they're part of a newspaper article, you'll have no problem.

E. Use Subheadings for Lengthy, Complicated Facts

As we have discussed before, you should use subheadings to help guide your reader. When the factual background of the litigation is complex or lengthy, subheadings will help keep your reader on track and, hopefully, help avoid confusion. For the car accident case discussed above, you don't need subheadings since the facts are short and straightforward. For a more complicated case, such as a real estate dispute or litigation over a business divorce, you will probably want to use subheadings in your factual allegations. Your subheadings may be simple:

- The Parties
- The Land
- The Dispute

Or they may be drafted to tell a story:

- Tisdale and Urban Form The Tisdale-Urban Law Group
- The Tisdale-Urban Law Group Earns $50 Million in Eight Years
- Tisdale Unilaterally Dissolves the Partnership

As always, strive to make the complaint as easy as possible to understand. If subheadings will help you do that, use them.

F. Attaching and Incorporating Documents

You generally should attach documents that form the basis of or relate to the facts or claims outlined in your complaint. For example, in a breach of contract action, you likely want to attach the contract or the writings you contend created a contract to the complaint. In a dispute over the boundary-line between two pieces of property, you'd want to attach a survey of the properties and the legal descriptions contained in the real estate records, or both. If there are prerequisites to filing suit against a specific defendant (a government entity, for example), you likely would want to attach documents to your complaint showing that you have satisfied the prerequisites.

Attach the documents as exhibits to your complaint and reference them just as you would in any other pleading. For example:

10.

On March 27, 2012, Francis Hassleman, in his capacity as executor of Ms. Reading's estate, signed a contract to sell the Vanderbilt residence to Highland Property Trust. A copy of the March 27, 2012 contract is attached as Exhibit A.

*   *   *   *   *

G. Asserting Causes of Action

A cause of action is the legal claim or theory you believe entitles your client to recover from the defendant. In some cases, your cause of action will sound in tort; in others, in contract. Sometimes your cause of action will be violation of a statute, such as 42 U.S.C. § 1983, or violation of a state constitutional provision.

After you assert your factual allegations, you should assert your client's cause or causes of action. You must be sure you have alleged sufficient facts to satisfy the elements of the cause of action you are going to assert. Thus, you must have done your research and know what you must allege to state a cause of action. If you need to go back and add additional facts, you should do that before drafting your causes of action.

Your causes of action will track the elements of each claim you assert, but generally shouldn't contain any black-letter law, like cases or statutes. Thus, you'll allege facts to support each element of your claim, but you won't outline the elements themselves.

Let's take an easy example — breach of fiduciary duty. In most jurisdictions, to assert a claim for breach of fiduciary duty, you must allege: (1) the defendant owed the plaintiff a fiduciary duty; (2) the defendant breached that fiduciary duty; and (3) the plaintiff was damaged as a result of the breach of fiduciary duty.

There are many types of fiduciary relationships, but let's look at the attorney-client relationship, since that's something we're all familiar with. Assume you represent a client, Jeremy Black, who wants to sue his former lawyer, Heather Mueller. Mueller represented Black in a personal injury suit. The defendant in that suit, International Trucking Company, offered to settle Black's claims for $300,000, but Mueller failed to tell Black about the offer. Black would have accepted the $300,000 offer if he had known about it. Instead, the case was tried and Black was awarded only $50,000. How would you draft a cause of action against Mueller for breach of fiduciary duty?

Count I — Breach of Fiduciary Duty

14.

Black incorporates the allegations made in paragraphs 1–13 of his complaint.

15.

As Black's attorney, Mueller owed Black a fiduciary duty.

16.

By failing to communicate International's offer to settle the case for $300,000, Mueller breached the fiduciary duty she owed to Black.

17.

Black was injured as a result of Mueller's breach of fiduciary duty because he would have accepted the $300,000 settlement offered by International had he known about the offer.

* * * * *

The allegations in each cause of action will necessary mirror — to some extent — your factual allegations. In general, you should give factual details in your factual allegations, then simply say that the standard is met in the allegations for each cause of action.

That's what the author of the passage above did. In the factual allegations, the author would have outlined the relationship between the parties, the prior litigation, the offer from International, and the trial judgment. Then, in the count for breach of fiduciary duty, the author simply alleges that each element is met — (1) there was a fiduciary duty because Black and Mueller had an attorney-client relationship; (2) Mueller breached that duty by failing to communicate the offer; and (3) Black was harmed because he would have accepted $300,000 and, instead, received a judgment for only $50,000.

"Okay," you say, "I think I understand. But what is that "incorporates the allegations" language in paragraph 14?" Many drafters of complaints include an incorporation statement at the beginning of each cause of action. The incorporation statement is a signal that the drafter isn't going to restate the factual allegations but intends to incorporate them as support for each cause of action. We have mixed feelings about whether the incorporation language is necessary, but it is very common. And we always feel it is better to err on the side of caution and include it, lest the lack of incorporation language cause confusion or ambiguity.

H.   Draft a Separate Count for Each Cause of Action

Sometimes, you'll only have one cause of action to assert. In the auto accident complaint above, you might only assert a cause of action for negligence. In many cases, though, you'll want to assert multiple causes of action, and each cause of action should be outlined in a separate count in the complaint. In the attorney-client case discussed above, the lawyer likely would want to assert causes of action for both breach of fiduciary duty and legal malpractice. The counts would look like this:

Count I — Breach of Fiduciary Duty

14.

Black incorporates the allegations made in paragraphs 1–13 of his complaint.

15.

As Black's attorney, Mueller owed Black a fiduciary duty.

16.

By failing to communicate International's offer to settle the case for $300,000, Mueller breached the fiduciary duty she owed to Black.

17.

Black was injured as a result of Mueller's breach of fiduciary duty because he would have accepted the $300,000 settlement offered by International had he known about the offer.

Count II — Legal Malpractice

18.

Black incorporates the allegations made in paragraphs 1–17 of his complaint.

19.

Black employed Mueller to represent Black in his lawsuit against International.

20.

In failing to communicate International's $300,000 settlement offer to Black, Mueller failed to exercise the level of ordinary care, skill, and diligence expected of a reasonable, prudent attorney. *See* **Affidavit of**

Michelle R. Johnson, Esq., attached as Exhibit A.[34]

21.

Black was injured as a result of Mueller's negligence because he would have accepted the $300,000 settlement offered by International and, instead, he was awarded only $50,000 by a jury in the *International* litigation.

*   *   *   *   *

As a reminder — the allegations in each count should track the elements of each specific cause of action. The allegations in Count I track the elements of a breach of fiduciary duty claim and the allegations in Count II track the elements of a legal malpractice claim.

If the facts do or might support alternative theories of recovery, be sure to draft a separate count for each of those theories as well. We're not talking about multiple causes of action, like the claims for breach of fiduciary duty and legal malpractice, above. Black could succeed in proving both those claims.

What we're talking about is alternative causes of action, only one of which is viable. For example, in a personal injury action, you may believe you have or can develop enough evidence to support a claim for intentional infliction of emotional distress, but you also want to make a claim for negligent infliction of emotional distress, just in case. Either the conduct was negligent or intentional — it can't have been both. In that situation, you would draft a count for intentional infliction of emotional distress and a separate count for negligent infliction of emotional distress, alleging the facts necessary to support each claim. Pleading rules almost always permit the pleading of alternative theories, and it is generally good practice to include them. You can almost always amend your complaint to remove a theory that you later discover is not viable, but you may not be able to go back and add a claim that was not made in the initial complaint. Just remember — your ethical duties as a lawyer do not permit you to make frivolous or unsupported claims. You must have some reasonable basis to believe the claims you're asserting could succeed or — at the very least — that the claims are not frivolous.

I. Heightened Pleading Standards

Certain claims are subject to heightened pleading standards in many jurisdictions, including the federal courts. To properly state a claim for fraud, for example, the plaintiff must make specific allegations in many jurisdictions — generally, who engaged in the fraud, when and where the fraud allegedly occurred, what statements or conduct constitute fraud, and how the statements or conduct constitute fraud. Thus, a plaintiff will not be able to overcome a motion to dismiss for failure to state a claim with only a blanket recitation that the defendant's conduct was fraudulent. For example, a well-pleaded complaint for fraud might look something like this:

---

[34] We'll talk about why an attorney's affidavit is attached to this pleading in the Expert Support subsection below.

FACTUAL BACKGROUND

4.

On or around February 12, 2014, Jacqueline Trent, a representative of the plaintiff-investors, met with Defendant Shoreline Realty Development Corporation's president, Sam Goldberg.

5.

At the meeting, Goldberg outlined a real estate development project, Chateau at the Shore, that Shoreline was about to undertake.

6.

According to Goldberg, Chateau at the Shore was to be a twenty-story, high-end condominium complex with on-site spa services, tennis, golf, swimming, and other recreational activities.

7.

At the February 12, 2014 meeting, Goldberg represented to Trent that Shoreline had already obtained permits for the Chateau at the Shore project and was simply waiting on $10 million additional funding before breaking ground on the project.

8.

At the February 12, 2014 meeting, Goldberg represented to Trent that the Chateau at the Shore project was an excellent investment opportunity for the investors and that Shoreline would be willing to re-pay the investment at a 30% return rate on or before May 31, 2016.

9.

In actuality, prior to the February 12, 2014 meeting between Trent and Goldberg, Shoreline had applied for a building permit to start construction on the Chateau at the Shore project, but that permit had been denied because the proposed building site was designated a wetland.

10.

Despite knowing that the permit had been denied, at the February 12, 2014 meeting, Goldberg represented to Trent that the permit had been issued, that Shoreline would break ground on this project soon, and that the Chateau at the Shore project was an excellent investment opportunity for the investors.

11.

Based on Goldberg's representations to Trent about the status of the Chateau at the Shore project and the large return rate, Trent recommended to the investors that they invest in the project.

12.

As a result of Trent's recommendation, the investors invested $10 million in the Chateau at the Shore project.

13.

Goldberg and Shoreline, however, did not use the $10 million from the investors for the Chateau at the Shore project.

14.

Goldberg transferred the funds into a personal off-shore bank account.

15.

Goldberg then shut down Shoreline's business operations and fled the country.

16.

Goldberg was captured in Istanbul by Interpol several months after fleeing the country and was extradited to the United States to face numerous charges, including federal racketeering charges.

17.

To date, federal authorities have been unable to locate or recover the $10 million the investors loaned Shoreline and Goldberg for the Chateau at the Shore project.

Count I — Fraud

18.

The investors incorporate the allegations made in paragraphs 1-17 of the complaint.

19.

At the February 12, 2014 meeting Goldberg represented to Trent that the Chateau at the Shore building permit had been issued, that Shoreline would break ground on the project soon, and that the project was an excellent investment opportunity for the investors.

20.

When he made the statements at the February 12, 2014 meeting, Goldberg knew the statements were false because he knew that the building permit for the Chateau at the Shore project had been denied and that the permit likely would never be granted.

21.

Goldberg made these representations to Trent at the February 12, 2014 meeting to induce the investors to invest in an essentially defunct project.

22.

The investors invested $10 million in the Chateau at the Shore project based on Goldberg's fraudulent misrepresentations to Trent about the viability of the project and the potential to recoup a substantial amount from the investment.

23.

The investors were damaged in the amount of at least $10 million as a result of Goldberg's fraud.

*   *   *   *   *

This example meets the heightened pleading standard for fraud claims — it gives the Who (Sam Goldberg), the When (February 12, 2014), the What (the building permit had been issued for the Chateau at the Shore project and the project was a good investment opportunity), and the how (the building permit hadn't been issued and Goldberg knew it likely wouldn't be issued).

The depth of information necessary to properly state a fraud claim varies from case to case. And remember — other claims may be subject to a heightened pleading standard as well, so check statutes and cases in your applicable jurisdiction to ensure you comply. When it comes to heightened pleading, err on the side of providing too much, rather than too little information.

J. Expert Affidavits and Support

In many jurisdictions, a plaintiff must offer an expert affidavit or some other testimony from an expert to support certain claims, such as professional malpractice claims (e.g., medical malpractice, legal malpractice). Generally, the expert must aver that the expert has reviewed the client's case and, in the expert's professional opinion, the defendant's conduct did not meet the standard of care for members of the defendant's profession. For example, in a medical malpractice case, you would need a medical expert to testify that the defendant-doctor's conduct was below the standard of care expected of doctors in the defendant's field.

If expert support is required, *do not* forget to attach it to or file it with your complaint. In some jurisdictions, the failure to provide the required expert support is a non-amendable defect, meaning that the court must dismiss the complaint with prejudice, which prevents you from re-filing.

III. CAUSES OF ACTION FOR SPECIAL TYPES OF DAMAGES, SUCH AS PUNITIVE DAMAGES

In many jurisdictions, a litigant can obtain an award of punitive damages to punish a defendant for exceptionally bad conduct. Litigants also may be able to recover attorney fees and costs they incurred in having to bring an action if, for example, the defendant should have realized the defendant was liable to the plaintiff and should have settled the case rather than force the plaintiff to go to the expense of filing suit. To obtain an award of punitive damages or attorney fees, the plaintiff must allege and prove that the defendant engaged in bad (generally) intentional conduct above mere negligence.

If you are seeking to recover punitive damages or fees and costs, you must make allegations in your pleading about what bad conduct by the defendant entitles you to those damages or costs. For example, in many jurisdictions, a plaintiff may recover punitive damages for willful misconduct, malice, fraud, or wantonness of care. If you are seeking punitive damages, be sure to allege facts sufficient to show you're entitled to them — some act by the defendant that rises to the level of willful misconduct.

Let's look at an example. Suppose you represent the family of a worker killed when the worker fell into an industrial compacting machine. The machine had a guard that was supposed to prevent these types of accident, but the guard malfunctioned. You believe you will be able to prove the manufacturer knew the guard was defective and did nothing to replace the guard or warn end-users to use extra caution when working near the machine. How would you draft the allegations necessary to state a claim for punitive damages?

COUNT III — PUNITIVE DAMAGES

35.

Hancock incorporates the allegations made in paragraphs 1-34 of the Complaint.

36.

Industrial knew or should have known that the Guard over which Hancock fell was defective.

37.

Industrial failed to remove the defective Guard and replace it with a non-defective guard.

38.

Industrial failed to warn users of the Compactor, including Hancock, that the Guard was defective.

39.

Industrial's conduct was wanton, willful, and done with conscious disregard for the safety of Compactor users, including Hancock.

40.

Hancock is entitled to recover punitive damages for Industrial's wanton, willful conduct.

*   *   *   *   *

IV. REQUESTING RELIEF

You should finalize your complaint with your prayer for relief. In the prayer, you should outline what it is you're asking for from the Court or finder of fact. Are you asking for monetary damages? Are you seeking an injunction? Are you looking for a declaratory judgment? Whatever it is you want, request that relief in your prayer for relief.

Just remember — you need to have done your research ahead of time to know what type of relief you're entitled to obtain. Most of the time there is no question, but sometimes there is. For example, take wrongful foreclosure cases. In some states, the only remedy for wrongful foreclosure is monetary damages. An attorney who hasn't done his research may not realize that and ask for rescission of the foreclosure, thinking that the client will be entitled to get his or her home back if the defendant is deemed to have wrongfully foreclosed on the client's home.

With respect to monetary damages, your jurisdiction may require that you include the specific amount you're seeking (e.g., $100,000) or may allow you to ask for an unspecified amount "left up the enlightened conscience of an impartial jury" (or some similar language). And in most jurisdictions, punitive damages are not available, are capped, or are set at a percentage of the underlying damages for certain causes of action (e.g., medical malpractice). Don't make the mistake of asking for $1.5 million in punitive damages if those damages are capped at $500,000. No matter the type of relief you're seeking, be sure to ask only for relief your client may legally be entitled to obtain.

Also, if you request damages that are subject to specific legal criteria — punitive damages or attorney fees, for example — track the standard you must prove in your prayer for relief. Your prayer for relief in the industrial accident involving Mr. Hancock might look something like this:

Hancock prays that he be awarded:

1. **$10 million in compensatory damages for Industrial's negligence;**

2. **$50 million in punitive damages for Industrial's deliberate and wanton failure to replace the defective Guard or warn end-users that the Guard was defective, or both;**

3. **Reasonable attorney fees and costs incurred for Industrial's stubborn litigiousness in forcing Hancock to file this action; and**

4. **Any other damages that the Court deems just and proper.**

Oh, and if you want a jury trial, be sure to request that as well. Some jurisdictions will allow you to make a jury demand in the prayer for relief, while others require a separate count requesting a jury trial or even a separate document altogether. Defer to the local rules to ensure you preserve your right to have a jury hear the case.

*   *   *   *   *

Waters v. Harrison, Complaint

Below is the complaint filed by Waters in the Northern District of California, alleging that Harrison's comments on www.justtellthetruth.com were defamatory and invaded her privacy under California law. As you'll see, Waters' well-pleaded Complaint sets forth cognizable causes of action. This might not stop Harrison from filing Motion to Dismiss, however, which you will see in the next chapter.

*   *   *   *   *

COMPLAINT

Kirsten Waters files this Complaint against Simon Harrison to recover for injuries Waters sustained as a result of Harrison's publication of false, defamatory, and injurious statements about Waters on Harrison's website. Waters alleges as follows:

PARTIES, JURISDICTION, AND VENUE

1. Plaintiff Kirsten Waters ("Waters") is a resident of San Jose, California. Waters received her Bachelor of Arts degree from Stanford University and Juris Doctorate from the University of California-Berkeley School of Law. Waters is licensed to practice law in the State of California.

2. Defendant Simon Harrison ("Harrison") is a resident of Erie, Pennsylvania. Harrison received his Bachelor of Arts degree from Stanford University. Harrison is a computer programmer and operates a well-known blog at www.justellthetruth.com.

3. This Court has personal jurisdiction over Harrison because the false and defamatory statements made by Harrison were published in this district and Waters, who was the target of these defamatory statements, was and remains a resident in this district.

4. Jurisdiction is proper pursuant to 28 U.S.C. § 1332(a)(1) as this action involves parties of different states and the amount in controversy exceeds $75,000.00, exclusive of interest and costs.

5. Venue is proper pursuant to 28 U.S.C. § 1391(b)(2) because a substantial part of the events or omissions giving rise to Waters' claim occurred in this District.

6. Pursuant to Civil Local Rules 3-5(b)(2), 3-2(c), and 3-2(e), this action should be filed in the San Jose Division of the United States District Court for the Northern District of California because a substantial part of the events or omissions occurred in Santa Clara County.

FACTUAL ALLEGATIONS

7. In 2012, Waters, a successful lawyer, decided to run for a seat in the United States Senate.

8. Waters acknowledged during the campaign that, while in college, she struggled with alcohol and prescription drug abuse.

9. Five days before the election, the final debate between Waters and then-Senator Robert Larson was held at the Shrine Auditorium in Los Angeles, California before a sold-out crowd and nationally televised audience.

10. During the debate, in response to a question from the moderator, Waters discussed her past history of drug and alcohol abuse and outlined the reasons her personal history made her an ideal candidate to serve as a California senator.

11. Immediately after the debate, Harrison posted the following statement about Waters on his website, www.justtellthetruth.com:

"Kirsten Waters blatantly lied at the final debate . . . details coming shortly."

12. Approximately thirty minutes later, Harrison published the following statements concerning Waters:

Sadly, I have uncovered yet another politician who cannot tell the truth. Kirsten Waters intentionally lied during her debate with Senator Larson. Kirsten's statements about her past struggle with substance abuse — obviously designed to sway California voters — are fabrications. I was Kirsten's friend during college and I unconditionally supported Kirsten while she struggled to overcome addiction. I am shocked that Kirsten would exploit her past for political gain. More specifically, while Kirsten was arrested for Driving under the Influence of Alcohol and possession of a controlled substance, **she was neither incarcerated nor ordered to spend even a single day in a residential treatment program. After pleading guilty, Kirsten was sentenced to 90 days probation and 100 hours of community service. Additionally, as part of the plea deal, the controlled substance charge was dropped. Kirsten only sought residential treatment because her parents threatened to stop paying her tuition at Stanford. Kirsten's lies show that she is not fit for public office.**

In addition, because I am committed to telling the whole truth, I must disclose that, while at Stanford, Kirsten engaged in highly questionable conduct. During our last two years at Stanford, Kirsten was engaged to a mutual friend (who I will not reveal at this time). Kirsten suddenly broke off the engagement and admitted to having a lengthy affair with another man throughout the duration of the relationship. I will soon release a letter Kirsten wrote to our friend admitting the affair. The whole truth is that Kirsten reluctantly sought treatment — only to save herself — while repeatedly lying to and eventually betraying a very decent man.

I would like to add one final comment. While at Stanford, Kirsten performed poorly in her studies. Kirsten was not a good student and I doubt she has the abilities to effectively serve in any elected capacity. I don't know how she was accepted by the University of California-Berkeley School of Law. I do know this: her dad is one of Berkeley's most generous donors. Kirsten's admission to Berkeley wasn't about merit. It was about favoritism and money. I also question how Kirsten ever graduated from Berkeley. I can't imagine her passing all of those difficult law school classes without receiving significant help from her family.

13. Five days after the debate, Waters defeated then-Senator Larson by 314 votes, the closest margin in California's history.

14. Shortly after the election, Harrison published a letter on his blog allegedly written by Waters' former probation officer. The letter, dated November 10, 1994 and addressed to Waters, contained the following statement:

As you know, the court sentenced you to a probation term of 90 days, and 100 hours of community service. Having complied fully with these responsibilities, your sentence is hereby complete and this matter now concluded.

Harrison has not provided information supporting this document's authenticity.

15. The statements Harrison posted on www.justtellthetruth.com were reported and re-published by news media organizations throughout the country.

16. Once the statements and accusations made on Harrison's website were widely reported by the media, Waters' approval rating plummeted. As a result of Harrison's tortious conduct, Waters was forced to resign her Senate seat.

COUNT ONE

TORTIOUS INVASION OF PRIVACY

17. Plaintiff incorporates the allegations made in paragraphs 1–16 as if set forth herein.

18. Harrison's disclosure of Waters' criminal background, including his disclosure of the criminal sentence she received as a result of 1994 charges of driving under the influence of alcohol and possession of a controlled substance, constitutes an invasion of Waters' privacy under California law.

19. Harrison disclosed information on Waters' criminal background on his website, www.justtellthetruth.com, a nationally known website viewed by thousands of people daily.

20. The facts about Waters disclosed by Harrison on his website were private facts.

21. The disclosure made by Harrison was objectionable to Waters and would have been objectionable to a reasonable person in Waters' position.

22. The information disclosed by Harrison was private information that was not of legitimate public concern.

23. Waters sustained injury, including injury to her reputation, as a result of Harrison's disclosure of information about Waters' criminal history.

COUNT TWO

CONSTITUTIONAL INVASION OF PRIVACY

24. Plaintiff incorporates the allegations made in paragraphs 1–23 as if set forth herein.

25. Harrison's disclosure of Waters' criminal background, including his disclosure of the criminal sentence she received as a result of 1994 charges of driving under the influence of alcohol and possession of a controlled substance, constitutes an invasion of Waters' right to privacy under the California constitution.

26. Waters had a legally protected privacy interest in the information Harrison disclosed about Waters' criminal history.

27. Waters had a reasonable expectation of privacy in the facts Harrison disclosed about Waters' criminal history.

28. Harrison's disclosure of information about Waters' criminal history constituted a serious invasion of Waters' privacy.

29. Waters sustained injuries, including injury to her reputation, as a result of Harrison's disclosure of facts about Waters' criminal history.

COUNT THREE

DEFAMATION — LIBEL PER SE

30. Waters incorporates herein the allegations contained on Paragraphs 1–29.

31. Harrison intentionally and knowingly published the above statements to third parties on his website, www.justtellthetruth.com.

32. The statements Harrison published on www.justtellthetruth.com, including statements that Waters lied to and was unfaithful to a former fiancé, that Waters sought treatment for substance abuse for her own personal gain, that Waters cheated her way through law school, and that Waters would not have graduated from law school had it not been for her father's status as a substantial donor to the law school Waters attended, were false and defamatory.

33. The statements Harrison published about Waters were unprivileged and were not made by Harrison pursuant to any official duty.

34. Harrison's statements directly injured and continue to injure Waters with respect to her office, profession, trade or business, either by imputing to her general disqualification in those respects which the office or other occupation peculiarly requires, or by imputing something with reference to her office, profession, trade, or business that has a natural tendency to lessen its profit.

35. Harrison's statements have exposed, and continue to expose, Waters to hatred, contempt, ridicule, or obloquy, caused Waters to be shunned or avoided, and have a tendency to injure Waters in her occupation.

36. The average listener can understand Harrison's statements to convey the intended defamatory meaning. They do not require explanatory or extrinsic evidence.

37. Harrison's statements were made with actual malice or reckless disregard for the truth and with the specific intent to injure Waters.

38. Waters has suffered, and continues to suffer, general, special, and exemplary damages. Harrison's statements directly and proximately caused injury to Waters' reputation, and deprived Waters of, among other things, the opportunity to pursue political office and obtain gainful employment in the legal profession. Additionally, Waters has suffered, and continues to suffer, psychological and emotional trauma.

<u>COUNT FOUR</u>

DEFAMATION — LIBEL PER QUOD

39. Waters incorporates herein the allegations contained on Paragraphs 1–38.

40. To the extent required, Waters can demonstrate by clear and convincing evidence that Harrison's statements were false, defamatory, unprivileged, injurious, and made with actual malice or reckless disregard for the truth.

<u>COUNT FIVE</u>

PUNITIVE DAMAGES

41. Plaintiff incorporates the allegations made in paragraphs 1–40 as if set forth herein.

42. Harrison's conduct in posting false, defamatory, and injurious statements about Waters on his website was done with actual malice and in willful disregard for the rights and privacy of Waters.

43. Waters is entitled to recover punitive damages as a result of Harrison's conduct.

WHEREFORE, Plaintiff demands:

1. Judgment against Harrison in the amount of $5,000,000 for his tortious invasion of Waters' privacy;

2. Judgment against Harrison in the amount of $5,000,000 for his violation of Waters' constitutional right to privacy;

3. Judgment against Harrison in the amount of $5,000,000 for his defamation of Waters; and

4. Judgment against Harrison in the amount of $5,000,000 for punitive damages to punish Harrison and to deter him from similar future conduct.

*   *   *   *   *

What makes this a well-pleaded complaint?

▶ *Jurisdiction and Venue.* The author alleges that the court has personal jurisdiction over Harrison, that the court has subject matter jurisdiction pursuant to 28 U.S.C. § 1332, and that venue is proper. The author cites the relevant code sections and even cites the local rules that show why the San Jose division is the proper one in the Northern District of California.

▶ *Factual Allegations.* The author drafts a "short and plain" statement of the factual background, outlining the Who (Harrison), the When (after the debate), and the What (the detailed statements made by Harrison). Note that the author includes the specific statements made by Harrison, not just a summary of those statements. There may be several reasons for this. First, by including the specific quotes, instead of a summary, Waters makes it difficult for Harrison to deny the allegations. Second, Waters seeks to avoid the possibility that Harrison would file a motion to dismiss for failure to state a claim. Third, Waters gets Harrison's allegedly defamatory statements in front of the court at the first opportunity.

► *Causes of Action.* The author asserts five separate claims — four substantive claims and one for punitive damages. The author tracks the elements of each of those types of claims. For example, as you know from the memos you previously reviewed, to prove tortious invasion of privacy under California law, Waters must prove: (1) public disclosure; (2) of a private fact; (3) the disclosure would be objectionable to a reasonable person; and (4) the fact disclosed is not of legitimate public concern. The allegations in Count One track the elements. Waters alleges that Harrison made a public disclosure of a private fact about Waters, the disclosure would be objectionable to a reasonable person, and the information disclosed by Harrison was not of legitimate public concern.

► *Punitive Damages.* Waters asks for punitive damages and tracks the relevant authority, which permits a plaintiff to recover punitive damages when a defendant acts with actual malice or in willful disregard for the rights of others.

► *Prayer for Relief.* Waters' prayer for relief is specific — she asks for monetary damages for defamation and invasion of privacy and punitive damages for what Waters alleges was actual malice on Harrison's part. These are appropriate, available damages for Waters' claims.

► *The Local Rules.* The author follows the Federal Rules of Civil Procedure (which govern filings in federal courts) and the local rules in the Northern District of California. For example, Rule 38 of the Federal Rules of Civil Procedure requires a written demand for jury trial and permits the plaintiff to include that demand with another pleading. The author complies by including the written demand at the conclusion of the complaint. The author also complies with the local rules of the Northern District of California which, for example, require that the attorney's contact information be included in the upper left corner of the first page of the complaint. The author wouldn't know this without consulting the local rules.

Chapter 7

THE MOTION TO DISMISS

THE MOTION TO DISMISS CHECKLIST

√ Use a short introduction
  - √ State the legal remedy you're seeking
  - √ Briefly outline the law on which you are relying
  - √ Perform a short analysis, explaining why your motion should be granted
√ Outline the facts in an accurate but persuasive manner
  - √ A court generally must accept facts alleged in complaint (but not the legal conclusions) as true, so do not try to contest factual allegations
  - √ You may assert additional facts (or lack of facts) for certain 12(b) motions to dismiss, but check the local rules or cases from your jurisdiction to determine what types of facts the courts will consider
  - √ Generally avoid providing facts other than those pertinent to the motion to dismiss
  - √ Support your recitation of the facts with an affidavit, if permitted and necessary
√ Know the standard you must meet and craft an accurate but persuasive explanation of the standard
  - √ Present the standard in a way that makes the court want to rule in your favor
√ Present the relevant law accurately but persuasively
  - √ Outline the law generally then discuss more specific information about elements, prongs, or considerations
  - √ Cite relevant statutory language
  - √ Cite relevant, binding cases, if available
  - √ Cite relevant, persuasive cases
√ Perform a convincing analysis of the facts in light of the law
  - √ Make your strongest argument first
  - √ Determine whether and to what extent to address counterarguments
  - √ Consider saving some arguments for a reply brief
√ Wrap up the brief with an effective conclusion
  - √ Remind the court what you want
  - √ Reiterate the reason you think you're entitled to it
√ Don't forget to check the local rules
  - √ Ensure that your motion is timely

    ✓ Ensure you comply with all font, formatting, and other requirements in local rules

    ✓ Check to see if reply briefs are permitted

I. WHEN — AND WHY — TO FILE A MOTION TO DISMISS

The Motion to Dismiss is a powerful weapon in any lawyer's arsenal. It protects clients against non-meritorious lawsuits, promotes judicial economy, and facilitates the speedy resolution of frivolous cases. Rule 12(b) of the Federal Rules of Civil Procedure provides specific grounds upon which an attorney may move to dismiss a complaint. Many state-specific rules of civil procedure mirror of the federal rules, but be sure to check your jurisdiction's rules on motions to dismiss before drafting one.

Under federal law (and in most jurisdictions), you may move to dismiss a complaint under Rule 12(b) for the following reasons:

- Lack of subject matter jurisdiction;

- Lack of personal jurisdiction;

- Improper venue;

- Improper service; and

- Failure to state a claim upon which relief may be granted. The attorney who moves to dismiss on this ground argues that even if the plaintiff's allegations are accepted as true, they do not support the requested relief.

You may file a motion to dismiss for a number of other reasons as well. For example, you might file a motion to strike a complaint and motion to dismiss on the ground that the plaintiff spoliated evidence. But we are not talking about those types of motions to dismiss here — we are talking about the typical 12(b) motions to dismiss.

You may seek to have a complaint dismissed for more than one reason; for example, lack of service of process and failure to state a claim. That's fine, so long as you adequately support each ground. And you may move to dismiss the entire complaint or only specific causes of action. If you are only asking the Court to throw out certain claims, make sure you clearly specify what claims you are moving to dismiss.

But think hard about the likelihood of success before filing a motion to dismiss. Through a motion to dismiss, you are asking a judge to singlehandedly throw out the plaintiff's case without allowing the plaintiff to obtain any discovery whatsoever and without allowing a jury to decide whether the plaintiff is entitled to a legal remedy. If you were a judge, you'd be skeptical too, wouldn't you? But motions to dismiss are granted regularly, so they are clearly appropriate in some cases. Follow these tips to increase your chance of success.

II. MAXIMIZING PERSUASION

A. Use an introduction to outline your strongest arguments

Be sure to use introductions in motions to dismiss, just as you would in any other motion. Your introduction needn't be long, but it should provide some general facts and analysis and let the court know that you are asking it to dismiss the plaintiff's complaint. In your introduction, you can choose to discuss the applicable legal principles generally and avoid having to provide cites to statues or cases. Since you will provide cites later in your document, it is not necessary to provide them in your introduction. Of course, if you quote specific language of cases or statutes in your introduction, you will need to provide citations.

Courts deal with motions to dismiss frequently, so you are probably safe to leave out a detailed explanation of "the law" in the introduction of your motion to dismiss; however, you should at least mention the applicable law. Let's look at an example introduction where the defendant is moving to dismiss the complaint for lack of subject matter jurisdiction:

> **Long Construction Company files this motion to dismiss, asking the Court to dismiss Eastern States Construction Company's complaint for lack of subject matter jurisdiction. Eastern alleges that the Court has subject matter jurisdiction over this case pursuant to 28 U.S.C. § 1332, which vests a federal court with jurisdiction over state-law claims when there is diversity of citizenship. While Long admits that the amount in controversy exceeds the $75,000 statutory minimum, Long and Eastern are not citizens of different states; thus, there is no diversity of citizenship. Long and Eastern are both citizens of Virginia. Long is a Delaware corporation; however, its principal place of business is in Virginia. And Eastern is a Virginia corporation with its principal place of business in Virginia. Because Long and Eastern are both residents of Virginia, this Court lacks subject matter jurisdiction. Thus, Long's motion to dismiss should be granted.**

This introduction tells the court what Long wants (a dismissal), tells the court the facts that support Long's motion (Long and Eastern are citizens of the same state), tells the court what law Long is relying on (but doesn't go into great detail about the law, since federal courts know the requirements of § 1332), and reminds the court again what Long is asking the court to do. Introductions are extraordinarily helpful for judges and their clerks, so don't forget to use them.

B. Use Strong Headings and Subheadings

Use headings and subheadings to guide the reader through your motion to dismiss, just as you would in any other motion. You can choose "standard" main headings if you'd like or tailor your headings depending on the case. The authors generally use some variation of these main headings:

- Introduction;

- Factual Background (or Factual and Procedural Background);
- Motion to Dismiss Standard;
- Authority and Legal Analysis; and
- Conclusion;

Your subheadings, of course, will depend on the basis of your motion to dismiss. For example, if you are filing a motion to dismiss for lack of personal jurisdiction, your authority and analysis subheadings might mirror the three-part test the federal courts employ in determining whether a federal court may exercise specific jurisdiction over a non-resident defendant. Or, as in some of the examples you will see below, if the facts and law are relatively uncomplicated, you might not need subheadings at all. Just remember that you use headings and subheadings to help your reader, and if headings and subheadings will aid readability and understanding, you should use them.

C. Know the Standard and State It Persuasively

The standard for granting a motion to dismiss, no matter the basis for the motion, is high. You've got to know what you need to prove to show your client is entitled to dismissal. As we've said before, you must present the law honestly, but you also want to state the standard in a way that favors your position. Let's look at how you might do that for a motion to dismiss for failure to state a claim.

To survive a motion to dismiss under Rule 12(b)(6) of the Federal Rules of Civil Procedure, the complaint must "state a claim to relief that is plausible on its face." *Bell Atlantic Corp. v. Twombly*, 550 U.S. 544, 570 (2007). A motion to dismiss should be granted when the plaintiff "can prove no set of facts in support of [the plaintiff's] claims which would entitle [the plaintiff] to relief." *Conley v. Gibson*, 355 U.S. 41, 45-46 (1957). The Seventh Circuit Court of Appeals, has interpreted this standard to mean that, to survive a motion to dismiss for failure to state a claim, the plaintiff's complaint "must contain either direct or inferential allegations respecting all the material elements necessary to sustain a recovery under *some* viable legal theory." *Car Carriers, Inc. v. Ford Motor Co.*, 745 F.2d 1101 (7th Cir. 1984) (quoting *Sutliff, Inc. v. Donovan Cos.*, 727 F.2d 648, 654 (7th Cir. 1984)) (emphasis in original).

A grant of dismissal pursuant to Rule 12(b)(6) "serves the very valuable function of saving judicial and party resources in cases where it simply would not be productive to proceed." *Worthington v. Subaru-Isuzu Auto., Inc.*, 868 F. Supp. 1067, 1068 (N.D. Ind. 1994). If every claim were allowed to proceed to trial, "the costs generated thereby would be enormous and there would be little benefit in the way of increased accuracy in the results." *Gomez v. Illinois State Board of Educ.*, 811 F.2d 1030, 1039 (7th Cir. 1987). When it is "obvious well before trial that the defending party is entitled to judgment . . . there is no need to expend further the resources of the parties and the court." *Id.*

This is a good, defendant-friendly explanation of the general standard as interpreted by the Seventh Circuit. Notice how the author turns the focus around — instead of focusing on what the defendant must prove to get the motion granted, the author drafts the standard in terms of what the plaintiff must have done to survive the motion, making it appear as if the plaintiff bears the burden of proof. Look at the language the author uses to shift the focus:

- "To survive a motion to dismiss, the complaint must . . . ."
- "A motion to dismiss should be granted when the plaintiff . . . ."
- "The plaintiff's complaint must . . . ."

Now what about the second paragraph? What does that paragraph add to the explanation of the standard? A lot, for the defendant. The author uses the second paragraph to emphasize the importance of 12(b)(6) motions — the author is essentially saying to the court: "I'm helping you out by filing this motion. I'm trying to preserve judicial resources, avoid wasting money, and prevent this fruitless case from clogging up the court docket." While you must be accurate in explaining the standard to the court, this passage is a great example of how you can present the standard in a way that favors dismissal.

D. State the Facts Persuasively — But Only the Facts That Are Relevant

Now, listen closely. We're about to tell you something that you might never have heard before and might never hear again. With the *very* important exception of motions to dismiss for failure to state a claim, Statements of Fact in motions to dismiss are generally not very important — and here's why. Under the Federal Rules and the rules of most (if not all) jurisdictions, in deciding the propriety of a motion to dismiss, the court must assume the allegations in the complaint are true. In your motion to dismiss, you can still briefly outline the factual contentions in the case (and you can ever refer to them as "contentions" rather than "facts"), but you cannot dispute that they are true for purposes of the motion to dismiss. Thus, unless you are filing a motion to dismiss for failure to state a claim, don't spend much time "telling the story"— it won't help your client's position.

What you must do in your Statement of Facts, however, is include facts that you will use in your brief to support your motion to dismiss. Many times, these facts will have nothing to do with the substance of the complaint. For example, the necessary supporting facts might be your client's state of incorporation or the amount in controversy (if you are challenging a federal court's subject matter jurisdiction), your client's state of residency (if you are challenging personal jurisdiction), or the "non-fact" that the client has not been served with process in the action (if you're filing a motion based on lack of service of process).

And a reminder: for each fact you offer in your Statement of Facts, you must cite the complaint, the answer, an exhibit to the complaint or answer, an affidavit (discussed in more detail below), or some other admissible evidence that supports your position.

Let's look at an example of how you might draft a good Statement of Facts. Suppose you represent a defendant-corporation and you want to file a motion to dismiss the plaintiff's personal injury action on the basis of lack of service of process. The plaintiff attempted to perfect service on your client by serving the corporation president's administrative assistant, but you have authority from your jurisdiction that service on an administrative assistant who is not authorized to accept service is not sufficient. How might you present the facts?

Dean filed this personal injury action against Jackson Management Company, Inc. on February 15, 2013, just one day before the two-year statute of limitations expired. *See* Personal Injury Complaint.

On February 28, 2013, Dean attempted to perfect service on Jackson by delivering a copy of the summons and complaint in an envelope to Elizabeth Ronald, the administrative assistant of Jackson's president, Ryan Winston. Affidavit of Elizabeth Ronald ("Ronald Aff.") ¶ 4. That day, Dean's process server, who did not identify himself, entered Jackson's headquarters and asked Ronald if she worked for Winston. *Id.* at ¶ 6. When Ronald told the process server that she did work for Winston, he handed her the envelope and walked out of Jackson's office. *Id.* at ¶ 7. In fact, Ronald was not even aware that Dean's process server was attempting service until Ronald opened the package, which bore Winston's name, and saw the summons and complaint. *Id.* at ¶ 8.

Ronald is not an officer of Jackson and is not Jackson's registered agent for service. *Id.* at ¶ 10; Affidavit of Ryan Winston ("Winston Aff.") ¶ 5. Ronald had no authority to accept service of process on behalf of Jackson and did not represent to the process server that she had such authority. Ronald Aff. at ¶ 11; Winston Aff. at ¶ 6.

Out of an abundance of caution, Jackson filed an answer within 30 days of the date Jackson was purportedly served. *See* Answer of Defendant Jackson Management Company.

This passage contains very little information about the underlying factual allegations; in fact, the only information the reader learns is that the suit is a personal injury action. That's because the allegations in the complaint aren't important for purposes of Jackson's motion to dismiss — the only "facts" that matter are those that bear on the issue of whether service on the administrative assistant was valid service, so those are the only facts the writer outlines.

And Jackson's decision not to mention the underlying allegations also is a strategic one. Jackson wants the court to focus on the Dean's "bad" conduct in waiting until the last minute to file the complaint then failing to properly perfect service, not the "bad" conduct Jackson allegedly committed that injured Dean. By declining to detail the underlying facts, Jackson seeks to avoid giving the court a reason to feel sorry for Dean and allow him another opportunity to perfect service.

If your motion to dismiss is one for failure to state a claim, however, the underlying allegations are *critically* important. Why? In filing a motion to dismiss, the filer basically says: "For purposes of the motion, I'll concede that the plaintiff's allegations are true. But even if they are, the plaintiff still can't state a claim."

As we said above, in deciding a motion to dismiss, the court will accept the plaintiff's factual allegations as true. Thus, in outlining the Statement of Facts in a motion to dismiss for failure to state a claim, you must truthfully and accurately report the allegations. Again, you can call them "allegations," rather than "facts," but the court still must have an accurate understanding of the plaintiff's allegations in order to determine the propriety of the motion to dismiss. And remember — do not attempt to "fudge" the plaintiff's allegations to make it appear the plaintiff has failed to make certain allegations that the plaintiff has, in fact, made. You'll lose credibility with the court — credibility that is critical if the court is to dismiss the plaintiff's complaint.

Let's look at an example of the Statement of Facts in a motion for dismiss for failure to state a claim. Assume you represent a client defending a breach of contract action. The plaintiff claims he had an oral employment agreement with your client. You don't think there was an agreement and, even if there were, you don't believe the agreement is enforceable because it does not comply with the statute of frauds. How would you draft your statement of facts?

> **Plaintiff Brian Green filed this breach of contract action against High Tech Solutions, Inc., a company that provides computer engineering services to private businesses, public companies, and governments around the world.** *See* **Complaint for Breach of Contract ("Complaint"). Green, a computer engineer, claims that he had a long-standing professional relationship with High Tech's president, Jennifer Lindon.** *Id.* **at ¶ 10. From 2008–2012, Green, pursuant to a written agreement, worked as an independent contractor for High Tech, performing computer engineering services for High Tech's customers.** *Id.* **at ¶ 12; Answer of High Tech Solutions, Inc. ("Answer") ¶ 12. Green claims that during that period, he also performed services for other people and businesses, including business that competed directly with High Tech. Complaint at ¶ 13.**

> **Green alleges that in 2012, Lindon offered him a full-time employment position with High Tech in exchange for Green's promise to cease performing services for any of High Tech's competitors.** *Id.* **at ¶ 14. According to Green, Lindon guaranteed him full-time employment with High Tech for at least 24 months at a salary of $10,000 per month.** *Id.* **at ¶ 15. Green claims his employment was to begin on May 1, 2012 and, if his contract were not renewed, would cease on April 30, 2014.** *Id.* **at ¶ 16.**

> **Green alleges that he began full-time employment with High Tech on May 1, 2012 but less than two weeks later, on May 12, 2012, Lindon fired him after the two disagreed about the way Green had written a program for a long-time High Tech client.** *Id.* **at ¶ 18. Green admits he was paid for the services he provided from May 1, 2012 to May 12, 2012 but seeks $236,500 in damages, the amount he claims he would have been paid over the 24-month period, for breach of contract.** *Id.* **at ¶¶ 20, 31.**

This example offers a thorough explanation of the plaintiff's allegations because the motion to dismiss is one for failure to state a claim. Don't forget, you want to give the court all the information it will need to decide the motion and you can't contest the factual allegations. This example does a good job of honestly and accurately outlining the plaintiff's claims in the least damaging way. You wouldn't for example, want to quote Green's complaint in which Green alleges Lindon "had no intention of employing Green on a full-time basis and simply lied to Green about offering him a full-time job with High Tech to prevent Green from taking a full-time job with one of High Tech's biggest competitors." That makes High Tech and its president look really bad. You want to strike the proper balance, like this example does, of accurately summarizing the plaintiff's allegations in a way that minimizes your client's conduct or involvement.

These are good examples of the types of short fact statements you'll likely draft when you file a motion for summary judgment. Remember, though, that each case is different. While some cases lend themselves to short fact statements, others require a more detailed explanation. The amount of detail you need to include in your Statement of Facts will differ from case to case.

E.   Supporting the Brief with an Affidavit

Some courts will accept affidavits in support of 12(b) motions to dismiss. Acceptable affidavits, however, must generally contain only limited information relevant to the basis for the motion to dismiss (e.g., an averment that the client has not been served with process). If you attempt to add additional facts, dispute alleged facts, or attach documents that relate to the underlying substantive allegations to an affidavit, the court likely will decline to dismiss the complaint.[35] The court might also convert your motion to dismiss to a motion for summary judgment, and you don't want that to happen, because a summary judgment motion is a different type of motion with different standards and requisite proof. Again, the rules in your jurisdiction (or the local rules) will govern this issue, so don't forget to check them.

F.   Outline the Law Accurately, Focusing on Law That Is Favorable

As we outlined in Chapter 3, good legal writers generally start with a broad explanation of the relevant legal principles (often known as the umbrella section) and work their way down to an explanation of the more minute details. You should use this method when drafting the Authority and Analysis section of your motion to dismiss.

For this section and the next section, we'll focus on the Virginia diversity of citizenship case that we drafted an introduction for above. How would you outline the law, going from broad principles to more specific ones? Here is an example we think is pretty good:

Federal courts are courts of limited jurisdiction, and the burden of proving jurisdiction rests with the party asserting it. *Kokkonen v.*

---

[35] Some federal courts recognize a "narrow exception" to this rule in which the courts will consider certain extrinsic documents, such as documents of undisputed authenticity, official public records, and documents sufficiently referred to in the complaint, in deciding motions to dismiss. *See, e.g., Freeman v. Town of Hudson*, 714 F.3d 29 (1st Cir. 2013).

Guardian Life Ins. Co. of Am., 511 U.S. 375, 377 (1994).When a plaintiff seeks to litigate a state law claim in a federal court, the plaintiff must prove the federal court has subject matter jurisdiction pursuant to 28 U.S.C. § 1332. Under that statute, a federal court has original subject matter jurisdiction over litigation (1) where the amount in controversy exceeds $75,000, excluding interest and costs; and (2) the parties are citizens of different states. 28 U.S.C. § 1332(a).

A corporation is deemed to be a resident of both the state in which it is incorporated and the state where its principal place of business is located. 28 U.S.C. § 1332(c)(1). Thus, 28 U.S.C. § 1332(c) provides "dual, not alternative, citizenship" to a corporation that is incorporated in one state and maintains its principal place of business in another. *Johnson v. Advance America*, 549 F.3d 932, 935 (4th Cir. 2008).

A corporation's principal place of business is its "nerve center"; that is, the place "where a corporation's officers direct, control, and coordinate the corporation's activities." *Hertz Corp. v. Friend*, 559 U.S. 77, 92 (2010). The nerve center is generally the location of the corporation's headquarters, so long as that headquarters is the "actual center of direction, control, and coordination." *Id.* In determining a corporation's nerve center, courts will look to the location of corporate oversight and strategic decision-making. *Central West Virginia Energy Co., Inc. v. Mountain State Carbon, LLC*, 636 F.3d 101, 105 (4th Cir. 2011). The principal place of business analysis is performed on a case-by-case basis. *Long v. Silver*, 248 F.3d 309, 315 (4th Cir. 2001).

For example, in *Central West Virginia*, the Fourth Circuit Court of Appeals considered whether a defendant's principal place of business was located in Michigan or West Virginia. The offices of the defendant's CEO, COO, CFO, and general counsel were in Michigan, while only one corporate officer, who was a vice president and general manager, maintained a West Virginia office. *Id.* at 105. The Michigan officers were responsible for "significant oversight and strategic decision-making," but the day-to-day company management and operations, such as purchasing materials, selling products, and administering payroll, occurred in West Virginia. *Id.* The defendant's corporate filings in several states, including West Virginia and Michigan, listed Michigan as the company's principal place of business. *Id.*

The Fourth Circuit held that the defendant's principal place of business for purposes of the Section 1332 jurisdictional analysis was Michigan. *Id.* at 102. The Court held that under the *Hertz* test, the defendant's principal place of business was Michigan because corporate policies were set in Michigan, high-level corporate decisions were made in Michigan, and corporate oversight occurred in Michigan. *Id.* at 103. The court acknowledged that employees who made day-to-day decisions were located in West Virginia, and that the company was "active in the West Virginia business community"; however, the court held that under

the *Hertz* analysis, the defendant's "nerve center" was in Michigan. *Id.* at
102; *see also Kansas City Life Ins. Co. v. Citicorp. Acceptance Co., Inc.*, 721
F. Supp. 106, 107 (S.D. W. Va. 1989) (company's principal place of business
was Missouri, where CEO's office was located in Missouri and board of
directors meetings were held there).

In this example, the author outlines the broad subject matter jurisdiction principles
(federal courts are courts of limited jurisdiction), then focuses on the elements of
federal subject matter jurisdiction analysis (the amount in controversy and diversity of
citizenship of the plaintiff and defendant), explains how courts determine citizenship of
corporations (the nerve center test), and then offers a case illustration of how the
courts apply that test (the *Central West Virginia* case).

Obviously, the facts of each case are different and, depending on the specific facts
of your case, you may have to go into further explanation or detail of the applicable law.
As you'll see below, this Section 1332 case is relatively straightforward, so there is no
reason for the author to analyze numerous cases.

One other point — you may have noticed that the *Hertz* case, in which the Supreme
Court formally adopted the nerve center test, is a recent case. Numerous prior cases
that haven't explicitly been overruled may still rely, at least to some extent, on the
"place of operations test" that is no longer good law. Thus, in explaining how the courts
apply the nerve center test, the author of this authority section chooses, we think
wisely, to rely primarily on a post-*Hertz* case that explicitly applies the "nerve center"
test as that test was outlined in *Hertz*. Although pre-*Hertz* cases that applied to the
nerve center test are still "good law," by choosing a post-*Hertz* case the author avoids
any counterargument that the author's primary authority has been overruled. This
technique is not what you would think as a classic way to address a counterargument,
but it is an effective way to prevent a potential counterargument from ever being made.

G. Analyze the Facts

The legal arguments in a motion to dismiss must be extremely persuasive and
amply supported by the relevant facts. If the court has any doubts about your client's
entitlement to dismissal, those doubts will be resolved in the plaintiff's favor, and your
motion will be denied. Thus, the Legal Analysis section of your motion to dismiss is
very important.

As we discussed in Chapter 3, your analysis must consist of more than a conclusory
summary of the facts or a blanket statement that the statute or cases offered, or both,
apply and support your position. The analysis should answer the question: Why
should your client prevail in light of the facts and law? Remember some of the
questions you should ask yourself to guide your analysis:

- Why is a statute/regulation/ordinance applicable or inapplicable?
- How are favorable cases factually similar?
- Does a comparison between recent cases and older cases suggest a trend that
  supports your position?
- How are unfavorable cases factually distinguishable?

- Was an unfavorable case decided under a different statute with different language?

- Was an unfavorable case decided under common law principles but a statute now applies?

- Are there policy arguments that support my position or disfavor my opponent's position?

And don't forget — while you don't want to be overly repetitive, you should err on the side of over-analyzing rather than under-analyzing. How would you draft a good legal analysis of the Virginia subject matter jurisdiction case?

In this matter, the requirements of Section 1332 are not met, and this Court has no subject matter jurisdiction over this case. Long admits that the amount in controversy exceeds the $75,000 statutory minimum; however, Long and Eastern are not citizens of different states and, therefore, there is no diversity of citizenship between the parties.

Under subsection (c)(1) of Section 1332, Long, a corporation, is a citizen of both the state in which it was incorporated and the state in which its principal place of business is located. Long was incorporated in Delaware and, thus, is indisputably a citizen of Delaware. Long, however, is also a citizen of Virginia because, under the *Hertz* nerve-center test, Long's principal place of business is in Virginia.

As outlined above, Long maintains a small office in Delaware that serves as a central "call center" for the company, and Long's accounting operations occur in Delaware. Eight of Long's three hundred employees work from the Delaware office, but not one of those eight employees has any decision-making authority. Long's headquarters is located in Roanoke, Virginia. The office of Long's owner and president, the single person who makes all corporate-level decisions and has sole control over the operation of the company, is located in Roanoke as well, and even the day-to-day operations of the company occur in Roanoke. Further, Long's corporate filings with the Secretaries of State in both Delaware and Virginia list Long's Roanoke, Virginia address as its principal place of business. There can be little question that Roanoke, Virginia is the place where Long's owner and president "direct[s], control[s], and coordinate[s] [Long's] activities." *Hertz*, 559 U.S. at 92.

Evidence that Long's principal place of business is in Virginia is even stronger than the evidence presented in *Central West Virginia*. In *Central West Virginia*, the defendant's officers, who were responsible for company oversight and strategic decision-making, were located in Michigan, but the day-to-day operations occurred in West Virginia. Here, Long's headquarters and president, the single decision-making authority in the company, are both located in Virginia, and Long's corporate filings represent to all interested persons that its principal place of business is in Virginia. And, unlike in *Central West Virginia*, where day-to-day operations and decision-making occurred in different states, the vast majority of all of Long's company operations, including the day-to-day operations, occur in Virginia. Under the *Hertz* nerve-center test, Long's principal place of business is located in Virginia and Long, therefore, is a resident of this state.

There is no question that Central is a Virginia resident because Central's state of incorporation is Virginia. And, as outlined above, Long is also a Virginia resident because its principal place of business is located here. Thus, because Long and Central are both citizens of Virginia, there is no diversity of citizenship between them, and the requirements of Section 1332 are not met. This Court, therefore, lacks subject matter jurisdiction over this matter, and should grant Long's motion to dismiss.

The author of this section does a good job of analyzing the legal issue in light of the facts and answering the question: Why should Long prevail in light of the facts and law? The author begins the analysis by summarizing the relevant facts about Long's corporate structure and the location of its headquarters to reach the conclusion that Long's principal place of business in is Virginia under the nerve center test. The author then compares and contrasts the facts to those in *Central West Virginia*, explaining how the facts are similar to — and even stronger than — those present in *Central West Virginia*. Importantly, the author concludes the analysis by answering the initial question: Is there subject matter jurisdiction? The author explains that the court lacks subject matter jurisdiction because Long is a citizen of Virginia, and Long is a citizen of Virginia because its principal place of business, per the *Hertz* nerve-center test, is located in Virginia.

Because the legal analysis is such an important part of any brief, be sure your legal analysis is thorough and convincing.

H.   If You Get a Reply Brief, Consider Waiting to Address Certain Counterarguments

In many jurisdictions, a motion filer may file a reply brief in addition to the initial brief in support of a motion to dismiss. Thus, if you are the movant, you will file your initial brief in support of your motion to dismiss, the respondent will file a response brief, and you will then be permitted to file a reply brief. This is true in many jurisdictions, but not all, so be sure to check your local rules to see if reply briefs are permitted.

For strategic reasons, you may want to save some of your arguments, especially responses to counterarguments, for the reply brief. First, by saving an argument for your reply brief, you'll get the last word. Second, if you don't know whether your opponent will raise a particular argument and you don't want to address the argument unless it's raised, you can choose not to address it in your initial brief. If your opponent raises the argument in the response brief, you'll still have your reply brief to address the issue. Third, if you have too many arguments to address in your initial brief, you can save some of your arguments for the reply brief. Generally, though, as we have discussed before, you should limit briefs to your best arguments, and those "best arguments" should fit in the number of pages you're allotted in your initial brief. And keep in mind — if you make "new" arguments in your reply brief, the opposing party may move to file a sur-reply brief to address those arguments.

*   *   *   *   *

Waters v. Harrison, Motion to Dismiss

In *Waters v. Harrison*, should Harrison's attorney, Warren G. Bell, file a motion to dismiss? If yes, on what grounds? Harrison lives in Erie, Pennsylvania, more than 2,500 miles from San Jose, California, where Waters resides and filed suit. Harrison resided in California while he was a student at Stanford but has not lived in California since then. Harrison made his blog posts about Waters from his residence in Pennsylvania, but those posts were read by California residents. Is that enough to subject Harrison to personal jurisdiction in a California court? Given these facts, Harrison has a reasonable chance of success in filing a motion to dismiss for lack of personal jurisdiction. Can you think of any additional grounds to dismiss the complaint?

SIMON HARRISON'S MOTION TO DISMISS

Note: All briefs must include the following: (1) a caption; (2) a notice of motion; (3) a Table of Contents and Authorities; (4) an Affidavit by each party certifying to all facts relied on in support of the motion; and (5) a certificate of service. We didn't include them here (or in our other examples) because they do not contribute significantly to the substantive discussion of persuasive writing.

INTRODUCTION

Plaintiff Kirsten Waters ("Waters") alleges that the online posting of allegedly defamatory statements — involving non-commercial and purely political speech — justifies haling into the Northern District of California a defendant who resides 2,594 miles away in Erie, Pennsylvania. Decisions from the Ninth Circuit and the Northern District of California do not support this proposition.

To begin with, "it is beyond dispute in this circuit that maintenance of a passive website alone," even "though the website [is] viewed by forum residents," cannot confer personal jurisdiction over a non-resident defendant. *Brayton Purcell LLP, v. Recordon & Recordon*, 606 F.3d 1124, 1129–1130 (9th Cir. 2010) (Brayton II) (brackets added);[36] *see also Fiore v. Walden*, 688 F.3d 558, 578 (9th Cir. 2012). As the Ninth Circuit recognizes, "something more" is required, namely, "express aiming" through "conduct targeted directly at the forum." Brayton II, 606 F.3d at 1129-1130 (*quoting Pebble Beach Co. v. Caddy*, 453 F.3d 1151, 1158 (9th Cir. 2006)).

Websites expressly aim at the forum by engaging in "commercial use" or, as the Northern District recently held, interacting with viewers in ways that encourage

---

[36] *Brayton II* superseded the Ninth Circuit's earlier decision in *Brayton Purcell LLP. v. Recordon & Recordon*, 575 F.3d 981, 988 (9th Cir. 2009).

"residents of the forum state to access the website." *Vanity.com, Inc. v. Vanity Shop of Grand Forks, Inc.,* . . . [2012 U.S. Dist. LEXIS 144088, at *10–*11] (Slip Copy) (N.D. Cal. October 4, 2012) (citation omitted).

Thus, merely, "making information available to those who are interested in it," even with "knowledge of an individual's residence," does not constitute the "something more" required for express aiming. *Advanced Skin & Hair, Inc. v. Bancroft*, 858 F. Supp. 2d 1084, 1088 (C.D. Cal. 2012). Accordingly, "the intentional posting of defamatory statements on the internet," is not sufficient to confer personal jurisdiction on an out-of-state defendant. *Xcentric Ventures, LLC v. Bird*, 683 F. Supp. 2d 1068, 1073 (D. Ariz. 2010).

Defendant Simon Harrison ("Harrison") operates http://www.justtellthetruth.com, a passive blog (the "Website") that serves a core purpose of the First Amendment: exposing dishonesty and corruption in various areas of public life. The Website does nothing other than make information available to a general audience of interested viewers. It does not sell, advertise, promote, or endorse commercial products. It does not interact or exchange information with viewers.

The same is true here. The blog posts Harrison published about Waters — the sole contact Harrison has with California — does not target specific individuals, locations, or audiences. *Id.*

Consequently, exercising personal jurisdiction on the basis of blog posts that are merely made available to interested readers violates due process of law and is contrary notions of fair play and substantial justice. Pursuant to Fed. R. Civ. P. 12(b)(2), Harrison respectfully requests that Waters' Complaint be dismissed for lack of personal jurisdiction.

FACTUAL BACKGROUND

One week after defeating then-Senator Robert Larson by 314 votes — the closest election in California history — Waters held a press conference resigning from office. Complaint, ¶ 13. During the press conference, Waters admitted to making "inaccurate statements" during her final debate with then-Senator Larson:

> I made certain inaccurate statements at my final debate with Senator Larson. Some of the details regarding my past were inconsistent with the facts . . . . In the interest of sparing California any further attention to this matter I will resign as your Senator, yet continue to fight for the vital issues affecting all citizens of this state.

Waters' resignation occurred shortly after Harrison's online statements concerning Waters were reported by media organizations throughout the country. Complaint, ¶ 12. The statements focused on Waters' criminal history, educational background, and former engagement while a student at Stanford University. *Id.* After resigning from office, Waters filed this action alleging that Harrison's statements were defamatory and constituted an invasion of Waters' privacy under California law. Complaint, ¶¶ 18, 25, 32, 40.

The Complaint's sole basis justifying personal jurisdiction over Harrison rests upon the statements Harrison made on his blog. *Id.*, ¶ 3. Significantly, however, neither the Website nor the allegedly defamatory statements: (1) target California; (2) exchange information with California residents; (3) allow viewers in California to contact Harrison, post comments, or interact with other users; (4) send messages, electronically or otherwise, to California residents; (5) directly appeal to California's residents; (6) encourage California residents to visit the Website; or (7) engage in other activity expressly aimed at California.

In fact, the Website does nothing more than make information available to an untargeted audience of interested viewers. It does not advertise or sell commercial products. The Website does not offer services, solicit donations, or provide endorsements of any kind. Additionally, Harrison does not own or lease property in California, and does not pay or owe taxes. Harrison does not have employees, officers, or agents in California and has not sponsored events or promotions in California. The Website is, in all respects, passive.

DISCUSSION

PLAINTIFF'S COMPLAINT DOES NOT ALLEGE FACTS SUFFICIENT TO SUPPORT A PRIMA FACIE SHOWING OF PERSONAL JURISDICTION

Harrison's blog posts did not target California's residents. Importantly, it is not sufficient to show that the blog posts targeted *Waters*; there must also be a showing that they were aimed at residents of California. Waters has not alleged any facts to support such a conclusion, making the exercise of personal jurisdiction inappropriate — and unreasonable.

"When a defendant moves pursuant to Rule 12(b)(2) to dismiss a complaint for lack of personal jurisdiction, the plaintiff bears the burden of demonstrating that jurisdiction is appropriate." *Kountze v. Kountze*, . . . [2013 U.S. Dist. LEXIS 24663, at *4–*5] (N.D. Cal. February 22, 2013) (Slip Copy); *see also Love v. Assoc. Newspapers, Ltd.*, 611 F.3d 601, 608 (9th Cir. 2010). In so doing, the plaintiff "cannot simply rest on the 'bare allegations of its complaint' if controverted by evidence incorporated into defendant's motion." *Kountze* . . . [2013 U.S. Dist. LEXIS 24663, at *5] (brackets added) (*quoting Schwarzenegger v. Fred Martin Motor Co.*, 374 F.3d 797, 800 (9th Cir.2004)); *see also Data Disc, Inc. v. Systems Technology Associates, Inc.*, 557 F.2d 1280, 1284 (9th Cir. 1977) (a court "may not assume the truth of allegations in a pleading which are contradicted by affidavit").

"A federal court sitting in diversity applies the personal jurisdiction rules of the forum state and the Due Process Clause of the Fifth Amendment." *Xcentric Ventures*, 683 F. Supp. 2d 1068, 1070 (D. Ariz. 2010). In California, as in other states, personal jurisdiction "may be either general or specific." *Gator.com Corp. v. L.L. Bean, Inc.*, 341 F.3d 1072, 1076 (9th Cir. 2003).

A. Harrison does not have sufficient contacts with California to support general
jurisdiction.

Harrison's sole contact with California — two blog posts that were equally available
to residents of any state — does not remotely approach the contacts necessary to
establish general jurisdiction.

General jurisdiction is appropriate only where the defendant has a "continuous and
systematic presence" in the forum, thereby allowing the defendant to "be haled into
court in that state in any action, even if the action is unrelated to those contacts."
Piping Rock Partners, Inc. v. David Lerner Assocs., Inc. . . . [2012 U.S. Dist. LEXIS
161643, at *8] (N.D. Cal. Nov. 9, 2012) (Slip Copy); *Bancroft and Masters, Inc. v.
Augusta Nat'l, Inc.*, 223 F.3d 1082, 1087 (9th Cir. 2000).

Indeed, "[t]he standard for establishing general jurisdiction is fairly high and
requires that the defendant's contacts be of the sort that approximate physical
presence." *Piping Rock Partners,* . . . [2012 U.S. Dist. LEXIS 161643, at *9] (citations
omitted). Courts focus on the "economic realities" of the defendant's activities, such as
"whether the defendant makes sales, solicits or engages in business in the state, serves
the state's markets, designates an agent for service of process, holds a license, or is
incorporated there." *Gates Learjet Corp. v. Jensen*, 743 F.2d 1325, 1331 (9th Cir. 1984);
Piping Rock Partners, . . . [2012 U.S. Dist. LEXIS 161643, at *9] (citations omitted).

Harrison's contacts with California do not constitute a "continuous and systematic
presence." *Piping Rock Partners, Inc.,* . . . [2012 U.S. Dist. LEXIS 161643, at *8].
Harrison does not, for example, own property in California or pay or owe taxes. He
does not have employees or agents in California. Harrison does not perform print,
radio, or television advertising in California and has not sponsored events or
promotions in California. Harrison's sole contact with California consists of website
that makes information available to an untargeted audience. This contact is not
sufficient to establish general jurisdiction.

B. Harrison does not have sufficient contacts with California to support specific
jurisdiction.

Harrison's sole contact with California (apart from attending college at Stanford)
consists of two untargeted messages that were posted on a passive website. Without
more, the exercise of specific jurisdiction would be inconsistent with decisions from
this district, the Ninth Circuit, and due process of law.

To exercise specific jurisdiction, "a nonresident defendant must have 'minimum
contacts' with the forum state such that the assertion of jurisdiction 'does not offend
traditional notions of fair play and substantial justice.'" *Vanity.com, Inc.,* . . . [2012
U.S. Dist. LEXIS 144088, at *6] (N.D. Cal. Oct. 4, 2012) (*quoting Pebble Beach Co., v.
Caddy*, 453 F.3d 1151, 1155 (9th Cir. 2006)) (citation omitted). "[R]andom," "fortuitous," or "attenuated" contacts do not constitute minimum contacts. *Glencore Grain
Rotterdam B.V. v. Shivnath Rai Harnarain Co.*, 284 F.3d 1114, 1123 (9th Cir. 2002)
(*quoting Burger King Corp. v. Rudzewicz*, 471 U.S. 462, 475 (1985)).

The Ninth Circuit uses a three-part test to determine whether a non-resident defendant has the requisite minimum contacts. *Vanity.com, Inc.,* . . . [2012 U.S. Dist. LEXIS 144088, at *6–*7]. First, the "nonresident defendant must do some act or consummate some transaction with the forum or perform some act by which he purposefully avails himself of the privilege of conducting activities in the forum." *Cybersell, Inc. v. Cybersell, Inc.,* 130 F.3d 414, 418 (9th Cir. 1997) (*quoting Ballard v. Savage,* 65 F.3d 1495, 1498 (9th Cir. 1998)).

Additionally, "the 'non-resident defendant must purposefully direct his activities or consummate some transaction with the forum or resident thereof . . . thereby invoking the benefits and protections of the forum state.' " *Vanity.com, Inc.,* . . . [2012 U.S. Dist. LEXIS 144088, at *7] (*quoting Cybersell, Inc.,* 130 F.3d at 418). This analysis "turns upon whether the defendant's contacts are attributable to 'actions by the defendant himself,' or conversely to the unilateral activity of another party." *Hirsch v. Blue Cross, Blue Shield of Kansas City,* 800 F.2d 1474, 1478 (9th Cir.1986) (*quoting Burger King Corp.,* 471 U.S. at 475).

Finally, "the claim must 'arise[ ] out of or result[ ] from the defendant's forum-related activities,' " and "the exercise of personal jurisdiction over the defendant must be reasonable." *Vanity.com, Inc.,* . . . [2012 U.S. Dist. LEXIS 144088, at *7] (brackets in original) (*quoting Pebble Beach Co.,* 453 F.3d at 1155).

Importantly, "[a] 'purposeful direction analysis . . . is most often used in suits sounding in tort,' whereas purposeful availment applies to suits in contract." *Piping Rock Partners,* . . . [2012 U.S. Dist. LEXIS 161643, at *11] (*quoting Schwarzenegger,* 374 F.3d at 802). Purposeful direction is present where the defendant: "(a) committed an intentional act, (b) expressly aimed at the forum state, (c) causing harm that the defendant knows is likely to be suffered in the forum state." *Piping Rock Partners,* . . . [2012 U.S. Dist. LEXIS 161643, at *11–*12] (*quoting Fiore v. Walden,* 688 F.3d 558, 576 (9th Cir. 2012); *see also Calder v. Jones,* 465 U.S. 783, 788-791 (1984).[37]

1. Passive Websites Do Not Satisfy The Express Aiming Requirement

Harrison's website engaged in non-commercial, constitutionally protected speech of matters of public importance. It is a textbook example of a passive website, which does not "satisfy the express aiming requirement, even though the website [is] viewed by forum residents." *Fiore,* 688 F.3d at 578 (*quoting Brayton II,* 606 F.3d at 1129–1130) (brackets added) ("it is beyond dispute in this circuit that maintenance of a passive website alone cannot satisfy the express aiming prong").

In *Advanced Skin & Hair, Inc.,* the court explained that "a passive website 'does little more than make information available to those who are interested in it,' " and does not support a finding of specific jurisdiction. 858 F. Supp. 2d at 1088 (*quoting Zippo Manufacturing Co., v. Zippo Dot Com, Inc.,* 952 F. Supp. 1119, 1123 (W.D. Pa. 1997)). Thus, a "website that is viewable in California is not sufficient to establish the purposeful availment [or direction] element of the specific jurisdiction analysis." *Katzenbach v. Grant,* . . . [2005 U.S. Dist. LEXIS 46756, at *20] (E.D. Cal. June 7,

---

[37] For purposes of this motion, Harrison concedes that Complaint's allegations satisfy the first and third elements.

2005) (Unreported) (brackets added); *see also Panavision, Int'l, L.P. v. Toeppen*, 141 F.3d 1316, 1321 (9th Cir. 1998) (posting information online and making it accessible to viewers does not establish purposeful direction).

Using a "sliding scale" approach, courts have found express aiming when a website has commercial aspects or interacts with viewers. *Advanced Skin & Hair, Inc.*, 858 F. Supp. 2d at 1088. In these cases, "the constitutionality of exercising personal jurisdiction is 'directly proportionate to the nature and quality of commercial activity that an entity conducts over the internet.'" *Id. (quoting Zippo*, 952 F. Supp. at 1124) (emphasis added); *see also Cybersell*, 130 F.3d at 418 ("Courts that have addressed interactive sites have looked to the level of interactivity and commercial nature of the information that occurs on the Web").

In *Cybersell*, for example, the Ninth Circuit refused to exercise personal jurisdiction where a defendant's website — accessible in California — contained allegedly infringing trademarks. 130 F.3d at 416. Since the website did not allow parties to transact business, the Ninth Circuit concluded that the defendant had "done no act and consummated no transaction, nor had it performed any act by which it purposefully availed itself of the privilege of conducting activities, in Arizona, thereby invoking the benefits and protections of Arizona law." 130 F.3d at 419; *see also Bancroft and Masters*, 223 F.3d at 1086 (finding that the defendant's website was passive because viewers could not make purchases). The Ninth Circuit explained that interactivity consists of, among other things, earning income, selling products or services, receiving telephone calls, forming contractual relationships, and sending messages over the internet. 130 F.3d at 419.

Moreover, in *Vanity.com, Inc.*, the Northern District held that websites are considered "interactive" when, in addition to online advertising, "they have 'something more,' such as conducting commercial activity over the internet with forum residents, encouraging residents of the forum state to access the website, or earning income from residents in the forum state." . . . [2012 U.S. Dist. LEXIS 144088, at *10–*11] *(quoting Cybersell, Inc.*, 130 F.3d at 419). The "additional connection" requirement was implicitly acknowledged in *Brayton I*, where the Ninth Circuit found personal jurisdiction "over a non-resident law firm that allegedly created a website that willfully copied portions of another law firm's website." *Xcentric Ventures*, 683 F. Supp. 2d at 1074 (*discussing Brayton I*, 575 F.3d at 988). In *Brayton I*, the majority, responding to Judge Reinhart's dissent, stated:

> Assuming the dissent is correct that something more than knowledge of the residence of the plaintiff is required for there to be express aiming at the Forum, such a requirement is satisfied here; the parties are competitors in the same business so that the intentional infringement will advance the interests of the defendant to the detriment of the Forum interests of the Plaintiff.

Brayton I, 575 F.3d at 988. (emphasis added). Furthermore, the defendant "targeted Brayton Purcell's business, and entered direct competition with Brayton Purcell." *Brayton II*, 606 F.3d at 1130 (emphasis added).

Similarly, in *Lang v. Morris*, the Northern District refused to exercise personal jurisdiction over a New York resident who — with knowledge of the Plaintiff's residency — posted a series of origami paintings online that allegedly infringed on the Plaintiff's copyrights. 823 F. Supp. 2d 966, 968 (N.D. Cal. 2011). In its holding, the Northern District stated that "[t]his Court has been unable to find any case in which a court relied only on the defendant's knowledge of the plaintiff's residency (coupled with an allegation of copyright infringement or other tortuous [sic] conduct) in finding specific personal jurisdiction." Id. at 972, fn.2 (emphasis added); *see also Mavrix Photo, Inc. v. Brand Technologies, Inc.* 647 F.3d 1218, 1229 (9th Cir. 2011) (specific jurisdiction was proper over a celebrity gossip website that "used Mavrix's copyrighted photos as part of its exploitation of the California market for its own commercial gain") (emphasis added); *CollegeSource, Inc. v. AcademyOne, Inc.*, 653 F.3d 1066, 1077 (9th Cir. 2011) (jurisdiction was found where the defendant competed with Plaintiff "in the market to assist students and educational institutions with the college transfer process," and expressly targeted Plaintiff's business as "direct competitors in a relatively small industry").

By contrast, "personal jurisdiction is 'not appropriate when a website is merely . . . passive' because, unlike interactive websites, it neither 'function[s] for commercial purposes' nor allows users to exchange information." *Allstar Marketing Group, LLC v. Your Store Online, LLC*, 666 F. Supp. 2d 1109, 1121 (C.D. Cal. 2009) (*quoting Stomp, Inc. v. NeatO, LLC*, 61 F. Supp. 2d 1074, 1078 (C.D. Cal. 1999)) (brackets added).

Harrison's website is entirely passive. The Website exists solely for the purpose of uncovering dishonest and, in some cases, unlawful behavior by public figures. To his credit, Harrison's website has been credited with exposing a bribery scandal involving the mayor of Philadelphia, Pennsylvania and raising awareness about the use of performance-enhancing drugs among professional athletes. The Website, however, does not target specific audiences, individuals, or forums. Viewers — in California and elsewhere — cannot contact Harrison, post comments, or interact with other users. Furthermore, the Website does not send messages, electronically or otherwise, to individual users. The Website merely makes information available to an untargeted audience of interested individuals.

Additionally, the Website neither sells nor advertises commercial products, and does not offer services, solicit donations, or provide endorsements. It earns no income whatsoever. Thus, by focusing solely on political speech that is made available to a general audience, the Website does not conduct "commercial activity over the internet with forum residents," or encourage "residents of the forum state to access the website." *Vanity.com, Inc.*, . . . [2012 U.S. Dist. LEXIS 144088, at *10–*11] (*quoting Cybersell, Inc.*, 130 F.3d at 419). The Website therefore lacks the requisite "interactivity" to justify specific jurisdiction, making Waters' allegations, which allege nothing more than the "defendant's knowledge of the plaintiff's residency (coupled with an allegation of . . . tortuous [sic] conduct)," insufficient. *Lang*, 823 F. Supp. 2d at 972, fn.2.

2. POSTING ALLEGEDLY DEFAMATORY STATEMENTS ONLINE DOES NOT CONSTITUTE EXPRESS AIMING UNLESS THE STATEMENTS DIRECTLY TARGET VIEWERS.

Although Harrison's blog posts refer to Waters, they were made on a passive website and did not target a single California resident. Individuals throughout the country — and world — had access to these posts, and Harrison did nothing to entice, make aware, or encourage California residents to read them.

Admittedly, the "express aiming" requirement is generally satisfied when a defendant engages "in wrongful conduct targeted at a plaintiff who the defendant knows to be a resident of the forum state." *Bancroft and Masters*, 223 F.3d at 1087. Importantly, however, its application to cases involving websites — particularly online defamation — is unsettled.

The Northern District, however, recently acknowledged this standard risks conflating the "foreseeability" and "express aiming" prongs of purposeful direction. *See Lang v. Morris*, 823 F. Supp. 2d 966, 968 (N.D. Cal. 2011) (a "defendant's knowledge of the plaintiff's residency goes to the 'foreseeable effects' prong of the *Calder* test and is not sufficient on its own to establish the 'express aiming' prong." 823 F. Supp. 2d at 972 (*citing Pebble Beach Co.*, 453 F.3d at 1154); *see also Fiore*, 688 F.3d at 577 (express aiming is not satisfied "when it is merely foreseeable that there will be an impact on individuals in the forum") (*citing Pebble Beach Co.*, 453 F.3d at 1156).

Likewise, in *Xcentric Ventures*, the district court expressed doubt about whether express aiming could be satisfied simply because the defendant engages "in wrongful conduct targeted at a plaintiff who the defendant knows to be a resident of the forum state." 683 F. Supp. 2d at 1073 (*quoting Bancroft and Masters*, 223 F.3d at 1087). As the court explained, "[s]ince most intentional torts are acts that involve 'individually targeting' a victim, a literal reading of this holding would appear to result in a rule that, practically speaking, means that an intentional tort plus knowledge of the victim's residence amounts to 'express aiming.' " *Xcentric Ventures*, 683 F. Supp. 2d at 1073 (brackets added) (*quoting Bancroft and Masters*, 223 F.3d at 1087). Such a result compromises the "purposeful direction" analysis by improperly conflating the "express aiming" and "knowledge" requirements. *See Xcentric Ventures*, 683 F. Supp. 2d at 1073.

In other words, "the distinction between 'express aiming' and 'foreseeability' suggests that mere knowledge of an individual's residence, combined with the intentional posting of defamatory statements on the internet" does not constitute express aiming. *Id.* Rather, it "appears to demand a showing that there is at least some additional connection between the defamatory act and the forum." *Id.*

In *Piping Rock Partners*, the Northern District echoed this concern, stating that "the mere act of using the internet to defame a target has the potential to lead to expanded jurisdiction." . . . [2012 U.S. Dist. LEXIS 161643, at *16]. Accordingly, the court held that "express aiming is not present if the plaintiff only alleges that the defendant has committed an intentional tort over the internet with knowledge that the defendant resides in the forum state." *Id.* (*citing Continental [Appliances], Inc. v. Thomas*, . . . [2012 U.S. Dist. LEXIS 119871] (N.D. Cal. August 23, 2012)). Three District Courts within the Ninth Circuit agree. *Xcentric Ventures*, 683 F. Supp. 2d at 1074 (*citing Lange v. Thompson*, . . . [2008 U.S. Dist. LEXIS 60731]) (W.D. Wash. August 6, 2008) (Unreported); *Medinah Mining, Inc. v. Amunategui*, 237 F. Supp. 2d 1132, 1138 (D. Nev.2002)); *U-Haul, Int'l, Inc. v. Osborne*, 1999 U.S. Dist. LEXIS 14466 (D. Ariz. 1999)).

Thus, express aiming is not present absent "allegations that the defendant *targeted a forum-state audience* or that the corporate plaintiff had its primary place of business in the forum state." *Piping Rock Partners*, . . . [2012 U.S. Dist. LEXIS 161643, at *15] (emphasis added) (the defendant's internet posts included "San Francisco, California" in "the titles or subheads of the posts, as well as the mailing address of plaintiffs in San Francisco and their local phone number with the area code") (*citing Continental [Appliances], Inc.*, . . . [2012 U.S. Dist. LEXIS 119871]; *see also Nicosia v. De Rooy* 72 F. Supp. 2d 1093, 1097-1099 (N.D. Cal. 1999) (personal jurisdiction was appropriate where the defendant posted a defamatory article concerning a California resident and sent emails directly to California residents).

Other jurisdictions follow this rule. *See Young v. New Haven Advocate*, 315 F.3d 256, 263 (4th Cir. 2002) ("the fact that the newspapers' websites could be accessed anywhere, including Virginia, does not by itself demonstrate that the newspapers were intentionally directing their website content to a Virginia audience"). In *Young*, the court held that "[t]he websites "must, through the Internet postings, manifest an intent to target and focus on Virginia readers." *Id.*

None of these facts are present here. Harrison's blog posts did not target a single California resident. For example, Harrison did not send electronic messages, letters, make telephone calls, or otherwise engage California residents. In fact, the Website does not even allow individuals to contact Harrison, post comments, or exchange information on his website. Unlike *Piping Rock Partners*, Harrison's statements did not directly appeal to California residents or manifest "an intent to target and focus on" California viewers. *Young*, 315 F.3d at 263.[38] Without more, Harrison's untargeted posting of allegedly defamatory information does not support a finding of specific jurisdiction.

C. Exercising Jurisdiction Over Harrison is Unreasonable

Courts consider seven factors in determining whether the exercise of personal jurisdiction is reasonable: (1) the extent of the defendant's purposeful interjection into the forum state's affairs; (2) the burden on the defendant of defending in the forum; (3) the extent of conflict with the sovereignty of the defendant's state; (4) the forum state's interest in adjudicating the dispute; (5) the most efficient judicial resolution of the controversy; (6) the importance of the forum to the plaintiff's interest in convenient and effective relief; and (7) the existence of an alternative forum. *CE Distribution, LLC v. New Sensor Corp.* 380 F.3d 1107, 1112 (9th Cir. 2004).

The first factor has been discussed in detail above. Concerning the second factor, Harrison would face an extraordinary burden if required to defend in this forum. Harrison is a computer programmer who resides 2,597 miles from the Northern District in the small town of Erie, Pennsylvania. With a stable but modest income, a costly and time-consuming litigation in the Northern District will jeopardize Harrison's financial security. First, it will likely require Harrison and his attorneys to make

---

[38] Unlike *Righthaven LLC*, where the defendant allegedly plagiarized a Las Vegas Journal article that focused on matters specifically related to Nevada, the results in Waters's senatorial campaign impacted a variety of economic and social issues on a national scale.

numerous trips across the United States. Furthermore, the attorneys' fees associated with defending a defamation case — involving an arguably public figure — are substantial and rarely recoverable.[39] Considering that Waters is an attorney and former managing partner at a well-known San Jose law firm, the burden Waters will face by litigating in an alternative forum is considerably less.

The third factor is less relevant because choice-of-law rules will mitigate concerns regarding state sovereignty. With respect to the fourth factor, California admittedly has an interest in this adjudication because Waters is a California resident and alleges substantial harm to her reputation. California's interest, however, should be considered within the context of this case. By her own admission, Waters made "inaccurate statements" during her debate with then-Senator Larson, and these misstatements were arguably responsible, at least in part, for Waters' abrupt resignation from the United States Senate. The harm that Waters alleges is, to some extent, attributable to her own conduct. While California has a strong interest in protecting its citizens from reputational injury, it has a less pronounced interest when that injury is caused by the allegedly aggrieved party.

Regarding the fifth factor, an alternative forum would not compromise the efficient resolution of this matter. The most relevant and possibly dispositive evidence will likely consist of: (1) Harrison's statements; (2) Harrison's state of mind; (3) Waters' state of mind when making "inaccurate statements" during the final debate; and (4) testimony tending to prove or disprove Harrison's statements. It is unlikely that this will require extensive testimony from witnesses located in California, and documentary evidence will not be voluminous or located solely within California.

Finally, although the Northern District is an efficient forum for Waters, a resident of San Jose, California, it would require Harrison, a resident of Erie, Pennsylvania, to travel more than 2,400 miles at a considerable, if not insurmountable, cost. This would not only be inefficient, but fundamentally unfair and contrary to due process of law. [40]

CONCLUSION

Based on the foregoing, Harrison respectfully requests that this Court dismiss Plaintiff's Complaint for lack of personal jurisdiction.

*   *   *   *   *

---

[39] *See* James Windon, *Fee Shifting in Libel Litigation: How the American Approach to Costs Allocation Inhibits the Achievement of Libel Law's Substantive Goals*, 3 J. INT'L MEDIA AND ENTERTAINMENT LAW 175, 180–182 (2010) (discussing fee-shifting statutes in the United States and noting that Alaska is the only state currently permitting fee-shifting for victorious defendants).

[40] The Ninth Circuit had adopted and applied the "sliding scale" test set forth in *Zippo Manufacturing Co.*, 952 F. Supp. at 1123, when examining, for personal jurisdiction purposes, the sufficiency of website-based contacts.

Waters' Response to Harrison's Motion to Dismiss for Lack of Personal Jurisdiction

PLAINTIFF'S RESPONSE AND OBJECTION TO MOTION TO DISMISS

Plaintiff Kirsten Waters files this response and objection to Defendant Simon Harrison's motion to dismiss. Harrison is subject to jurisdiction in California, and the exercise of jurisdiction over Harrison comports with due process requirements of the U.S. Constitution. Harrison targeted this forum by publishing false, defamatory statements about California resident Waters on his blog — statements made for the purpose of harming a California resident and influencing a California election. Harrison expressly aimed his conduct at California and, therefore, is subject to personal jurisdiction in this Court. Thus, Harrison's motion to dismiss should be denied.

FACTUAL BACKGROUND

Waters brings this action for invasion of privacy and defamation against blogger Harrison to recover for injuries Waters sustained when Harrison published statements and information about Waters on his blog, www.justtellthetruth.com. *See* Complaint and Demand for Jury Trial ("Complaint").

In 2012, Waters, a successful lawyer, decided to run for one of the two California seats in the United States Senate. *Id.* at ¶ 7. During her campaign, Waters acknowledged she had struggled with alcohol and prescription drug abuse in college. *Id.* at ¶ 8.

Five days before the election, Waters and then-Senator Robert Larson participated in their final debate. *Id.* at ¶ 9. During that debate, in response to a question from the moderator, Waters discussed her past history of drug and alcohol abuse, detailed her 1994 arrest and punishment for DUI and possession of a controlled substance, and outlined the reasons her personal history made her an ideal candidate to serve as a California senator. *Id.* at ¶ 10. Waters' personal story made her popular among voters. *Id.*

Immediately after the debate, Harrison, who had known Waters when the two were in college, posted a false, malicious statement about Waters on his website, telling readers that Waters "blatantly lied at the final debate." *Id.* at ¶ 11.

That statement wasn't Harrison's last attack on Waters, however. Less than an hour later, Harrison's assault on Waters escalated when he posted the following statements on his blog:

> Sadly, I have uncovered yet another politician who cannot tell the truth. Kirsten Waters intentionally lied during her debate with Senator Larson. Kirsten's statements about her past struggle with substance abuse — obviously designed to sway California voters — are fabrications. I was Kirsten's friend during college and I unconditionally supported Kirsten while she struggled to overcome addiction. I am shocked that Kirsten would exploit her past for political gain. More specifically, while Kirsten was arrested for

Driving under the Influence of Alcohol and possession of a controlled substance, she was neither incarcerated nor ordered to spend even a single day in a residential treatment program. After pleading guilty, Kirsten was sentenced to 90 days probation and 100 hours of community service. Additionally, as part of the plea deal, the controlled substance charge was dropped. Kirsten only sought residential treatment because her parents threatened to stop paying her tuition at Stanford. Kirsten's lies show that she is not fit for public office.

In addition, because I am committed to telling the whole truth, I must disclose that, while at Stanford, Kirsten engaged in highly questionable conduct. During our last two years at Stanford, Kirsten was engaged to a mutual friend (who I will not reveal at this time). Kirsten suddenly broke off the engagement and admitted to having a lengthy affair with another man throughout the duration of the relationship. I will soon release a letter Kirsten wrote to our friend admitting the affair.

The whole truth is that Kirsten reluctantly sought treatment — only to save herself — while repeatedly lying to and eventually betraying a very decent man.

I would like to add one final comment. While at Stanford, Kirsten performed poorly in her studies. Kirsten was not a good student and I doubt she has the abilities to effectively serve in any elected capacity. I don't know how she was accepted by the University of California-Berkeley School of Law. I do know this: her dad is one of Berkeley's most generous donors. Kirsten's admission to Berkeley wasn't about merit. It was about favoritism and money. I also question how Kirsten ever graduated from Berkeley. I can't imagine her passing all of those difficult law school classes without receiving significant help from her family.

Id. at ¶ 12. Despite Harrison's vicious attack on Waters and her reputation, Waters defeated Larson by 314 votes, the closest margin in California's history. *Id.*

Even after Waters' impressive victory, Harrison's onslaught against her continued. Shortly after the election, Harrison published a letter on his blog allegedly written by Waters' former probation officer. In this supposed letter, the writer confirms that Waters completed her sentence for her 1994 arrest — probation of 90 days and 100 hours of community service. *Id.* at ¶ 13. The details of Waters' sentence contained in the alleged letter from her probation officer differ from those outlined by Waters at the final debate. *Id.* at ¶¶ 10, 13.

After the election, the statements Harrison posted on www.justtellthetruth.com were reported and re-published by news media organizations throughout the country. *Id.* at ¶ 14. Once the statements and accusations made on Harrison's website were widely reported by the media, Waters' approval rating dropped. *Id.* at ¶ 15. As a result of Harrison's tortious conduct, Waters was forced to resign her senate seat. *Id.* at ¶ 16. This suit followed.

MOTION TO DISMISS STANDARD

When a defendant files a motion to dismiss for lack of personal jurisdiction, the plaintiff "bears the burden of demonstrating that jurisdiction is appropriate." *Schwarzenegger v. Fred Martin Motor Co.*, 374 F.3d 797, 800 (9th Cir. 2004). The plaintiff's burden, however, is low, and the plaintiff "need only make a prima facie showing of jurisdictional facts." *Id.* (*quoting Sher v. Johnson*, 911 F.2d 1357, 1361 (9th Cir.1990)). Where the "undisputed facts reveal sufficient contacts to support jurisdiction," the plaintiff's burden is satisfied. *Sher*, 911 F.2d at 1361.

ARGUMENT AND CITATION TO AUTHORITY

This suit was filed in a federal court on the basis of diversity of citizenship. In cases such as this one, a court may exercise personal jurisdiction over a non-resident defendant if: (1) the forum's long-arm statute confers jurisdiction; and (2) the exercise of jurisdiction accords with the federal limits of due process. *Lake v. Lake*, 817 F.2d 1416, 1420 (9th Cir. 1987). The California Civil Code permits California courts to exercise personal jurisdiction to the full extent of the Due Process Clause. *See* Cal. Civ. Code § 410.10. Therefore, the California and federal limits of due process are "coextensive," and the analysis is the same under both the first and second elements. *Lake*, 817 F.2d at 1420.

In order for the exercise of personal jurisdiction over a non-resident defendant to comply with federal due process requirements, the defendant must have certain "minimum contacts" with the forum state. *Int'l Shoe Co. v. Washington*, 326 U.S. 310, 316 (1945). The personal jurisdiction inquiry is not subject to any mechanical test but, instead, focuses on the "relationship among the defendant, the forum, and the litigation with the particular factual context of each case." *Gordy v. Daily News, L.P.*, 95 F.3d 829, 834 (9th Cir. 1996) (*quoting Core-Vent Corp. v. Nobel Industries AB*, 11 F.3d 1482, 1487 (9th Cir. 1993)).

A state may exercise either general or specific jurisdiction over a defendant. *Lake*, 817 F.2d at 1420. General jurisdiction exists where the defendant's contacts with a state are "continuous and systematic" or "substantial." *Perkins v. Benguet Consol. Mining Co.*, 342 U.S. 437, 445, 447 (1952). However, even if a state cannot exercise general jurisdiction over a non-resident defendant, it can still exercise specific jurisdiction if the defendant's contacts with and relationship to the forum state are such that the defendant "should reasonably anticipate being haled into court" in the forum and the litigation arises out of those contacts. *World-Wide Volkswagen Corp. v. Woodson*, 444 U.S. 286, 297 (1980). Specific jurisdiction exists where: (1) the defendant has "performed some act or consummated some transaction within the forum or otherwise purposefully availed himself of the privileges of conducting activities in the forum"; (2) the claim against the defendant arises out of the defendant's "forum-related activities"; and (3) the exercise of jurisdiction over the defendant is reasonable. *Bancroft & Masters, Inc. v. Augusta Nat'l Inc.*, 223 F.3d 1082, 1086 (9th Cir. 2000).

Waters does not contend that this Court may exercise general jurisdiction over Harrison. Harrison's conduct, however, gives this Court specific personal jurisdiction over him.

I. California courts have specific jurisdiction over Harrison.

A. The purposeful availment requirement is met because Harrison's conduct and statements were expressly aimed at California.

Under the first prong of the specific jurisdiction analysis, the "purposeful availment" prong, a defendant need not have physically entered a forum to be subject to jurisdiction there. *Gordy*, 95 F.3d at 832. The purposeful availment prong of the analysis is met where the "effects test" is met, and the effective test is satisfied when: (1) the defendant engages in intentional conduct; (2) the conduct is "expressly aimed" at the forum state; and (3) the defendant's conduct causes harm, the brunt of which is suffered — and the defendant knows will be suffered — in the forum state. *Bancroft*, 223 F.3d at 1087.

Harrison admits that his conduct was intentional and that he knew Waters would suffer harm in California. Thus, the only question remaining is whether Harrison expressly aimed his conduct at California. The answer to that question is yes.

A defendant expressly aims conduct at a forum when the defendant engages in conduct "targeted at a plaintiff whom the defendant knows to be a resident of the forum state." *Id.* Furthermore, " 'express aiming' encompasses wrongful conduct individually targeting a known forum resident." *Id.*

In considering whether non-resident owners of websites are subject to specific personal jurisdiction, courts have developed a "sliding scale" approach. Operators of passive websites who merely make information available are on one end of the scale and are not deemed to have expressly aimed their conduct at a forum. Persons who use websites to do business over the internet by soliciting orders from or entering into contracts with forum residents are at the other end of the scale. *See Cybersell, Inc. v. Cybersell, Inc.*, 130 F.3d 414 (9th Cir. 1997) (following *Zippo Mfg. Co. v. Zippo Dot Com, Inc.*, 952 F.Supp. 1119, 1123 (W.D. Pa. 1997)). The former are not subject to personal jurisdiction in a foreign forum while the later are. *Id.*

This case, however, is distinguishable from those website sliding scale cases. Here, Harrison neither passively made information available nor used his blog to do business. Instead, Harrison published defamatory statements about Waters on his blog and targeted those statements at California residents and voters. Harrison's conduct, therefore, is more akin to that of newspapers and other publishers who publish potentially defamatory pieces. Relevant defamation cases involving publishers show why Harrison is subject to personal jurisdiction in this Court.

The outcome of this case is controlled by *Calder v. Jones*, 465 U.S. 783 (1984), the seminal personal jurisdiction case in this area of law. In *Calder*, the United States Supreme Court found that a non-resident author and editor who published allegedly defamatory statements about a California resident in a nationwide publication were subject to jurisdiction in California. The plaintiff, an actress, sued the non-resident defendants in California for libel and invasion of privacy after the defendants wrote an article impugning on the plaintiff's professionalism. *Id.* at 784.

In finding the defendants were subject to personal jurisdiction in California, the

Supreme Court noted that the article "concerned the California activities of a California resident," was "drawn from California sources," and "the brunt of the harm, in terms both of the [plaintiff's] emotional distress and injury to her professional reputation, was suffered in California." *Id.* at 788–89. Because the defendants "were not charged with mere untargeted negligence," and because they wrote an article they knew would have an impact on the plaintiff in the state where she lived and worked, the Court held they should have reasonably anticipated being haled to court in California. *Id.* at 789. Thus, California courts could properly exercise personal jurisdiction over the author and editor. *Id.*

Like *Calder*, *Gordy* is indistinguishable from the case at hand and supports Water's position that this Court can and should exercise personal jurisdiction over Harrison. The *Gordy* plaintiff, a California resident, sued the publisher-defendant for publishing allegedly defamatory statements about the plaintiff in a New York-based newspaper. 95 F.3d at 831. The paper primarily covered events that occurred in New York but routinely included entertainment features of national interest. *Id.* Only 13 to 18 copies of the newspaper were distributed in California. *Id.* at 832. The Ninth Circuit Court of Appeals held the defendant was subject to personal jurisdiction in California courts. *Id.* at 836.

The Ninth Circuit noted that while the defendant distributed only a small number of newspapers in California, those papers were distributed to regular subscribers and their receipt of the papers was not "random or fortuitous." *Id.* at 833. Furthermore, the court found that the small number of distributions was sufficient to enable a California court to exercise jurisdiction where the papers were sent to the state in which the plaintiff lived and the place where he would suffer the biggest impact to his reputation. *Id.* at 834. Finally, the court concluded that the defendants had sufficiently targeted California by publishing material about a California resident when it was "reasonable to expect the bulk of the harm from defamation of an individual to be felt in his domicile." *Id.* at 833.

Harrison is like the *Calder* defendants, who expressly aimed their conduct at California by publishing an allegedly defamatory article about a California resident with knowledge that the publication would negatively impact the plaintiff there. Harrison published false, defamatory statements about Waters, a California resident, with the express purposes of encouraging California voters not to cast votes for Waters and harming Waters' personal and professional reputation in the state in which she lives and works. Harrison's conduct was both aimed at and had an effect in California.

And like the *Gordy* defendant, the relationship between Harrison's conduct and California is not merely "random or fortuitous." The defamatory, untrue statements Harrison posted on his website did not randomly or fortuitously reach California — Harrison expressly directed his comments about a California resident to other California residents for the purpose of influencing the California election. His intentional conduct was done not simply to provide information to a broad class of people but specifically to reach California voters and influence their votes in a California election. Given his intentional conduct, targeted at a California resident and done with the purpose of harming her political career in California, it is "reasonable" for Harrison to expect he might be haled into court in California.

Because Harrison made defamatory statements about California resident Waters, directed those statements at California voters, and because the brunt of the damage to Waters' reputation and political career have occurred and continue to occur in California, Harrison expressly aimed his conduct at California. The first prong of the three-pronged specific jurisdiction analysis, purposeful availment, is met.

B. WATERS' CLAIM AGAINST HARRISON AROSE OUT OF HARRISON'S FORUM-RELATED ACTIVITIES.

In determining whether the claims against a defendant arose out of the defendant's forum-related activities, the courts use a "but for" test. *Ziegler v. Indian River Cnty.*, 64 F.3d 470, 474 (9th Cir. 1995). Where, but for the defendant's forum-related activities, the cause of action would not exist, the test is met. *Id.*

Under the but for test, Waters' claims against Harrison arose out of Harrison's forum-related conduct. But for Harrison's publication of defamatory statements about Waters, Waters would not have been forced to resign her Senate seat and would not have brought this action. Waters has not sued Harrison in California over an issue that bears no relationship to the state. To the contrary, Waters brought this suit in California to recover for injuries Waters sustained to her reputation and emotional harm she suffered as a result of statements about her that Harrison directed at California residents with the purpose of influencing the California senatorial election. Harrison's conduct meets the second prong of the specific jurisdiction analysis.

C. THE EXERCISE OF PERSONAL JURISDICTION OVER HARRISON IS REASONABLE.

For the exercise of jurisdiction over a defendant to be reasonable, it must comport with traditional notions of fair play and substantial justice. *Bancroft*, 223 F.3d at 1088 (citing *Burger King Corp. v. Rudzewicz*, 471 U.S. 462, 476 (1985)). Once the first two prongs of the analysis have been met, the defendant is required to "present a compelling case that the presence of some other considerations would render jurisdiction unreasonable." *Burger King*, 471 U.S. at 477.

Courts consider several factors in determining whether the exercise of jurisdiction is reasonable, including: (1) "the extent of the defendant's purposeful interjection into the forum"; (2) the burden the defendant will bear by being sued in a foreign forum; (3) "the extent of the conflict with the sovereignty" of the state in which the defendant resides; (4) the forum state's interest in adjudicating the matter; (5) "the most efficient judicial resolution of the controversy"; (6) the forum's importance to the plaintiff's interest in "convenient and effective relief"; and (7) the availability of an alternative forum. *Bancroft*, 223 F.3d at 1088 (*citing Burger King*, 471 U.S. at 476-77). This list of factors, however, is not exhaustive, and courts are given flexibility to determine whether the exercise of jurisdiction over a defendant is reasonable under the facts and circumstances of each individual case. *Gordy*, 95 F.3d at 835-36. The reasonableness analysis under the third prong inevitably "duplicate[s] to a large degree" the "express aiming" analysis under the first prong. *Id.* at 836.

For example, in *Gordy*, discussed above, the court outlined the numerous reasons the exercise of jurisdiction over the defendant-newspaper by a California court was reasonable. The court noted that the defendant knew the plaintiff lived in California and "had good reason to expect that a substantial impact of [its] actions would be felt in California." 95 F.3d at 836. Furthermore, the court concluded a California resident should not be forced to go to a foreign jurisdiction to "seek redress from persons who . . . knowingly caused injury in California." *Id.* For those reasons, and because California "maintains a strong interest in providing an effective means of redress for its residents tortiously injured," the exercise of jurisdiction over the foreign defendant was reasonable. *Id.*

Each of the reasons outlined by the *Gordy* court is equally applicable here. Harrison, like the *Gordy* defendant, knew Waters lived in California, knew she was running for a California senate seat, and not only knew the effects of his conduct would be felt in California but actually intended to influence voters in California. Waters, a California resident, should not be forced to file suit against Harrison in Pennsylvania to recover for injuries she sustained and felt in California.

Furthermore, California has a particularly strong interest in the outcome of this case above the state's interests in either *Calder* or *Gordy*. As a result of Harrison's wrongful, malicious conduct, Waters was forced to resign her position. This resignation impacted the California electoral system and, therefore, all California citizens, not just Waters. A defendant who intentionally publishes false information about a California political candidate with the express purpose of influencing California voters cannot be heard to complain if he is sued in a California court. Harrison has not and cannot present a compelling case that this Court's exercise of personal jurisdiction over him is unreasonable. The third prong of the analysis is met. Thus, this Court has specific personal jurisdiction over Harrison and his Motion to Dismiss should be denied.

II. HARRISON WAS NOT MERELY OPERATING A "PASSIVE" WEBSITE BUT INTENTIONALLY AIMED HIS STATEMENTS ABOUT A CALIFORNIA CITIZEN AT OTHER CALIFORNIA RESIDENTS WITH THE PURPOSE OF IMPACTING A CALIFORNIA ELECTION.

Waters does not believe the sliding scale line of cases applies here; however, Harrison is correct that "maintenance of a passive website alone cannot satisfy the express aiming prong." *Brayton Purcell LLP v. Recordon & Recordon*, 606 F.3d 1124, 1129 (9th Cir. 2010). Where the defendant operates a passive website, though, the defendant may still be subject to personal jurisdiction if he engages in conduct "directly targeting the forum." *Id.* Even if Harrison's blog is passive, which Waters denies, Harrison directly targeted the forum when he posted the statements about Waters on his blog.

Despite Harrison's arguments to the contrary, he was not merely operating a "passive," untargeted website that made information available to California residents. Harrison's posts about Waters not only encouraged California residents to visit his website, they encouraged California voters to vote against Waters. Harrison did far more than "mak[e] information available to those who are interested in it." *Advanced Skin & Hair, Inc. v. Bancroft*, 858 F. Supp. 2d 1084, 1088 (C.D. Cal. 2012).

Further, Harrison did more than "intentionally plac[e] defamatory information on the internet"; he "expressly aimed" his conduct at California with the purpose of causing harm to Waters there and influencing the California election. This case is distinguishable from *Xcentric Ventures, LLC v. Bird*, 683 F. Supp. 2d 1068 (D. Ariz. 2010), cited by Harrison in support of his motion to dismiss. In *Bird*, the defendant did not know the plaintiff was an Arizona resident or that the plaintiff's company was based in Arizona and did not seek to influence the conduct of other Arizonans, but merely posted an article about the plaintiff on a website. *Id.* at 1072.

Unlike the *Bird* defendant, Harrison knew Waters was a California resident, knew the brunt of harm to her reputation would be felt in California, where she lives and works, and acted for the express purpose of influencing California voters. This situation is more akin to *Righthaven LLC v. South Coast Partners, Inc.*, No. 2:10–CV 01062, . . . 2011 U.S. Dist. LEXIS 12802 D. Nev. February 8, 2011), where the district court concluded it could exercise personal jurisdiction over a defendant whose conduct implicated on issues related to Nevada and was of special interest to Nevada citizens. Here, as in *Rightaven*, Harrison's statements about Waters were made to impact the California election and were of special interest to Californians.

As Harrison himself acknowledges, when a defendant has targeted both an individual resident of a forum as well as other residents of that forum, the defendant is deemed to have expressly aimed his conduct at the forum. Harrison's Motion p. 19. That is exactly what happened here. Harrison admits he targeted Waters. Harrison also, however, targeted California residents by disseminating information to encourage those residents not to vote for Waters.

This situation also is distinguishable from *Young v. New Haven Advocate*, 315 F.3d 256 (4th Cir. 2002), a Fourth Circuit Court of Appeals Case cited by Harrison. There, the plaintiff, a Virginia resident, brought suit in Virginia against a Connecticut newspaper. According to the plaintiff, the paper had defamed him in an article about a Connecticut program that transferred prisoners to Virginia for incarceration. *Id.* at 258. In finding the Virginia district court lacked jurisdiction, the Fourth Circuit noted that the newspaper did not direct the article that mentioned the plaintiff to a Virginia audience. *Id.* at 264. The court held that the article, which was both printed in a Connecticut newspaper and posted on the newspaper's website, was directed at a local Connecticut audience and the article was written to encourage debate by Connecticut residents about the Connecticut prison transfer policy. *Id.* at 263–64. Thus, the newspaper did not intentionally aim its conduct at Virginia, and the Virginia court had no jurisdiction over the newspaper.

Here, California was the focal point of Harrison's blog post — he published information about a California resident and directed that information to other California residents to encourage debate about whether Californians should elect Waters to the United States Senate.

Harrison concedes that California citizens have a "special interest" in the election, but claims the election wasn't "local" because it "impacted a variety of economic and social issues on a national scale." Harrison's Motion p. 21. What Harrison fails to say, however, is that not only did California residents have a "special interest" in the election, they are the *only* citizens of any state who could vote either for or against Waters. While citizens of other states may have some interest in the California election, Waters' campaign was "local" to California. To claim the election was not "local" because the elected official would be working in the United States Senate on national issues is ludicrous.

Furthermore, the information Harrison provided about Waters, while not "uniquely associated with California," was of unique interest to California citizens who, as outlined above, were the only people who had any power to "do anything" with the information Harrison disseminated — they were the only people who could vote to elect or not elect Waters.

When he published the statements about Waters on his blog, Harrison targeted a California resident and California citizens, thereby subjecting himself to personal jurisdiction in this Court. Harrison published the highly defamatory statements about Waters knowing she was a California resident and would be harmed here. Furthermore, Harrison published the statements for the express purpose of convincing California citizens not to vote for Waters. He cannot have acted for the purpose of convincing citizens of any other state not to vote for Waters — California residents were the only people with the power to vote for or against Waters. Harrison expressly aimed his conduct at a California resident and its citizens and is subject to jurisdiction in this Court. Harrison's motion to dismiss should be denied.

CONCLUSION

This Court may exercise personal jurisdiction over Harrison. Harrison intentionally aimed his conduct at California for the express purpose of affecting a California election and harming a California resident, Waters. Harrison did not merely operate a passive website to make information generally available — he posted an article about Waters and encouraged California residents not to vote for Waters, all while knowing the article would cause substantial harm to Waters and her reputation in California. Harrison's conduct targeted California, and he should expect to be haled into court here. Harrison is subject to specific personal jurisdiction in this Court, and the court should deny his motion to dismiss.

*   *   *   *   *

Reasons why these briefs were effective.

- ► *Introductions.* Both briefs use short introductions to let the court know the issues the parties will address. Each author briefly lays out the facts that support the author's position then moves on to the meat of the brief. Waters' introduction is a mere four sentences but lets the court know the issue before it, the relevant law, a few of the most important facts, and what Waters seeks from the court.

- ► *Clear and Concise Writing.* How long did it take you to know what each side wants and why? Maybe a few sentences, or a paragraph at most? The parties get to the point quickly and don't waste time expounding on the history of the due process clause or the importance of *International Shoe* to constitutional jurisprudence.

- ► *Know The Standard.* The motion to dismiss requires the movant to meet a high standard. Waters only needs to make a *prima facie* showing that jurisdiction is proper, and the court will assume, unless Harrison demonstrates to the contrary, that jurisdiction is proper. Harrison's does not misrepresent or try to "argue around" the standard of review. Instead, Harrison sets forth compelling case law — from the Northern District of California and Ninth Circuit Court of Appeals — to persuasively argue that this standard is satisfied. Don't try to circumvent the applicable standard of review or pretend that it doesn't exist because a court will rely on this standard when making its decision. As you'll see in the upcoming chapters, different standards of review apply at different stages of the litigation process. A motion that might be denied under one standard might be granted under another. Writing your brief in light of the standard of review is critical if you want to have a reasonable chance of success.

Waters also demonstrates that she knows the standard and outlines it in a way that makes the Court want to rule in her favor. Do you see how she does that? By framing the evidentiary requirements as low, she suggests to the Court that she has easily met the standard and Harrison's motion should be denied.

► *Effective use of persuasion.* Both writers transition well from their roles as lawyers to storytellers. In doing so, the writers use effective persuasive techniques. Look at how Waters frames Harrison's conduct in Waters' Statement of Facts. She uses war-themed words to describe Harrison's "attack," "assault," and "onslaught" against her. She describes herself, however, in much more favorable terms — as a "successful lawyer" and a "popular" candidate.

Do you see how Waters describes the case she relies most heavily on — *Calder* — as the "seminal" case. And look at how Waters uses certain words: According to Waters, Harrison didn't simply "direct" his conduct at California; instead, he "expressly directed" his conduct. Likewise, Harrison didn't just engage in bad conduct, he engaged in "intentional" bad conduct that targeted Waters in California. Notice how Waters describes Harrison as having "subjected" himself to suit in California through his conduct. Harrison talks extensively how it would be unfair to make him litigate the case in California. Waters' use of the term "subjected" implies that Harrison himself is responsible for getting sued in California — how can it be unfair for the court to exercise jurisdiction over Harrison if Harrison "subjected" himself to suit in California?

Waters also uses every opportunity she has to remind the court of the reason she filed the suit — Harrison's statements were defamatory and untrue. She doesn't just refer to them as "statements"— she reminds the reader why she filed the action in the first place and she reiterates her position that Harrison shouldn't be able to avoid suit in California when he engaged in such "bad" conduct against a California resident.

Notice that Harrison begins his brief with a strong introduction. The first sentence highlights Harrison's strongest argument: Merely posting allegedly defamatory statements on a non-commercial website is not sufficient to exercise personal jurisdiction over a non-resident defendant. Harrison wants the reader to react by thinking, "that shouldn't happen." It's a good example of winning the case from the beginning.

In addition, Harrison takes the somewhat unusual step of including law in the introduction. Sometimes, there may be language from a case that highlights the strength of your argument or exposes weaknesses in the adversary's argument. Don't be afraid to "break the rules" if doing so will maximize persuasion.

► **Word choice.** The authors of both briefs choose appropriate language and avoid over-the-top words likely to detract from the substance of their arguments. The authors use the space to show — rather than tell — the court why their position is the correct one.

You might have noticed, however, that in Waters' response, she calls one of Harrison's arguments "ludicrous." While it's not typical to use a word such as "ludicrous," that word has a powerful impact based on where it is placed in the brief and the context within which it is used (to highlight Harrison's weakest argument). Waters doesn't call all of Harrison's arguments ludicrous — just the weakest one. Notice, too, that Waters doesn't call Harrison or his attorney "ludicrous," she calls their argument "ludicrous." Remember — you can break the rules if doing so helps to maximize persuasion. Paper chess doesn't require you to blindly adhere to formulas.

► **Strategic concessions.** The parties each make strategic concessions to avoid wasting the court's time on issues that are either clear losers or that they aren't arguing. Waters, for example, concedes up front that the court can't exercise *general* jurisdiction over non-resident Harrison. She instead focuses her time and energy on the better argument — that it can exercise *specific* jurisdiction over Harrison. Likewise, Harrison concedes that the only element in dispute is the "express" aiming requirement, thus avoiding unnecessary length and argument and properly focusing the court's attention on the relevant issue.

► **Effective organization.** The briefs are organized in a user-friendly way, with roadmaps to guide the reader and headings and subheadings to separate the different legal issues. In addressing the three-prong specific jurisdiction analysis, Waters and Harrison use a separate subheading for each prong so the reader won't be confused. Waters also separates her argument, under section I, from her response to Harrison's argument, under section II.

► **Paragraph and sentence length.** The writers avoid overly long paragraphs and even use short paragraphs when appropriate. Waters' brief contains several paragraphs that are only two or three sentences long. Each of those paragraphs addresses a separate legal issue and, so, is properly separated from the other arguments contained in their own paragraphs. The authors also use short sentences effectively — consider Waters' sentence "The answer to that question is yes." Do you notice how less really can be more?

► **Addressing unhelpful law and facts.** Both briefs acknowledge but effectively de-emphasize the law and facts that are not favorable to them. Notice that Waters de-emphasizes her conduct and focuses instead on what Harrison did.

Unlike Harrison's brief, which outlines Waters' exact statements at the debate, Waters' brief provides only that she "discussed her past history of drug and alcohol abuse." Notice, too, that Waters does not include her post-election statement about making unintentional misrepresentations about her 1994 arrest and criminal sentence. That statement is neither helpful to Waters nor essential to the court's personal jurisdiction analysis, so Waters chooses to leave it out.

We've previously talked about the importance of making your strongest argument first and then addressing actual or potential counterarguments. In her response brief, Waters does a good job of outlining her position and the helpful law that supports her argument first *then* addressing the reasons she believes Harrison's arguments are incorrect and the cases he cites are inapplicable. By making her strongest argument first, then addressing Harrison's arguments, she de-emphasizes the strength of Harrison's position.

▶ *Flow.* Notice how both briefs use transitions to ensure a smooth flow. Words such as further, furthermore, here, for example, and, but, and the like are all used to help the authors connect paragraphs and ensure the reader understands the relationships between the legal principles discussed.

▶ *Authority and Legal Analyses:* The authors of these briefs do a good job of analyzing the facts in light of the law they have presented. Look at subsection A of Waters' brief, where Waters addresses the purposeful availment prong. Waters:

   ○ Outlines the three elements of purposeful availment generally;

   ○ Explains that two of the three elements of that prong are met;

   ○ Delves deeper into an explanation of the element at issue, express aiming;

   ○ Uses two cases, *Calder* and *Gordy*, to explain how courts analyze the express aiming element;

   ○ Analyzes the facts in light of the law she has just explained, comparing the facts of her case to those in *Calder* and *Gordy* to explain how Harrison expressly aimed his conduct at California; and

   ○ Concludes by noting that because Harrison expressly aimed his conduct at California, the purposeful availment prong of the 3-pronged specific personal jurisdiction analysis is met.

▶ *Conclusions.* Each brief contains a short, to-the-point conclusion. The authors succinctly summarize the arguments they have made in the brief and remind the court what they want it to do.

After reading the briefs, who do you think should win, and why?

Is there anything you would do to improve either or both briefs? If so, what?

Chapter 8

THE ANSWER

The answer is not the place to offer lengthy explanations or justifications, or passionately argue the merits of your case. All you should do in your answer is respond to the allegations in the complaint. When answering a complaint, you'll take an approach similar to the approach for drafting a complaint: be concise, direct, professional, and make sure that you have complied with the relevant rules.

I. LOCAL RULES — THEY'RE BACK

Yep. Again. Your jurisdiction's rules and statutes will control when your client's answer is due. But the local rules, including those of the specific judge hearing the case, may govern the form of your answer, whether you can make a general denial of the entire complaint (more on that later), and the requirements for pleading affirmative defenses. Check all relevant rules before you draft your answer.

A. Do Your Research

Like the plaintiff's attorney who should perform legal research before filing a complaint, you also should perform research before filing an answer. You should check the elements of each cause of action asserted by the plaintiff to ensure the plaintiff has adequately stated a claim. If those elements haven't been pleaded, you may be able to get the case dismissed without ever having to file an answer.

Additionally, some affirmative defenses must be made in the defendant's first pleading, which is often the answer, or they are waived. Many of the Federal Rule of Civil Procedure 12(b) defenses, for example, must be raised in the first pleading or they are waived. Other affirmative defenses may be asserted later in the litigation. Legal research will help you know what affirmative defenses you should assert in your answer.

Legal research will also help you determine if your client can assert counterclaims (against the plaintiff), crossclaims (against a co-defendant), or third-party claims (against a yet-unnamed party). In some jurisdictions, claims arising from the same set of the facts as those alleged in the plaintiff's complaint cannot be asserted in a later action. Research will help you determine whether your client can and should assert a cross, counter, or third-party claim.

Finally, legal research may help you decide whether your client should answer a complaint and litigate the case or try to settle with the plaintiff before expending too much time or money. We all know litigation is very expensive. Research may show that your client is dead in the water. If that occurs, your client likely will be better off trying to settle the case early, rather than pay your attorney fees and get hit with a large judgment later. Your legal research is very important.

B. Introduction

Your answer should include a brief introductory sentence, something like this:

Defendant Top Sails, Inc. files this answer to Plaintiff John-John Boats, Inc.'s complaint, alleging as follows:

*   *   *   *   *

You may notice many lawyers' introductions looks something like this:

COMES NOW Defendant Top Sails, Inc., by and through its counsel of record, Hood, Hatch, and Lynch, LLP, 3500 Peachtree Street, Suite 500, Atlanta, Georgia 30328, and files its answer to Plaintiff John-John Boats, Inc.'s complaint.

*   *   *   *   *

As you know by now, we're not big fans of legalese. The "COMES NOW" isn't necessary, nor is the "by and through its counsel of record . . . " These phrases add length but not substance. A simple, one sentence introduction is all you need.

C. Plead Affirmative Defenses

"I've heard the term 'affirmative defense' before," you say, "but what is an affirmative defense, exactly?" Broadly, an affirmative defense is one that will cut off the plaintiff's ability to recover anything from the defendant. The defendant bears the burden of proving any affirmative defense the defendant asserts. Affirmative defenses include the defenses outlined in Rule 12(b) (and similar state rules and statues) as well as defenses such as statute of limitations, laches, res judicata, accord and satisfaction, statute of frauds, and many others.

Often, you will want to assert multiple affirmative defenses. Rule 8 of the Federal Rules of Civil Procedure requires that a party responding to allegations must "state in short and plain terms its defenses to each claim asserted against it."

In many jurisdictions, your affirmative defenses should be pleaded before you respond to the factual allegations in the complaint. Generally, you need not include "law" with your affirmative defenses or be overly specific — you just need a "short and plain" statement of the defenses. Here's an example of how you would assert affirmative defenses.

Affirmative Defenses

1.

Plaintiff has failed to perfect service of process on Defendant, and Plaintiff's claim should be dismissed.

2.

Plaintiff has failed to state a claim against Defendant, and Plaintiff's claim should be dismissed.

3.

Plaintiff's complaint is barred by the doctrine of res judicata, and Plaintiff's claim should be dismissed.

4.

Plaintiff's complaint is barred by the doctrine of accord and satisfaction, and Plaintiff's claim should be dismissed.

*   *   *   *   *

The most difficult part about asserting affirmative defenses is knowing which defenses to assert. As we said above, legal research is critical. Your research will help you determine which defenses, if any, you should assert on behalf of your client. Just remember, your ethical obligations prohibit you from asserting frivolous defenses, just as they prohibit a plaintiff's lawyer from asserting frivolous allegations. You must have some basis to believe the affirmative defenses you assert might succeed — or at least that they aren't frivolous.

D.   Respond to Allegations in the Complaint

Rule 8 requires that a defendant responding to a plaintiff's complaint admit the allegations against the defendant, deny the allegations against the defendant, or respond that the defendant "lacks knowledge or information sufficient to form a belief about the truth of an allegation." Fed. R. Civ. P. 8(b)(5). Additionally, there may be room to state that the plaintiff's allegations are vague or unclear and, therefore, the defendant can't respond to them.

A defendant may also admit or deny allegations in part as well. However, to state that a defendant lacks knowledge or information in most, if not all jurisdictions, the defendant must have made a reasonable investigation into the truthfulness of the allegations.

In responding to the allegations in the complaint, you should provide a brief (usually one sentence) response. Remember, the answer is not the place to argue the merits of your client's case. The only thing you must do in the answer is respond to the allegations in the complaint by admitting them, denying them, partially admitting or denying them, or stating that you lack information to respond.

Let's look at how this might work in practice using the allegations in the *Turner v. Bean* litigation we talked about in the Complaint chapter. The allegations:

4.

On December 21, 2013, Plaintiff Marshall Turner was driving southbound on Highway 41A in Winchester, Tennessee.

5.

At the same time and place, Defendant Jason Bean was driving southbound on Highway 41A behind the vehicle driven by Turner.

6.

As Turner approached a traffic light at the intersection between Highway 41A and the Highway 41A Bypass Road, he slowed his vehicle because the traffic light was red.

7.

Bean, who was still travelling directly behind Turner, failed to slow or stop his vehicle and struck the rear-end of Turner's vehicle.

8.

Turner sustained injuries as a result of the accident.

*   *   *   *   *

Suppose you represent Bean. Bean admits he struck the rear-end of Turner's vehicle. Bean claims, however, that he wasn't travelling too closely to Turner's vehicle and that Bean struck Turner's vehicle because Turner slammed on his brakes suddenly. Your answer might look this this:

4.

Bean admits the allegations in paragraph 4 of the complaint.

5.

Bean admits the allegations in paragraph 5 of the complaint.

6.

Bean is without information sufficient to form a belief as to the truthfulness of the allegations in paragraph 6 of the complaint and therefore denies those allegations.

7.

Bean admits that he struck the rear-end of Turner's vehicle but denies the remainder of the allegations in paragraph 7 of the complaint.

8.

Bean is without information sufficient to form a belief as to the truthfulness of the allegations in paragraph 8 of the complaint and therefore denies those allegations.

*   *   *   *   *

Bean's responses to paragraphs 4 and 5 aren't complicated. Why might Bean have responded as he did to paragraph 6? Because Bean doesn't know why Turner slowed Turner's vehicle — only Turner knows that. What about paragraph 7? Bean admits he struck Turner's vehicle but doesn't want to admit anything else. What does travelling "directly" behind mean? Bean doesn't want to admit that he failed to slow or stop his vehicle because he claims Turner caused the accident by slamming on his brakes. So, Bean's response to paragraph 7 makes sense. As for paragraph 8, Bean doesn't have any idea what injuries, if any, Turner might have sustained; thus, his response is that he lacks information.

A word about admitting or denying allegations in part. If you do this, you must be very specific about what you are admitting and what you are denying. Under Rule 8(b)(3), "a party that does not intend to deny all the allegations must either specifically deny designated allegations or generally deny all except those specifically admitted." Notice how Bean does this in his response to paragraph 7. He clearly states what he is admitting (that he struck the rear-end of Turner's vehicle) and denies the rest.

And be sure you respond to every allegation in the complaint. In most jurisdictions, if you fail to respond to an allegation (or a portion of an allegation), you are deemed to have admitted the truthfulness of the allegation. If you're answering a complicated complaint and are concerned about unintentionally admitting an allegation, you might consider including a denial at the end of your answer like this one:

35.

Any allegation Defendant has not previously responded to in this answer is denied.

*   *   *   *   *

This denial of all allegations not previously responded to *may* protect your client from being deemed to have admitted an allegation the defendant didn't intend to admit.

E. Respond to Causes of Action

You should respond to the plaintiff's legal allegations just as you have to the factual allegations. You will generally want to deny the legal allegations. Even if you think your client likely is liable to the plaintiff, liability is determined by a trier of fact. So, you are safe to (and will want to) deny all allegations that your client is liable to the plaintiff. Let's go back to *Turner v. Bean*. Suppose the complaint alleges Bean was negligent in failing to avoid the accident with *Turner*:

<u>Count I — Negligence</u>

9.

Turner incorporates the allegations in paragraphs 1–8 of the complaint.

10.

On December 21, 2013, Bean had a duty to exercise reasonable care in operating his vehicle.

11.

Bean breached that duty by failing to stop his vehicle in time to avoid striking Turner's vehicle.

12.

Turner was injured as a result of Bean's negligence.

*   *   *   *   *

How would you respond?

<u>Count I — Negligence</u>

9.

Turner incorporates the allegations in paragraphs 1–8 of the complaint.

10.

Bean admits the allegations in paragraph 10 of the complaint.

11.

Bean denies the allegations in paragraph 11 of the complaint.

12.

Bean denies the allegations in paragraph 12 of the complaint.

*   *   *   *   *

Obviously, Bean wants to deny that he failed to exercise reasonable care and that Turner sustained injuries as a result of Bean's conduct. But why might Bean have admitted the allegation in paragraph 10? Because it is true — Bean did owe Turner a duty to exercise reasonable care. Bean's position, however, as his responses to paragraphs 11 and 12 make clear, is that he didn't breach the duty he owed to Turner. You'll gain credibility by responding honestly and truthfully rather than act like an obstructionist. If you're concerned the defendant or court might interpret Bean's response to paragraph 10 as an admission he was negligent in causing the accident, you could also respond like this:

10.

Bean admits that on December 21, 2013, he had a duty to exercise reasonable care in operating his vehicle. Bean denies he breached that duty.

*   *   *   *   *

F. General Denials

Some jurisdictions permit a defendant to file a general denial; that is, a blanket denial of all allegations in the complaint. You must check the rules in your jurisdiction — some jurisdictions do not permit general denials. Even if general denials are permitted in your jurisdiction, they likely aren't favored. A general denial suggests to the court that you or your client, or both, didn't take the complaint seriously — you glanced at it, drafted a general denial, and filed it without making any attempt to investigate the truthfulness of the allegations.

A general denial is not appropriate in the vast majority of cases. Most of the time, at least one allegation or part of an allegation in the complaint is true, even if the only true allegation is the state in which the defendant was incorporated or the defendant's registered agent for service of process. Think long and hard before filing a general denial.

If you decide a general denial is appropriate, it will look something like this:

1.

Defendant denies each and every allegation asserted in Plaintiff's complaint.

G. Filing a Special Appearance Answer

Some jurisdictions permit a party to file a special answer or a special appearance answer. A special appearance answer is appropriate only in limited situations; for example, where the defendant has been improperly named or the plaintiff hasn't properly perfected service on the defendant.

By filing a special appearance answer, the defendant basically says, "I'm not submitting myself to this court's jurisdiction, but I want to file an answer anyway, just in case the court determines the case can go forward." A special appearance answer is an opportunity for a defendant to maintain its right to dispute the court's exercise of jurisdiction over it while protecting itself from a default. A special appearance answer is no different from a traditional answer except in title. You will still want to assert affirmative defenses and respond to each allegation.

H.   Make Counterclaims, Crossclaims, and Third-Party Claims

Unless your jurisdiction's rules require otherwise, you should make any counterclaims, crossclaims, or third-party clams at the end of the answer, after you've offered your client's affirmative defenses and responded to the factual and legal allegations in the complaint. These claims generally should look just like the allegations of a complaint. You should make general allegations about the counterclaim, crossclaim, or third-party defendant and its status, make relevant factual allegations, then state your client's cause or causes of action.

Do not forget to make your counterclaims, crossclaims, and third-party claims. As we outlined above, in some jurisdictions, you must assert these in the answer (or through an amended answer, if permitted) or they will be lost.

*   *   *   *   *

Waters v. Harrison, Answer to the Complaint

As it turns out, the Northern District of California denied Harrison's motion to dismiss, finding that Harrison's blog posts were "expressly aimed" at Waters and posted with the intent to cause harm to Waters in California. Now, Harrison must file an Answer to Waters' Complaint. How would you draft the answer?

HARRISON'S ANSWER TO THE COMPLAINT

ANSWER AND DEFENSES OF SIMON HARRISON

Defendant Simon Harrison files this answer to Plaintiff Kirsten Waters' Complaint. Harrison denies this Court has personal jurisdiction over him and denies Waters may recover from him as a matter of law. Harrison responds to the allegations in Waters' complaint as follows:

AFFIRMATIVE DEFENSES

1. The Court lacks personal jurisdiction over Harrison, and the complaint should be dismissed.

2. Venue is improper in this Court.

3. Waters cannot state a claim against Harrison for tortious invasion of privacy, and the complaint should be dismissed.

4. Waters cannot state a claim against Harrison for constitutional invasion of privacy, and the complaint should be dismissed.

5. Waters cannot state a claim against Harrison for libel per se, and the complaint

should be dismissed.

6. Waters cannot state a claim against Harrison for libel per quod, and the complaint should be dismissed.

7. Harrison reserves the right to assert additional affirmative defenses as they become known.

PARTIES, JURISDICTION, AND VENUE

1. Harrison is without information sufficient to form a belief as to the truth of the allegations in paragraph 1 of the complaint and therefore denies those allegations.

2. Harrison admits the allegations in paragraph 2 of the complaint.

3. Harrison denies the allegations in paragraph 3 of the complaint.

4. Harrison admits he and Waters are citizens of different states. Harrison denies the remaining allegations in paragraph 4 of the complaint.

5. Harrison denies the allegations in paragraph 5 of the complaint.

6. Harrison denies the allegations in paragraph 6 of the complaint.

FACTUAL ALLEGATIONS

7. Harrison is without information sufficient to form a belief as to the truth of the allegations in paragraph 7 of the complaint and therefore denies those allegations.

8. Harrison admits the allegations in paragraph 8 of the complaint.

9. Harrison admits the allegations in paragraph 9 of the complaint.

10. Harrison admits Waters discussed her past history of drug and alcohol abuse at the debate at the Shrine Auditorium in Los Angeles, California. Harrison is without information sufficient to form a belief at to the truth of the remaining allegations in paragraph 10 of the complaint and therefore denies those allegations.

11. Harrison admits the allegations in paragraph 11 of the complaint.

12. Harrison admits the allegations in paragraph 12 of the complaint.

13. Harrison admits Waters defeated Larson in the election. Harrison is without information sufficient to form a belief as to the truth of the remaining allegations in paragraph 13 of the complaint and therefore denies those allegations.

14. Harrison admits he published a November 10, 1994 letter on www.justtelltthet-ruth.com written by Waters' former probation officer that contained the statement:

> As you know, the court sentenced you to a probation term of 90 days, and 100 hours of community service. Having complied fully with these responsi-bilities, your sentence is hereby complete and this matter now concluded.

Harrison denies that that the document is inauthentic and denies that he has failed to provide information supporting this document's authenticity.

15. Harrison admits the allegations in paragraph 15 of the complaint.

16. Harrison admits that after the information on www.justtellthetruth.com was widely reported by the media, Waters' approval rating dropped. Harrison denies the remaining allegations in paragraph 16 of the complaint.

COUNT ONE

TORTIOUS INVASION OF PRIVACY

17. Harrison incorporates his defenses and responses to paragraphs 1–16 of the complaint as if set forth fully herein.

18. Harrison denies the allegations in paragraph 18 of the complaint.

19. Harrison admits the allegations in paragraph 19 of the complaint.

20. Harrison denies the allegations in paragraph 20 of the complaint.

21. Harrison denies the allegations in paragraph 21 of the complaint.

22. Harrison denies the allegations in paragraph 22 of the complaint.

23. Harrison denies the allegations in paragraph 23 of the complaint.

COUNT TWO

CONSTITUTIONAL INVASION OF PRIVACY

24. Harrison incorporates his defenses and responses to paragraphs 1–23 of the complaint as if set forth fully herein.

25. Harrison denies the allegations in paragraph 25 of the complaint.

26. Harrison denies the allegations in paragraph 26 of the complaint.

27. Harrison denies the allegations in paragraph 27 of the complaint.

28. Harrison denies the allegations in paragraph 28 of the complaint.

29. Harrison denies the allegations in paragraph 29 of the complaint.

COUNT THREE

DEFAMATION — LIBEL PER SE

30. Harrison incorporates his defenses and responses to paragraphs 1–29 of the complaint as if set forth fully herein.

31. Harrison admits he published truthful statements about Waters on his website, www.justtellthetruth.com. Harrison is without information sufficient to form a belief as to what "above statements" means and therefore denies the remaining allegations in

paragraph 31 of the complaint.

32. Harrison denies the allegations in paragraph 32 of the complaint.

33. Harrison denies the allegations in paragraph 33 of the complaint.

34. Harrison denies the allegations in paragraph 34 of the complaint.

35. Harrison denies the allegations in paragraph 35 of the complaint.

36. Harrison denies the allegations in paragraph 36 of the complaint.

37. Harrison denies the allegations in paragraph 37 of the complaint.

38. Harrison denies the allegations in paragraph 38 of the complaint.

COUNT FOUR

DEFAMATION — LIBEL PER QUOD

39. Harrison incorporates his defenses and responses to paragraphs 1–38 of the complaint as if set forth fully herein.

40. Harrison denies the allegations in paragraph 40 of the complaint.

COUNT FIVE

PUNITIVE DAMAGES

41. Harrison incorporates his defenses and responses to paragraphs 1–40 of the complaint as if set forth fully herein.

42. Harrison denies the allegations in paragraph 42 of the complaint.

43. Harrison denies the allegations in paragraph 43 of the complaint.

44. Harrison denies the allegations made in Waters' prayer for relief.

45. Any remaining allegations not expressly admitted are denied.

*   *   *   *   *

Why is this Answer effective?

> ► *Preserves affirmative defenses.* Harrison's answer contains a separate section for his affirmative defenses that he will or might raise at trial, thus ensuring that none of them are waived. Notice paragraph 7 of the affirmative defenses in which Harrison reserves the right to raise additional defenses. This tells the Court that Harrison might raise additional defenses if they become available. This often occurs when additional facts and information come to light in the discovery process. The point: don't box yourself in — you don't yet know all of the facts.

▶ ***Plain, simple, and to the point.*** Sometimes, it's okay to be dry and boring. The answer is one of those times. Harrison's answer is a matter-of-fact, no-nonsense response to both the factual and legal allegations in Waters' complaint. Harrison briefly responds to each allegation by admitting or denying the allegation or claiming he lacks sufficient information to respond. Notice that Harrison doesn't include extensive explanation or justification for his responses or his conduct. You shouldn't either.

▶ ***Doesn't deny the undeniable.*** Harrison doesn't deny facts that are obviously true. For instance, look at his responses to paragraphs 15 and 16. In paragraph 15, Waters alleges: "The statements Harrison posted on www.just-tellthetruth.com were reported and re-published by news media organizations throughout the country." In paragraph 16, she alleges: "Once the statements and accusations made on Harrison's website were widely reported by the media, Waters' approval rating plummeted. As a result of Harrison's tortious conduct, Waters was forced to resign her Senate seat." Harrison admits the allegation in paragraph 15 because it is true — the statements were widely reported. And he admits part of the allegation in paragraph 16 because once Harrison's statements were widely reported Waters' approval rating did plummet. These admissions make Harrison and his lawyer appear honest and trustworthy. Don't be one of those lawyers who denies obviously true allegations.

▶ ***Effective organization.*** Each numbered paragraph in the answer mirrors the corresponding allegation in the complaint, making it easy for the reader to compare the allegations with Harrison's responses.

Chapter 9

DISCOVERY

THE DISCOVERY CHECKLIST

√ Know the number of interrogatories and RPDs you can submit

√ Provide thorough instructions and definitions

√ Draft interrogatories designed to elicit information related to the claims and defenses

- √ Witnesses and parties with knowledge
- √ Claimed damages
- √ Medical treatment
- √ Corporate information
- √ Insurance information
- √ Expert witnesses

√ Draft RPDs to obtain documents related to the claims and defenses

- √ Medical records and bills
- √ Wage records
- √ Documents that support claimed damages
- √ Corporate files and documents
- √ Insurance policies
- √ Expert witness CVs and files

√ Avoid requests that are vague, overbroad, or too narrow

- √ Limit requests in time and scope
- √ Draft requests broadly enough to obtain information sought

√ Respond to discovery

- √ Give yourself time to draft responses and gather and review documents
- √ Assert appropriate objections
- √ Provide responsive answers that aren't overly detailed

After the defendant has answered the complaint and any motion to dismiss has been denied, it's time to begin discovery. Often, the judge will hold a status conference, where the parties agree upon a timetable for completing discovery and a tentative date for trial.

Discovery is incredibly important. It's often long and very tedious, however. Discovery is the stage of the lawsuit where you cull information from your adversary and, sometimes, third parties through interrogatories, document requests, depositions, and subpoenas. You'll use this information to evaluate your client's chance of success, decide whether to file a motion for summary judgment or other dispositive motion, and determine whether your client should attempt to settle the case or go to trial. You also may present the evidence you develop during discovery at trial to convince the fact-finder that your client should prevail.

Since this is a legal writing book, when we talk about discovery, we're referring to written discovery; that is, interrogatories and requests for production of documents (often referred to as RPDs). In the discovery phase, you'll be drafting interrogatories and RPDs to the opposing party. Don't let these terms overwhelm you — Interrogatories and RPDs are nothing more than questions. The opposing party will then answer the questions and provide the documents requested.

Your objective is to draft strategic questions that probe the factual and legal bases of the adversary's claims or defenses and may reveal weaknesses in the adversary's case. So, what questions should you ask, and how should you ask them?

I. YOU GUESSED IT — THE RULES

A. Know the Number and Types of Questions You Can Ask

Before drafting interrogatories or RPDs, you must consult the relevant federal, state, or local rules, which provide information such as: (1) the maximum number of interrogatories and document requests you may send; (2) the format for asking questions or requesting documents; (3) the time within which the responding party must answer (often 30 days); and (4) the grounds upon which the responding party may object.

Many attorneys draft interrogatories and RPDs with subparts to attempt to evade the limit on the number of questions the party may ask. In some jurisdictions, this practice is accepted and rarely challenged. In others, litigants must stick strictly to the question limit. You should know the common practices in your jurisdiction as well as the relevant black-letter law.

B. Instructions and Definitions

You should provide a set of instructions and definitions for your interrogatories and RPDs. In the instructions and definitions, you can inform the opposing party when responses are due and to whom they should be sent and remind the party that your requests are ongoing and should be supplemented if the party later learns additional relevant information or acquires additional relevant documents.

In the definitions section, you should define all relevant terms the opposing party could construe as ambiguous. Understand that your adversary is looking for any reason to avoid answering, particularly where the adversary's response could reveal weaknesses in its case. Accordingly, you should clarify potential ambiguities in word choice, phrasing, and scope. If you're drafting interrogatories, for example, you can state that the word "you" refers not only to the party answering the interrogatories, but to the party's agents, employees, representatives, and other persons within the party's control or direction. You can — and should — define terms such as "accident" or "contract." You can even define the term "document" to include, for example, photos, videos, emails, and electronic versions of documents. Your instructions and definitions might look like this:

Instructions and Definitions

Plaintiff propounds these interrogatories on Defendant. Defendant is instructed to respond to these interrogatories within 30 days and to send responses to Plaintiff's counsel at 100 Main Street, Miami Beach, Florida 10000. These interrogatories are continuing in nature, and Defendant is under a duty to supplement his responses in the event he later learns information that could change his responses. The following definitions apply to these interrogatories:

1. **"You" and "your" means Defendant and any agent, employee, representative, attorney, or other person acting on behalf of Defendant.**

2. **"Accident" means the automobile accident that occurred on April 4, 2012 on Collins Avenue, Miami Beach, Florida that forms the basis of this litigation.**

3. **"Criminal Charges" means the charges filed against you by the State of Florida arising from the April 4, 2012 accident that forms the basis of this litigation.**

*   *   *   *   *

Of course, use discretion in drafting your instructions and definitions. Make sure to clarify your requests, but avoid being one of those lawyers who drafts pages and pages of introductory material.

C. Types of Questions and Requests

Obviously, the types of questions and requests you will make will depend greatly on the type of case. In most jurisdictions, discovery is broad. Generally, the information and documents requested need not themselves be admissible — the requests need only be "calculated to lead to the discovery of admissible evidence." Thus, so long as you think the information will lead to the discovery of admissible evidence, you can ask for information that would be inadmissible hearsay, for example. You generally are not, however, entitled to obtain information protected by a privilege, such as the attorney-client privilege.

Your questions should be short and easy to understand. The longer and more complicated they are, they more likely you are to get an objection rather than a response.

But what types of questions should you ask in your Interrogatories? Some common questions include:

- personal information of the party (name, address, occupation, etc.);

- personal information of all persons with knowledge relevant to the claims or defenses;
- the substance of knowledge those persons have regarding claims or defenses;
- personal information of all witnesses to the incident(s);
- the substance of knowledge of all witnesses to the incident(s);
- claimed damages;
- personal information of all persons providing answers to Interrogatories or culling documents to produce;
- identity of any expert witnesses;
- substance of expected testimony of any expert witnesses; and
- prior litigation in which the party has been involved.

If one party is a corporation, limited liability company, or similar entity you might also ask:

- corporate information (date of incorporation, corporate officers etc.);
- corporate structure; and
- corporate policies relevant to the claims and defenses.

If the case is a personal injury action, you might also consider Interrogatories such as:

- the injured party's relevant medical history;
- injuries sustained in the accident;
- treatment received subsequent to the accident;
- medical diagnoses;
- the amount of medical expenses claimed as a result of the accident; and
- prognosis.

This certainly is nowhere near an exhaustive list, but gives you an idea of the types of questions you will want to ask. You should think critically about what type of information you want to elicit from the opposing party.

And what types of documents should you ask for in your RPDs? Again, you can ask for any documents "calculated" to lead to discoverable evidence, which may include:

- any document the party consulted in responding to Interrogatories;
- any document referenced in the party's responses to Interrogatories;
- documents relevant to the claims or defenses;
- contracts or other writings that evidence a contract (if applicable);
- the CV of the expert witness;
- all documents reviewed by expert witnesses; and
- the contents of all expert witnesses' files.

If an entity is involved, you may also ask for:

- incident/accident reports and records;
- personnel files for employees involved in the incident/accident;
- corporate training manuals and materials; and
- other corporate records that might lead to the discovery of admissible evidence.

If your case involves personal injury, you likely will want to request the following documents as well:

- medical records and bills;
- wage records (if lost wages are claimed);
- other records of special damages; and
- photographs of injuries sustained.

Don't forget — Your interrogatories and RPDs should be simple, straightforward, and easy to understand. For example, your interrogatories might look like this:

1.

Please state your full name, address, telephone number, date of birth, and Social Security number.

2.

Were you married on the date of the Accident? If so, please state your spouse's name, address, and telephone number.

3.

Were you employed on the date of the Accident? If so, please state your employer's name, address, telephone number; your title or position with that employer on the date of the Accident; the name, address, and telephone number of your direct supervisor; and your compensation, salary, or hourly pay rate on the date of the Accident.

*   *   *   *   *

Your RPDs should be even more straightforward:

1.

Please produce medical records and bills for any medical treatment you received that you contend was related, in any way, to the Accident at the center of this litigation.

2.

Please produce photographs of the vehicles involved in the Accident at the center of this litigation.

3.

If you are seeking to recover lost wages, please produce your tax returns for the years 2010, 2011, 2012, and 2013.

*   *   *   *   *

II. KNOWING WHAT TO ASK, AND KNOWING HOW TO ANSWER

A. Avoid Unhelpful Responses, Non-Responses, and Objections

You must draft your interrogatories and RPDs to minimize the likelihood you'll receive: (1) unhelpful answers; (2) non-responsive or vague answers that lead to unnecessary motions practice; or (3) objections.

Typically you will have only a limited number of interrogatories and RPDs, so you should use your requests carefully and try to avoid asking questions that will result in unhelpful responses. Unless a question is otherwise objectionable, the opposing party will happily answer questions that do not probe areas where the party is vulnerable. Don't waste a question by seeking information that is unlikely to help you prove your client's case or disprove the opposing party's case.

Furthermore, be careful of questions that likely will result in objections. Common objections include:

- The request is overly broad and unduly burdensome;
- The request is not reasonably calculated to lead to the discovery of admissible evidence;
- The request seeks information protected by the attorney-client or work-product privilege, or both; and
- The information requested is equally available to the requesting party through reasonable investigation.

If the opposing party objects to the request and does not respond, you'll have to decide whether to make the request again in a way that won't elicit an objection — an option only available if you haven't exhausted the maximum number of interrogatories or RPDs — or challenge the grounds for objection by moving to compel the opposing party to respond. Either way, you'll have to spend additional time and money to attempt to get a response. Avoid drafting objectionable questions by following the tips below.

B. Avoid Overly Broad Questions

Just because broad categories of evidence are discoverable, you should not draft broad interrogatories and RPDs. If you do so, you'll likely get objections and no responses. Remember, a party is not required to respond to requests that are overly broad and would be unduly burdensome to respond to.

For example, if you are asking for information or documents about incidents that happened before or after the incident or accident in question, you'd probably be wise to limit the scope of your request in time. Assume you represent a slip-and-fall plaintiff and want to know of prior slip-and-fall claims made against the defendant grocery store. You generally should avoid drafting a request so broad that you essentially ask for information about any slip-and-fall accident that occurred at any of the defendant's stores anywhere in the country. You won't get a response — you'll only get an objection that the request is too broad.

Instead, you might consider narrowing your request to ask for information on accidents that occurred within five years before the accident in the same store in which the defendant slipped. Or, if the defendant slipped, for example, in the produce section, you might consider narrowing your request to ask for information about other slip-and-fall accidents that occurred in produce sections in any one of the defendant's grocery stores in the state in which your client's slip-and-fall accident occurred.

If you draft a narrow request but the opposing party still refuses to respond, you'll have to file a motion to compel to obtain a response. You'll look substantially better in front of the judge, however, if you've exercised discretion in drafting your request and the opposing party, for refusing to respond, will appear less credible for attempting to stymie the discovery process.

C. Avoid Overly Narrow Questions

You also, of course, want to avoid drafting interrogatories and RPDs that are overly narrow — you might not get all information relevant to the case. For example, suppose you represent a plaintiff in a car accident case. You want to know if the defendant intends to allege your client made any statements at the scene of the accident. Why might the following request be too narrow?

1.

Did you hear the plaintiff make any statements at the scene of the Accident about the cause of the Accident? If so, please state the substance of those statements.

*   *   *   *   *

What if the plaintiff made statements at the scene that aren't "about the cause of the Accident"? What if the plaintiff, an attorney, jumped out of her car after the accident and angrily yelled, "I'm going to sue your ass for everything you have." Your request wouldn't encompass that statement and you might not learn, until trial, about your client's damaging statement. "That never happens in real life," you say. It does. And it happened in a case in which one of the authors was involved. How might you have drafted this interrogatory to encompass the statement the plaintiff made at the scene?

1.

Did you hear the plaintiff make any statements to anyone at the scene of the Accident? If so, please state the substance of those statements.

*   *   *   *   *

That request would encompass the plaintiff's outburst and threat at the scene of the accident. Think carefully about what information you are trying to obtain and draft your request narrowly enough to avoid an objection and broadly enough to obtain the information you seek. Give yourself time to carefully draft questions that probe the factual basis for an opposing party's claims, but do not ask for unnecessary, irrelevant, or objectionable information.

D. Responding to Interrogatories

You aren't the only one who gets to ask questions — the opposing party will also propound Interrogatories on your client. In responding, you'll have to navigate through the tricky forest of under- and over-disclosure. In other words, you have to know how to provide responsive answers that don't inadvertently reveal your entire case. Given the breadth of possible questions and answers, we can't really teach you how to respond to every possible question or request you might receive. We can, however, give you some general tips that will serve you well.

You shouldn't wait until the last minute to look at or attempt to respond to interrogatories sent to your client. You must give yourself enough time to analyze precisely what information the adversary is seeking. You should also be familiar with all available objections and know when you can raise those objections. Remember, like you, the opposing party is required to ask specific, direct, and easy-to-understand questions. If even a single word creates uncertainty or confusion, you should object on the ground that the question is ambiguous. Should you decide, however, to respond despite an available objection, be sure to include this objection at the beginning of your response to ensure you do not waive it.

That said, if an interrogatory has been phrased properly, do not assert frivolous objections. And please do not cut and paste the same objections into every answer. Instead, answer the question, but be careful to limit your response to the specific information sought through the interrogatory. In addition, resist the urge to offer unnecessary explanation, and be careful not to misinterpret the question's scope. Doing so can result in the inadvertent disclosure of information that harms your case or prompts the adversary to propound — if the rules allow — additional discovery requests.

You should not go to unreasonable lengths to avoid disclosing information that harms your case where that information is properly requested and discoverable (e.g., not protected by a privilege). Do not, for example, lie or provide misleading responses, omit relevant information requested, or offer vague, politician-like answers. If a question asks you to provide all documentation supporting your request for $500,000 in damages, do not respond by saying, "Plaintiff has suffered terribly since the defendant's tractor-trailer demolished plaintiff's house while she was enjoying quality time with her family. Plaintiff cries every morning, has frequent nightmares, and claims that her life will never be the same." All of this might be true. But that answer says — and accomplishes — nothing. The adversary will hound you to provide the requested documentation, and if you continue playing the cat and mouse game, the adversary might file a motion with the court seeking to compel you to produce the requested documents. In some cases, you or your client might even face sanctions.

Stated simply, don't be a jerk. For example, if you were representing Waters, think about how you would answer this question from Harrison:

1.

Please describe in detail the factual basis for your belief that you spent 30 days in the Palo, Alto County Jail.

*   *   *   *   *

Don't respond with this:

1.

Please describe in detail the factual basis for your belief that you spent 30 days in the Palo Alto County Jail.

Response: Plaintiff believes that Harrison's comments on www.just-tellthetruth.com were defamatory. Plaintiff stands by her claims and will not answer any question designed to burden or harass.

*   *   *   *   *

Waters filed the case and put her statements at issue, so Harrison is entitled to ask the question and is entitled to a meaningful response. This nonsensical response above serves no purpose other than to provoke the adversary and unnecessarily protract the litigation. The truth may hurt, but successful litigators deal with it and win anyway. Thus, instead of offering a non-response to the above question, say something like this:

1.

Please describe in detail the factual basis for your belief that you spent 30 days in the Palo Alto County Jail.

Response: Plaintiff objects to this request to the extent it seeks disclosure of information protected by the attorney-client or attorney work product privileges. Plaintiff acknowledges that her representation that she spent 30 days in the Palo Alto County Jail was incorrect. However, Plaintiff believed that statement was true at the time she made it. Plaintiff concedes the statement was inaccurate and based on her unsupported belief that she did spend time in jail as a result of her arrest and conviction for DUI. Plaintiff will supplement this response as relevant information becomes available or is adduced through discovery.

*   *   *   *   *

In this answer, Waters does not reveal every thought or motivation that may have related to her representation that she spent 30 days in the Palo Alto jail. Waters simply admits that she made an honest mistake and that she does not know of a specific reason to explain her erroneous belief. Moreover, Waters' response does not attempt to mislead, conceal, or obfuscate the truth.

Do not forget to object if there is a reasonable basis to justify non-disclosure of information that might be more responsive. For example, if Waters told you in a private consultation that she intentionally lied to garner sympathy from the voters, this information is protected by the attorney-client privilege.[41] In the event that Harrison seeks a more detailed response, you will have preserved this objection and can re-assert it at that time.

Ultimately, the most important rule in responding to discovery is this: if the opposing party doesn't ask, you shouldn't show or tell. The opposing party is responsible for asking questions sufficient to obtain all relevant information—you aren't required to do that party's job for it. In short, don't ever provide information that the other party did not clearly and specifically request.

E.   Responding to RPDs

Once you have decided whether your client possesses responsive documents, responding to RPDs is easy. You simply outline your objections, if any, and respond that the documents are attached, or will be produced upon payment of copying costs, or some similar language. Again, the appropriate response likely will depend on the relevant rules or practices in your jurisdiction. For example:

1.

Please produce medical records and bills for any medical treatment Plaintiff received that Plaintiff contends was related, in any way, to the Accident at the center of this litigation.

Response: All responsive documents are attached to this response.

F.   Try to Avoid Discovery Disputes

Ultimately, a cantankerous approach to discovery may lead to unnecessary motions practice, be costly to the client, inject unnecessary discord into the litigation process, and harm your credibility. And judges really dislike having to resolve discovery fights. They have more important things on their plates. Don't try to rationalize this behavior: "I'm just being a zealous advocate for my client, and papering the adversary to death will stall the case or make the other party soften its position." The judge won't buy it. Try to avoid discovery disputes by drafting carefully worded discovery requests and providing appropriate, responsive answers.

*   *   *   *   *

Waters v. Harrison, Interrogatories and Document Requests

Below are interrogatories and document requests propounded by Harrison and Waters. As read them, notice how the requests are broadly phrased, yet seek specific information that is targeted at particular categories of evidence, and are unlikely to warrant a meritorious objection. Keep it simple, and be straightforward.

---

[41] Whether you would need to withdraw from representation after learning this information is beyond the scope of this text.

PLAINTIFF KIRSTEN WATERS' INTERROGATORIES TO DEFENDANT SIMON HARRISON

Plaintiff Kirsten Waters propounds the following interrogatories on Defendant Simon Harrison to be answered separately and fully, in writing, under oath, and in accordance with the Federal Rules of Civil Procedure:

GENERAL INSTRUCTIONS

1. If any of these interrogatories cannot be answered in full, you should answer to the extent possible and specify the reasons for your inability to answer the remainder.

2. The person or persons answering these interrogatories must furnish such information as is known or is available to him/her upon reasonable investigation regardless of whether you obtained this information directly, or whether this information was obtained by and made known to you by any of your attorneys or other agents or representatives.

3. If you object to any part of an interrogatory, state precisely your objection and answer, to the best of your ability, the remaining portion of that interrogatory. If you object to the scope or time period of an interrogatory and refuse to answer for that scope or time period, state your objection and answer the interrogatory within what you believe is the appropriate scope for the appropriate time period.

DEFINITIONS

As used in these interrogatories, the terms listed below are defined as follows:

1. "You," "your," "yourself," and "plaintiff" mean or refer to Plaintiff Kirsten Waters.

2. "Relates, directly or indirectly," means supports, evidences, describes, mentions, refers to, suggests, contradicts, or comprises.

3. "Person" means any natural or juridical person, firm, corporation, partnership, proprietorship, joint venture, organization, group of natural persons or other association separately identifiable, whether or not such association has a separate juristic existence in its own right.

4. "Identify," when referring to a natural person, means the following:

   a. The person's full name and present or last known home address, home telephone number, business address and business telephone number;

   b. The person's present title and employer or other business affiliation; and

   c. The person's home address, home telephone number, business address and business telephone number at the time of the actions at which each interrogatory is directed.

5. "Identify," when used to refer to a document, means the following:

   a. The subject of the document;

b. The title of the document;

c. The type of document (e.g., letter, memorandum, telegram, chart);

d. The date of the document, or if the specific date thereof is unknown, the month and year or other best approximation of such date with reference to other events;

e. The identity of the person or persons who wrote, contributed to, prepared or originated such document; and

f. The present or last known location and custodian of the document.

6. "Identify," when used to refer to oral communications means the following:

a. Identify the person making any statement, the person to whom the statement was made, and all persons present at the time the statement was made;

b. To state whether the statement was recorded, transcribed, or summarized by any person;

c. To summarize the contents of the communication or conversation;

d. To state the date of the communication; and

e. To identify any person having custody of any document evidencing the communication.

7. To state the "basis" for a claim or allegation, provide the following information:

a. Identify persons having information or knowledge about such incident or event about which such claim or allegation is made;

b. Identify documents pertaining to such incident or event about which such claim or allegation is made;

c. Identify documents providing information about such incident or event about which such claim or allegation is made;

d. Identify oral or verbal communications pertaining to such incident or event about which such claim or allegation is made;

e. Identify oral or verbal communications providing information about such incident or event about which such claim or allegation is made;

f. Describe the incident or event about which such claim or allegation is made; and

g. State the legal bases, including identifying contracts, agreements or other documents (including specifying the particular portions relied upon), statutes, rules, regulations and oral and verbal communications, underlying or supporting the claim or allegation or upon which the claim or allegation is based.

INTERROGATORIES

1. Please describe in detail your relationship with Waters, including, but not limited to, when and where you met Waters, your interaction with Waters while an undergraduate at Stanford University, and all other information relating, directly or indirectly, to the subject matter of this lawsuit.

2. Please identify the names of all individuals who may have knowledge that is related, directly or indirectly, to this matter, including telephone numbers, addresses, and other relevant information.

3. Please describe in detail your educational history, including, but not limited to, degrees obtained at secondary and post-secondary institutions, the dates on which those degrees were obtained, the institutions from which those degrees were obtained, and the years in which those degrees were obtained.

4. Please describe in detail your criminal history, including, but not limited to, arrests, convictions, and plea agreements.

5. Please describe in detail the basis for asserting, on www.justtellthetruth.com, that Waters "intentionally lied" during her final debate at the Shrine Auditorium in Los Angeles, California with then-Senator Robert Larson.

6. Please describe in detail the basis for asserting, on www.justtellthetruth.com, that, as part of her plea bargain, Waters was "neither incarcerated nor ordered to spend even a single day in a residential treatment program."

7. Please describe in detail the basis for asserting, on www.justtellthetruth.com, that "Kirsten only sought residential treatment because her parents threatened to stop paying her tuition at Stanford."

8. Please describe in detail the basis for asserting, on www.justtellthetruth.com, that "During our last two years at Stanford, Kirsten was engaged to a mutual friend."

9. Please describe in detail the basis for asserting, on www.justtellthetruth.com, that "Kirsten suddenly broke off the engagement and admitted to having a lengthy affair with another man throughout the duration of the relationship."

10. Please describe in detail the basis for asserting, on www.justtellthetruth.com, that "Kirsten was not a good student and I doubt she has the abilities to effectively serve in any elected capacity."

11. Please describe in detail the basis for asserting, on www.justtellthetruth.com, that "Kirsten's admission to Berkeley wasn't about merit. It was about favoritism and money."

12. Please describe in detail the basis for asserting, on www.justtellthetruth.com, that "her [Waters'] dad is one of Berkeley's most generous donors."

13. Please describe in detail the basis for asserting, on www.justtellthetruth.com, that Waters is "not fit for public office."

*   *   *   *   *

DEFENDANT SIMON HARRISON'S INTERROGATORIES TO PLAINTIFF KIRSTEN WATERS

(INSTRUCTIONS OMITTED FOR PURPOSES OF BREVITY)

INTERROGATORIES

1. Please describe in detail your prior and current use of alcohol and prescription, over-the-counter, and illegal drugs during your secondary, post-secondary, and professional career, including, but not limited to, the frequency with which you use those substances.

2. Please describe in detail your criminal history, including, but not limited to, your August, 1994 arrest, any convictions or pleas entered, and the length of any sentences imposed by a court, including sentences that resulted in probation.

3. Please identify the names of all individuals who may have knowledge that is related, directly or indirectly, to this matter, including their telephone numbers, home and business addresses, and the substance of their knowledge.

4. Please describe in detail your educational history including any degrees you have obtained, the dates on which you obtained those degrees, and the institutions from which they were obtained.

5. Please list any financial contributions you or any immediate family member have made to any educational institution you attended or obtained a degree from, including the amount on the contribution, the date on which the contribution was made, the institution to which the contribution was made, and the person who made the contribution.

6. Please describe in detail your employment history, including, but not limited to, positions within the legal profession and public offices held.

7. Please describe in detail the relationship with your former fiancé(s), including, but not limited to, your engagement to Jonathan Berman while an undergraduate student at Stanford University.

8. Please describe in detail your relationship with Harrison, including, but not limited to, where and when you met Harrison and conversations you had with Harrison that relate, directly or indirectly, to your claims.

9. Please describe in detail the basis for asserting, during your final debate with then-Senator Robert Larson at the Shrine Auditorium in Los Angeles, California, that the plea agreement, in connection with your August, 1994 arrest, required a thirty-day period of incarceration as well as treatment in a residential facility.

10. Please describe in detail the basis for asserting that your statements at the debate were "inconsistent" with the facts.

11. Please describe in detail the basis for your decision to resign from the United States Senate.

12. Please describe in detail the basis for your claim that the statements on Harrison's blog, www.justtellthetruth.com, caused you to suffer damages, including economic and non-economic damages.

13. Please describe in detail the basis for claiming that Harrison "lied" when posting the relevant statements on www.justtellthetruth.com.

14. Please describe in detail the basis for claiming that Harrison's statements were "intentionally and maliciously" false.

*   *   *   *   *

REQUESTS FOR PRODUCTION TO DEFENDANT SIMON HARRISON

(INSTRUCTIONS OMITTED FOR PURPOSES OF BREVITY)

1. All documents in your possession that relate to Waters' history of alcohol and substance abuse.

2. All documents in your possession that relate to Waters' criminal history, including any documents from criminal authorities regarding any criminal charges brought against Waters, any documents regarding Waters' convictions or plea agreements, and any documents relating to Waters' probation.

3. All documents in your possession that support the statement made on your website, www.justtellthetruth.com, that Waters "lied" during the final debate between herself and then-Senator Ted Larson.

4. All documents in your possession that support statements made on your website, www.justtellthetruth.com, regarding Waters' academic history, including any documents that support your claim that Waters engaged in academic dishonesty.

5. All documents in your possession that support statements made on your website, www.justtellthetruth.com, that Waters "only sought residential treatment because [Waters'] parents threatened to stop paying her tuition at Stanford."

6. All documents in your possession that support statements made on your website, www.justtellthetruth.com, that Waters is not fit for public office.

7. All documents in your possession that support statements made on your website, www.justtellthetruth.com, that Waters has ever been unfaithful to any person to whom she has been engaged.

8. All documents in your possession that support statements made on your website, www.justtellthetruth.com, that Waters "performed poorly in her studies" while an undergraduate student.

9. All documents in your possession that support statements made on your website, www.justtellthetruth.com, that Waters' admission to law school was not the result of Waters' academic merit.

10. All documents in your possession that support statements made on your website,

www.justtellthetruth.com, that Waters' admission to law school was the result of "favoritism and money."

11. The curriculum vitae of any person you have retained to serve as an expert in this matter.

12. Any report prepared by any person you have retained to serve as an expert in this matter.

13. Any documents reviewed by any person you have retained to serve as an expert in this matter.

14. The complete file related to this litigation developed by any person you have retained to serve as an expert in this matter.

*   *   *   *   *

REQUESTS FOR PRODUCTION TO PLAINTIFF KIRSTEN WATERS

(INSTRUCTIONS OMITTED FOR PURPOSES OF BREVITY)

1. All documents in your possession that relate to your history of alcohol and substance abuse.

2. All documents in your possession that relate to your criminal history, including any documents from criminal authorities regarding any criminal charges brought against you, any documents regarding your convictions or plea agreements, and any documents relating to your probation.

3. All transcripts or other documents in your possession that reflect your undergraduate academic history and credentials.

4. All transcripts or other documents in your possession that reflect your postgraduate academic history and credentials.

5. All documents in your possession that evidence the reason your relationship with Jonathan Berman ended.

6. All documents in your possession that reflect any relationship between you or any member of your family, including your mother and father, and Berkeley Law School.

7. All documents in your possession that support your claim for damages.

8. All documents in your possession that support your claim that the statements Harrison made on his website, www.justtellthetruth.com, are "intentionally and maliciously" false.

9. All documents in your possession that support your claim that you were forced to resign from the United States Senate as a result of Harrison's conduct.

10. All documents in your possession that reflect how statements you made during the final debate between you and then-Senator Larson were "inconsistent" with the facts.

11. The curriculum vitae of any person you have retained to serve as an expert in this matter.

12. Any report prepared by any person you have retained to serve as an expert in this matter.

13. Any documents reviewed by any person you have retained to serve as an expert in this matter.

14. The complete file related to this litigation developed by any person you have retained to serve as an expert in this matter.

*   *   *   *   *

Why are the parties' discovery requests effective?

▶ ***They don't re-invent the wheel.*** Discovery is not the place for you to show off your creativity and originality. While you should certainly ask penetrating and detailed questions that relate to the facts of the litigation (as opposed to sending the same form discovery in every case), the general character of your discovery requests should be pretty standard.

▶ ***Definitions guard against ambiguity.*** Notice that the parties' discovery requests have a "Definitions" section, where all relevant terms, even those that seem obvious, are defined. Why should you define what seems obvious? To ensure that both parties are on the same page about the type of information and documents sought. Did you intend the term "document" to encompass hard-copy as well as electronic versions of documents? Yes — but the opposing party might not know that. Be sure to cover all of your bases, and err on the side of being too detailed because the opposing party will look for any reason to object and not provide a response.

▶ ***The discovery requests are properly phrased.*** In *Waters v. Harrison*, the parties' discovery requests are specific, unambiguous, and generally phrased in broad but non-objectionable terms. For example, in her interrogatories, Waters requests that Harrison provide the factual basis to support each allegedly defamatory statement he made on www.justtellthetruth.com. In so doing, Waters is, among other things, probing Harrison's state of mind when he made the statements, which goes to the issue of malice. Harrison would have a difficult time objecting to this request because it involves relevant statements that he made on his website.

What if you don't have the luxury of blog posts like those Harrison posted? Review the opposing party's complaint and ask for the factual basis for every allegation made. Or look at the opposing party's answer to your complaint and ask about the factual basis for every allegation that was denied.

In addition, the parties' questions are simultaneously broadly *and* narrowly phrased. For example, Waters does not make the mistake of asking something like, "Please provide all email communications that support your assertion that Waters' lied at the final debate." That's too narrow — What if Harrison's allegations are based on letters, text messages, or a conversation he had with one of Waters' former campaign workers? Harrison would not have to mention these because Waters only asked for email communications, not all communications, whether oral or written. Be sure to phrase your questions in a broad and open-ended manner while being specific and unambiguous enough to avoid an objection.

▶ **Safeguard against meritorious objections.** Both parties propounded discovery requests that are unlikely to trigger meritorious objections. As an initial matter, let's get something straight. No matter what you ask or how you ask it, some attorneys will always object. Some attorneys cut and paste a standard objection into each response, obsessively trying to preserve every objection, no matter how frivolous that objection might be. You can't control what your adversary does, but you can make sure that your questions do not result in a *sustainable* objection.

▶ **Follow the rules regarding form and number.** Note that both parties drafted only a handful of interrogatories and RPDs and have "saved" some questions in case they need to use them later in the litigation. For example, it is very difficult to ask every relevant question of a deponent. Often, after you have deposed a party, you realize there were additional questions you should have asked at the deposition. If you haven't exhausted all your interrogatories, you can propound additional interrogatories after the deposition to obtain information you forgot to ask about at the deposition or to clarify statements the deponent made. If you practice in a jurisdiction that doesn't have an express limit on the number of discovery requests you may send, you shouldn't interpret this as a license to subject your adversary to hundreds of interrogatories or RPDs. If you serve 500 interrogatories on a party — no matter how straightforward those interrogatories may be — the opposing party is going to object to responding to them. And the more you annoy the opposing party, the more that party will fight you, and the more that party fights you, the harder it will be for you to get valuable information and make progress in the litigation. Remember that civility and ethics matters are important. Why do you think litigation sometimes goes on for years, even though the legal issues are relatively straightforward? Bickering between the parties. Unnecessary motion practice. Fighting over every little detail. That approach doesn't make you a good lawyer. It wastes time and money and tests the court's patience. Use discovery properly.

▶ **Don't accept less.** This tip is not related to the discovery requests above, but is very important. Don't *ever* accept *incomplete* or *partially responsive answers*. Your adversary is hoping that you will say "this is good enough. I don't want to deal with this nonsense anymore." Don't have that attitude because in some jurisdictions, a complaint may be dismissed *with prejudice* if, after repeated requests, a party does not provide fully responsive answers in discovery. Know the rules so you can enforce them on behalf of your client.

Chapter 10

THE MOTION FOR SUMMARY JUDGMENT

THE MOTION FOR SUMMARY JUDGMENT CHECKLIST

√ Don't file too early or too late

√ Know the standard

√ Draft a statement of undisputed material facts

  √ Keep the statement of facts as short as possible

  √ Lean toward objectivity in the statement of facts

  √ Use a one fact equals one paragraph approach

  √ Support each fact with evidence from the record (deposition transcripts, documents, etc.)

  √ Don't make legal conclusions

√ Attach exhibits, if permitted

√ Outline the summary judgment standard in an accurate but persuasive way

√ Make your case for summary judgment

  √ Focus on the facts

  √ Don't cite cases helpful to the opposing party

√ Consider filing a motion for partial summary judgment

√ Respond to a motion for summary judgment

√ File a reply brief

  √ Respond to counterarguments

  √ Don't regurgitate arguments already made in initial brief

  √ Use a one fact equals one paragraph approach

  √ Support each fact with evidence from the record (deposition transcripts, documents etc.) but don't disguise legal conclusions as facts

√ Consider filing a cross-motion for summary judgment

Motions for summary judgment filed in federal court are governed by Rule 56 of the Federal Rules of Civil Procedure. In a motion to dismiss, you're basically saying to the court: "Even if everything the plaintiff has alleged in the complaint is true, the defendant still can't recover." A motion for summary judgment is different. In filing a motion for summary judgment you're saying: "The plaintiff isn't entitled to have a jury consider his claims because he doesn't have any evidence to prove those claims." Motions for summary judgment differ in several respects from motions to dismiss, including that both plaintiffs and defendants can file motions for summary judgment.[42] Before you file a motion for summary judgment, you must be aware of some important rules governing summary judgment practice.

I. CHECK THE TIMING

Check your jurisdiction's rules about the timing of a motion for summary judgment. Generally, you won't be ready to file a summary judgment motion until discovery is complete, but in some circumstances, you might be able to file one earlier. Some jurisdictions allow litigants to file summary judgment motions at any time. Others do not allow motions for summary judgment until discovery is complete. Some, including federal courts, set deadlines that require parties to file summary judgment motions within 30 days after discovery expires. Make sure you know the appropriate time to file your motion.

II. YOU SHOULD KNOW THE STANDARD — IT'S HIGH

Before filing a motion for summary judgment, you must decide whether your argument can satisfy the high standard for granting a motion for summary judgment. Specifically, you must convince the court that, even when construing the relevant law and all available evidence in your adversary's favor, there is no genuine issue of *material* fact — not just any fact — concerning the legal sufficiency of a particular claim.

Rest assured that the court will give your adversary the benefit of every doubt. If the court can identify any reason to deny your motion, whether it is based on an interpretation of the law or a reasonable disagreement between the parties regarding a material fact, you will lose. Think about it: in filing a summary judgment motion, you are asking the judge to deprive the opposing party of a jury trial.

We cannot emphasize this point enough: if *any* material fact, relating to *any* element of a claim, is disputed, your motion will not be successful. If your legal argument does not meet this tough standard, then it is not a winning argument for purposes of summary judgment. It does not matter that there is a ninety-nine percent chance that a jury will rule in your favor. The only thing that matters to a court is whether, as a matter of law, a jury should even be *allowed* to hear the other party's claim. The point is, be sure that you have a strong argument that is supported by the law and undisputed facts when you seek summary judgment

Contract cases are particularly well-suited to summary judgment motions. Unless a contract is ambiguous, courts, not juries, will construe it. Negligence cases, on the other hand, often cannot be disposed of through summary judgment. This makes sense, because the question of whether a party was negligent is generally one of fact, not law. And questions of fact must be decided by the trier of fact.

---

[42] Motions for summary judgment from defendants are much more common, but plaintiffs file them as well.

III.   STATEMENT OF UNDISPUTED MATERIAL FACTS

Most courts require a *Statement of Undisputed Material Facts* with a motion for summary judgment, where the lawyer must outline every material fact that cannot be disputed by the opposing party. Don't make the mistake of: (1) including facts that are arguably contested (thereby creating an issue of material fact); (2) asserting legal conclusions; (3) listing irrelevant or immaterial facts; or (4) omitting facts that are undisputed and germane to your motion.

If you find yourself leaving out inconvenient facts, that's a red flag: your motion might not be ripe for summary judgment. Be sure to meticulously analyze the facts in light of the relevant law, and think about how the court — and adversary — will respond to your arguments.

What is a material fact, you might ask? Well, the term is a little hard to define, but, generally, a fact is material if it tends to prove or disprove a required element of a claim or defense. What constitutes a material fact will differ from case to case — and the same fact could be material in one case and immaterial in another.

A word of advice: the greater the number of material facts, the less likely the court is to grant a motion for summary judgment. If you think about it, this makes sense. The more facts, the more likely it is that at least one is contested.

Let's look at any easy situation. Suppose your client is an electronics store. The store's security manager suspected a man of shoplifting. The manager spoke with the man for a few minutes and did not find any stolen merchandise. The man left the store then filed a lawsuit for false imprisonment.

In most jurisdictions, false imprisonment is defined as the intentional, unlawful detention of a person that deprives the person of his liberty. As the defendant, you need only show that the plaintiff can't prove one element of his case to obtain a grant of summary judgment.

At his deposition, the manager testified that he did not detain the plaintiff and that he never told the plaintiff he could not leave. The manager spoke with the plaintiff on the floor of the store, not in a separate room. The plaintiff admitted at his deposition that he voluntarily chose to speak with the supervisor because he felt an obligation to clear himself.

These facts are all material because they tend to disprove an element of false imprisonment: detention.

But how do you draft your statement of material facts? Your statement of material facts will generally look similar to a complaint, but you'll have to support each allegation with a citation to some part of the record (answer, depositions, affidavits, discovery responses, documents produced in discovery, etc.). You generally should list a single "fact" per paragraph.

For example, assume you represent restaurant owners who claim a county wrongfully denied them an alcohol license. Your statement of material facts might look something like this:

1.

On May 1, 1980, Petitioners Mary and Charles Cole opened a Southern-style friend chicken restaurant, the Cluckin' Chick, in Anderson County, South Carolina. December 14, 2012 Deposition of Charles M. Cole (C. Cole Deposition), 27:5–23, attached as Exhibit A.

2.

Each year from 1980 until 2010, the Coles applied for and Anderson County issued them a license to serve alcohol at the Cluckin' Chick. C. Cole Deposition 39:8–25; 40:1–13; Copies of alcohol licenses issued to Mary and Charles Cole from 1980 through 2010, attached as Exhibit B.

*   *   *   *   *

You should generally err on the side of objectivity when writing statements of material fact. Save arguments for your brief. The more objective your statements are, the less likely your opponent will be able to dispute the truthfulness of the statements. Consider the difference between the second material fact above and this one:

2.

For 30 years, Anderson County issued the Coles an alcohol license for the Cluckin' Chick, but in 2011, the County wrongfully refused to issue the Coles an alcohol license, thereby crippling the business. C. Cole Deposition 39:8–25; 40:1–13; 58:3–25; 59:1–25; 60:1–19; 100:4–25.

*   *   *   *   *

As an initial matter, there is more than one "fact" in this second example — there are three facts: (1) the Coles were issued a license from 1980 through 2010; (2) in 2011 the County refused to issue the Coles a license; and (3) the denial of the license crippled the Cole's business. Second, you can make this point — that the County wrongfully denied the Coles an alcohol license — through offering objective evidence that the County cannot dispute.

For example, suppose the evidence you've gathered shows that Coles were denied an alcohol license in 2011 because a vengeful county commissioner, who was mad that the Cluckin' Chick prospered while her restaurant failed, ordered the licensing office to deny the Coles a license. Your objective statement of facts would look something like this:

12.

The Coles' 2011 application for an alcohol license was properly completed and supported with appropriate documents. January 20, 2013 Deposition of Jeremy Murray (Murray Deposition) 45:20–25; 46:1–24.

13.

An Anderson County licensing clerk, Jeremy Murray, reviewed the application in January 2011 and intended to issue a 2011 alcohol license to the Coles. Murray Deposition 47:6–13.

14.

Before Murray could issue the license, he received a call from his supervisor, Beverly Worthy. Worthy told Murray to deny the Coles' alcohol license. Murray Deposition 48:18–25; 49:1–25; 50:1–3.

15.

Murray informed Worthy that the license was complete and should be approved, but Worthy instructed Murray to deny the license. Murray Deposition 50:4–19; January 20, 2013 Deposition of Beverly Worthy (Worthy Deposition) 30:3–10.

*   *   *   *   *

Structuring the statement of facts in this way is much more effective than simply saying the denial was wrongful — you're actually showing the court how the objective, indisputable evidence proves the denial was wrongful. The County can dispute that the denial was wrongful — but it can't dispute the testimony of its own employees.

Just remember, don't try to slip legal arguments or conclusions into your statement of undisputed facts. This is not a statement of fact:

15.

The County wrongfully refused to issue the Coles an alcohol license. C. Cole Deposition 39:8–25; 40:1–13.

*   *   *   *   *

This "statement of fact" is a legal conclusion. Your statement of facts should contain "just the facts," and nothing else. Save legal arguments and conclusions for the argument section of your brief.

IV.   EXHIBITS

Unless the court prohibits exhibits, you should attach copies of all documents you cite to your statement of material facts. You generally must file original deposition transcripts with the clerk of court, but attaching copies of depositions to your statement of material facts will enable the judge or the judge's clerk to locate the cited materials more easily. Of course, if you are relying on photos, official or business records, surveys and plats, or similar evidence, you will want to attach copies of those documents to your statement of material facts as well.

V.   OUTLINING THE STANDARD

Courts routinely deal with motions for summary judgment and are familiar with the standard. However, you will still need to draft a short outline of the legal standard for summary judgment. Remember to draft the standard in a favorable but accurate way.

VI. MAKING YOUR CASE FOR SUMMARY JUDGMENT

In your summary judgment motion, you'll want to follow all the tips we have discussed throughout this book — craft a strong introduction, develop a theme, use every opportunity to persuade, etc.

In summary judgment motions, your discussion of the facts is very important. Remember — the summary judgment motion is dead in the water if there are any material facts in dispute. You must explain the undisputed material facts carefully and explain why the opposing party can't prove its case, using case law, statutes, and other relevant legal authority to support that position.

Assume you represent a plaintiff in a contract action. Contract interpretation is almost always a question of law for the court, unless the contract is ambiguous, so you're already off to a good start. In your argument section, outline all the steps the court must go through to determine the meaning of contract terms, and point out that where the contract is unambiguous "courts cannot revise the contract in order to change or make a better agreement for the parties."*Elliott v. Darwin Neibaur Farms*, 69 P.3d 1035, 1040 (Idaho 2003) (citation omitted).

Support your position with cases in which the courts have interpreted the same or similar language at issue in your case, focusing on recent, binding cases. And don't rely on cases where an appellate court upheld the findings of the trier of fact (as opposed to a judge's ruling on a motion for summary judgment). You'll sink your motion. Why? Because you are arguing the case should never get to the trier of fact. If you cite cases in which the fact questions were decided by the trier of fact, you're essentially admitting your client isn't entitled to a grant of summary judgment.

Be sure to use a conclusion to summarize your facts and your authority and explain again why your client is entitled to summary judgment.

VII. PARTIAL SUMMARY JUDGMENT

As with a motion to dismiss, you can file a motion for partial summary judgment. If a plaintiff has asserted numerous causes of action and you believe some, but not all, are subject to summary judgment, file a partial motion. Partial motions for summary judgment, if granted, narrow the issues for trial, decrease the scope of admissible evidence, and may lead to pre-trial settlement.

VIII. REPLY BRIEFS

If you are moving for summary judgment, remember that you get the last word. Most jurisdictions permit the moving party to file a reply brief, in which the party may respond to the arguments raised by the non-moving party in that party's response to the motion.

Generally, you should use your initial brief to make your strongest arguments and save your reply brief to address your adversary's counterarguments. Do not use your initial brief space to address all of your adversary's possible counterarguments — especially ones you are not even certain the adversary will raise. Use your reply brief to respond to those counterarguments and reinforce the reasoning outlined in your initial brief.

Just remember: don't regurgitate the arguments you presented in the initial brief. You might be tempted to break out those killer lines from your initial brief and "wow" the court again with your prose. That's a bad idea. An argument does not become more persuasive because you repeat it . . . and repeat it . . . and . . . repeat it. In fact, you'll lose credibility if your reply brief is nothing more than an encore performance of the original. Simply stated, don't waste the judge's time.

And, if you use your reply brief to re-make your initial arguments, you won't have any space left to address your adversary's counterarguments. Your initial brief is the place to make your strongest case. And your reply brief is the place to tear down the other party's counterarguments.

IX.   RESPONDING TO MOTIONS FOR SUMMARY JUDGMENT

In responding to a motion for summary judgment, you have one goal: to convince the Court that there is at least one issue of material fact that must be resolved by the trier of fact.

First, you need to respond to the moving party's statement of undisputed material facts. Your response will probably look similar to an answer — you'll either admit the undisputed facts or deny that a fact is undisputed and tell the court why the fact is disputed by referring to evidence in the record.

Let's look at the electronics store false imprisonment case we discussed above. The defendant has argued that your client, Wolfe, cannot prove false imprisonment because he cannot prove an element of false imprisonment — that he was detained. Your response to the defendant's statement of undisputed material facts might look like this:

5.

The security manager, Barnett, spoke with Wolfe on the floor of the store, not in a separate room. April 2, 2014 Deposition of Tyler Barnett ("Barnett Deposition") 39:2–13.

Response: It is true that Barnett did not take Wolfe to a separate room to speak about the alleged shoplifting. However, Barnett cornered Wolfe in the back, right corner of the store to speak to Wolfe about the alleged shoplifting. April 15, 2014 Deposition of Ryan Wolfe ("Wolfe Deposition") 9:4–20. Barnett, who is 6 feet, 4 inches tall and weighs more than 250 pounds, cornered the smaller, 5 foot, 8 inch Wolf in the back of the store and blocked Wolfe's access to the exit at the front of the store. Wolfe Deposition 10:6–19.

6.

Barnett never told Wolfe that Wolfe could not leave the store. Barnett Deposition 42:17–24.

Response: Barnett never told Wolfe that Wolfe could not leave the store, but Barnett's actions toward Wolfe indicated to Wolfe that he was not free to leave. Barnett, who is substantially larger than Wolfe, cornered Wolfe at the rear of the store and spoke to Wolfe in a loud, threatening manner. Wolfe Deposition 9:4–20; 10:6–19; 10:20–25; 11:1–17. At one point during the conversation, Wolfe attempted to walk toward the front of the store. Wolfe Deposition 29:18–24. Barnett then stepped toward Wolfe, put his hand on Wolfe's shoulder, and physically prevented Wolfe from walking toward the exit. Wolfe Deposition 29:25; 30:1–25; 31:1–14.

7.

Wolfe was free to leave the store at any time. Barnett Deposition 42:25; 43:1–22.

Response: Denied. Wolfe did not feel he was free to leave the store while Barnett questioned Wolfe about the alleged shoplifting. Wolfe testified:

Q: But Barnett never told you that you couldn't leave, right?

A: He never said "you can't leave," but his actions and tone of voice told me I wasn't free to leave the store and had to stay and talk to him.

Q: What do you mean his actions and tone of voice?

A: He's a lot bigger than I am. He cornered me in a very small space at the back of the store and towered over me. I had nowhere to go. I would have had to push him out of the way to get past him to leave. Like I told you earlier, when I tried to leave, he blocked my path. And he was in my face basically yelling at me, accusing me of stealing stuff from the store. I didn't know what he was talking about and when I said that, he yelled even louder, saying "You know exactly what the hell I'm talking about."

Wolfe Deposition 31:19–25; 32:1–4.

In an answer, you generally don't want to give too much information — you just want to admit or deny the allegations. In responding to a summary judgment motion, however, you want to clearly explain why you're denying what your adversary claims are "undisputed" material facts. Remember, your goal is to show the court that some material facts are disputed. The best way to do that is to cite evidence in the record that contradicts your adversary's version of the facts. If you have strong testimony, for example, you might even quote the testimony directly for an even greater impact, as the writer did in response to statement seven, above.

After you respond to the statement of undisputed material facts, you'll need to start making your case against summary judgment. In the false imprisonment example, assume the store has argued it is not liable for false imprisonment because of the "shopkeeper's privilege." Under Texas law, the privilege permits a store owner who reasonably believes a person is attempting to steal merchandise to detain the suspected shoplifter in a reasonable manner for a reasonable time to question the suspected shoplifter. *See Wal-Mart Stores, Inc. v. Resendez*, 962 S.W.2d 539 (Tex. 1998).

But you want to argue the evidence isn't one-sided, and the trier of fact must determine whether Barnett had reasonable cause to believe Wolfe was shoplifting and whether Barnett detained Wolfe in a reasonable manner and for a reasonable time. How do you do that? By citing cases such as *Dillard Department Stores, Inc. v. Silva*, 148 S.W.3d 370 (Tex. 2004), where the Texas court held that when testimony about the length and reasonableness of the detention is contradictory, the fact finder must decide whether the owner is protected by the shopkeeper's privilege. You'd point out how Wolfe's situation is similar to that of the plaintiff in *Dillard* and how he, like the plaintiff in *Dillard*, is entitled to have a jury consider whether his detention was reasonable.

Remember what we talked about earlier — make your best case first, then address your adversary's arguments. Once you've outlined the reasons the adversary is not entitled to summary judgment, then pick apart the adversary's supporting counter-arguments and case law. Did your adversary cite cases that actually support your position (i.e., ones where a jury decided whether the shopkeeper's privilege applied)? In your adversary's cited cases, did the plaintiff fail to offer contradictory evidence (unlike Wolfe, whose testimony creates a question of fact)? Did your adversary cite out-of-jurisdiction cases when binding authority supports your position? Be sure to address all the reasons your adversary's position is unsupported. Remember, while pointing out disputed facts is essential in responding to a summary judgment motion, addressing the law cited by the moving party is equally important.

X.   CROSS-MOTIONS FOR SUMMARY JUDGMENT

Sometimes the parties will file cross-motions for summary judgment. The parties may agree that the facts are undisputed but have different interpretations of the law or, for example, of the meaning of contract language.

If this happens, you'll need to respond to the opposing party's statement of material facts, even though you've already provided your own statement of material facts. And don't simply rely on your initial brief to advance your position — you need to file a response brief and respond to the opposing party's arguments.

If the parties do file cross-motions for summary judgment, you may find, however, that a reply brief is unnecessary. After all, you will have the opportunity to make your case in your initial brief and to respond to your adversary's position in your response brief. Think hard about whether you really need to file a reply brief. Remember — you don't want to beat a dead horse and burden the judge with unnecessary, repetitive documents. If you can't add anything new in a reply brief, don't file one.

*   *   *   *   *

Waters v. Harrison, Motion for Summary Judgment, Response, and Reply

Below are Harrison's motion for summary judgment, Waters' response, and Harrison's reply.

Note: *The authors did not include a supporting declaration of either Simon Harrison or Kirsten Waters because it would not add substantially to the persuasive writing techniques this chapter emphasizes. However, in many jurisdictions, all parties must file a declaration, signed by the party, swearing, under penalty of perjury, that all factual representations are true.*

HARRISON'S MOTION FOR SUMMARY JUDGMENT

INTRODUCTION

When a person's life has "ceased to be private," no cause of action for invasion of privacy will stand." *Gill v. Hearst Pub. Co.*, 40 Cal. 2d 224, 229 (1953). Plaintiff Kirsten Waters ("Waters") is a former candidate for the United States Senate. During her final debate with then-Senator Robert Larson — before a nationally televised audience and sold-out crowd at the Shrine Auditorium — Waters misled California voters about her criminal history. Waters later acknowledged making "inaccurate" statements, and resigned from office. Now, she claims that Simon Harrison ("Harrison"), the person responsible for exposing these inaccuracies, should be held liable for invasion of privacy. California law disagrees — unanimously.

During the campaign, Waters spoke openly about her past, including an admission that she was arrested on charges of Driving under the Influence of Alcohol and possessing a controlled substance. Waters also claimed that, following her guilty plea to charges relating to Waters' August 2, 1994 arrest, she was "ordered to serve 30 days in the Palo Alto County Jail, followed by a 90-day stay at a residential treatment facility." These statements were not true.

Waters did not spend a single day in prison, and the Court never ordered Waters to spend one day in a residential treatment facility. As evidenced by a letter that defendant Simon Harrison ("Harrison") posted on his website, www.justtellthetruth-.com, Waters' guilty plea only required her to perform 100 hours of community service. Waters does not dispute this fact, or any fact that is material to her invasion of privacy claim.

Nor can Waters dispute her status as a public figure, or the representations she made during the campaign. Waters portrayed herself as a person who valued honesty, integrity, and transparency. Harrison's comments simply exposed these statements as misleading and, in some cases, false. And that is exactly why ordinary citizens have wide latitude to comment on a politician's character, especially during an election season. It is a vital, if not indispensable, element of our political discourse — and the marketplace of ideas.

Finding an invasion of privacy under these circumstances would chill core First

Amendment freedoms and compromise the pursuit of truth. Neither the California courts — nor the California Constitution — permits such a result.

Harrison respectfully requests that this Court grant summary judgment dismissing Waters' invasion of privacy claims.

FACTUAL BACKGROUND

Waters received her undergraduate degree from Stanford University in Palo Alto, California, and graduated at the top of her class from the University of California, Berkeley School of Law. Prior to entering public life, Waters was an attorney with the law firm of Jones, Davis, Bartlett and Strom, LLP, where she became a managing partner in the firm's litigation department.

During her campaign for the United States Senate, Waters' personal struggles gained her substantial popularity among likely voters. Waters acknowledged that, while in college, she struggled with alcohol and prescription drug abuse. Waters has been forthright about her past, and discussed the consequences that substance abuse has had on her personal and professional life. Waters' apparent honesty during the campaign, coupled with her inspiring story of recovery, garnered support among voters across the political spectrum.

Five days before the election, with the race between Waters and then-incumbent Senator Larson considered a dead heat, the final debate was held at the Shrine Auditorium in Los Angeles. Before a sold-out crowd and nationally televised audience, the moderator, former governor Patricia Brown, began with the following question.

> "Ms. Waters, can you talk about your personal struggles, how they have changed your life, and what impact, if any, they may have on you as a United States Senator?"

Kirsten responded as follows:

> "Thank you, Governor Brown. I appreciate the opportunity to be here tonight with the voters of California and, of course, Senator Larson. As you know, I've been very forthcoming about my struggle — many years ago — with alcohol and prescription medication. It was the darkest period of my life. Perhaps the worst moment came on August 2, 1994, the summer of my junior year at Stanford when, due to a regrettable mistake in judgment, I was responsible for Driving under the Influence of Alcohol and possessing an unauthorized controlled substance. For me, this was rock bottom and a wake-up call that I had to make immediate changes in my life. My first step was to accept responsibility for my actions, which I did. **After being ordered to serve 30 days in the Palo Alto County Jail, followed by a 90-day stay at a residential treatment facility, I continued the life-changing process of taking my life back.** Looking back, I don't know if I would be here tonight without having faced the consequences of my actions. From this experience, I learned what it means to truly struggle in life. I learned how to cope with adversity and life's difficult challenges. I came to know the value of account-ability, hard work, and perseverance. These are values, in my opinion, to which

all of California's voters, regardless of background or political party, can relate.

(Emphasis added.) Five days later, in one of the closest elections in California history, Waters defeated then-Senator Larson by 314 votes.

Harrison operates a well-known blog, www.justtellthetruth.com, which seeks to expose corruption in all areas of public life. Harrison's website has been credited with, among other things, uncovering a bribery scandal involving Philadelphia's mayor and exposing the use of performance enhancing substances by several high-profile athletes.

Harrison also attended Stanford University and met Waters during their freshman year. While remaining friends throughout college, they each went their separate ways and no longer remain in contact.

Importantly, however, Harrison watched Waters' final debate. He was shocked to hear Waters' statements concerning her past, particularly because Harrison was very close to Waters at the time and knows the events in question well. After the debate, Harrison posted an urgent message on www.justellthetruth.com. His comments included the following:

> Kirsten's statements about her past struggle with substance abuse — obviously designed to sway California voters — are fabrications. I was Kirsten's friend during college, and I unconditionally supported Kirsten while she struggled to overcome addiction . . . . [W]hile Kirsten was arrested for Driving under the Influence of Alcohol and possession of a controlled substance, she was neither incarcerated nor ordered to spend even a single day in a residential treatment program. After pleading guilty, Kirsten was sentenced to 90 days probation and 100 hours of community service. Additionally, as part of the plea deal, the controlled substance charge was dropped. Kirsten only sought residential treatment because her parents threatened to stop paying her tuition at Stanford.

Harrison substantiated his comments by posting a letter Waters received from her probation officer, dated November 10, 1994. Among other things, the letter stated:

> Dear Kirsten:
>
> As you know, the court sentenced you to a probation term of 90 days, and 100 hours of community service. Having complied fully with these responsibilities, your sentence is hereby complete and this matter now concluded.

Harrison made additional comments related directly to Waters' character and moral fitness:

> [W]hile at Stanford, Kirsten engaged in highly questionable conduct. During our last two years at Stanford, Kirsten was engaged to a mutual friend (who I will not reveal at this time). Kirsten suddenly broke off the engagement and admitted to having a lengthy affair with another man throughout the duration of the relationship. I will soon release a letter Kirsten wrote to our friend admitting the affair. The whole truth is that Kirsten reluctantly sought

treatment — only to save herself — while repeatedly lying to and eventually betraying a very decent man.

While at Stanford, Kirsten performed poorly in her studies. Kirsten was not a good student, and I doubt she has the abilities to effectively serve in any elected capacity. I don't know how she was accepted by the University of California-Berkeley School of Law. I do know this: her dad is one of Berkeley's most generous donors. Kirsten's admission to Berkeley wasn't about merit. It was about favoritism and money.

One week after the election, Harrison's story became national news. Under extraordinary pressure from her party, coupled with damaging public opinion polls, Waters resigned. She released a statement containing the following admission:

I made certain inaccurate statements at my final debate with Senator Larson. Some of the details regarding my past were inconsistent with the facts. In the interest of sparing California any further attention to this matter, I will resign as your Senator, yet continue to fight for the vital issues affecting all citizens of this state.

Two days later, Waters filed a complaint against Harrison in the United States District Court for the Northern District of California alleging, among other things, that Harrison's comments constituted an invasion of privacy under the California Constitution and relevant law.

DISCUSSION

SUMMARY JUDGMENT SHOULD BE GRANTED BECAUSE HE INFORMATION HARRISON DISCLOSED WAS NOT PRIVATE.

Courts should grant summary judgment when the parties' submissions "show that there is no genuine issue as to any material fact and that the moving party is entitled to judgment as a matter of law." FED. R. CIV. P. 56(c). A genuine issue of material fact is present where the evidence would support a jury verdict in favor of the non-moving party. *See Anderson v. Liberty Lobby, Inc.*, 477 U.S. 242, 248 (1986).

The burden is on the non-moving party to demonstrate that a genuine issue of fact exists. *See Celotex Corp. v. Catrett*, 477 U.S. 317, 322 (1986). While the facts are construed in the non-moving party's favor, "metaphysical doubt as to the material facts," is insufficient. *Matsushita Elec. Indus. v. Zenith Radio*, 475 U.S. 574, 586-87 (1986). Instead, the non-moving party must, as a matter of law, produce more than a mere "scintilla" of evidence supporting its claims. *Anderson*, 447 U.S. at 252.

Invasion of privacy claims are governed by Article I, § I of the California Constitution, and California tort law. Based on the undisputed facts, including those in Waters' Complaint as well as information revealed in discovery, summary judgment is warranted.

A. UNDER THE CALIFORNIA CONSTITUTION, WATERS' INVASION OF PRIVACY CLAIM SHOULD BE DISMISSED BECAUSE SHE HAD NO REASONABLE EXPECTATION OF PRIVACY CONCERNING HARRISON'S COMMENTS.

To state a cause of action for invasion of privacy under the California Constitution, Waters must prove that she had: (1) a legally protected interest in the information disclosed; (2) a reasonable expectation of privacy in the information disclosed; and (3) that the defendant's conduct constituted a serious invasion of privacy. *Jeffrey H. v. Imai, Tadlock & Keeney*, 85 Cal. App. 4th 345, 353 (1st Dist. 2000). The right to privacy under the California Constitution protects "the individual's reasonable expectation of privacy against a serious violation." *Sheehan v. San Francisco 49ers, Ltd.*, 45 Cal. 4th 992, 998 (2009) (emphasis in original). Waters does not satisfy any of these elements.

1. WATERS DID NOT HAVE A LEGALLY PROTECTED INTEREST IN THE INFORMATION HARRISON DISCLOSED.

Waters does not have a legally cognizable interest in the statements Harrison posted on his blog. The statements related directly to Waters' fitness for political office, and contradicted Waters' express representations regarding her criminal history — which she later admitted were "inaccurate."

The right to be "let alone" must be "consistent with the democratic processes under the constitutional guarantees of freedom of speech and of the press." *Gill*, 40 Cal. 2d at 228. Importantly, conduct that "substantively furthers one or more countervailing interests," cannot sustain an invasion of privacy claim, which is a question of law for the court. *Sheehan*, 45 Cal. 4th at 998; *Life Tech. Corp. v. Superior Court*, 197 Cal. App. 4th 640, 644 (4th Dist. 2011).

A public figure and candidate for the United States Senate, Waters had no legal protected interest concerning information that she voluntarily disclosed, and which related directly to her character and fitness for political office. At her final debate with then-Governor Larson, Waters stated that, following her arrest and plea bargain, she spent "30 days in the Palo Alto County Jail, followed by a 90-day stay at a residential treatment facility." These representations were false, or as Waters acknowledged, "inaccurate." Either way, they are not protected. Getting caught red-handed does not give rise to an invasion of privacy claim under the California Constitution.

Furthermore, in exposing these untruths, Harrison exercised his constitutionally protected right to freedom of speech under the First Amendment, and provided California's voters with vital information about Waters' honesty and integrity. Neither Waters — nor any political candidate — are protected from relevant information that relates to the candidate's fitness for office. This is particularly true where, as here, Harrison's comments came in response to information that Waters intentionally disclosed — and misrepresented.

2. Waters Did Not Have a Reasonable Expectation of Privacy Because She Is a Public Figure

As a candidate for national political office, Waters had no expectation of privacy in statements that related to her honesty and moral fitness for political office.

An expectation of privacy "must be objectively reasonable under the circumstances, especially in light of the competing social interests involved." *Sheehan*, 45 Cal. 4th at 1000; *see also Jeffrey H.*, 85 Cal. App. 4th at 354. Courts properly consider "customs, practices, and physical settings surrounding particular activities" to determine whether the plaintiff had a reasonable expectation of privacy in the information disclosed. *Jeffrey H.*, 85 Cal. App. 4th at 354.

Harrison's comments simply exposed statements that Waters later admitted were inaccurate. Harrison substantiated his comments by posting a letter from Waters' probation officer, which Waters did not deny or challenge. Additionally, while Harrison's comments included information about Waters' educational and personal history, they related directly to Waters' character and integrity, qualities that voters value highly when choosing a candidate. In fact, without Harrison's disclosures, Waters would be in office today, having successfully misled California's voters. A ruling in her favor would increase the likelihood that other candidates would materially misrepresent their past conduct — and get away with it.

3. Waters Did Not Suffer A Serious Invasion of her Privacy.

Waters did not suffer any, much less a serious, invasion of her privacy.

An invasion of privacy must "constitute an egregious breach of the social norms underlying the privacy right. *Jeffrey H.*, 85 Cal. App. 4th at 355. The question of whether the invasion was serious is a mixed question of law and fact. *See Life Tech.*, 197 Cal. App. 4th at 644.

As a public figure, Waters knew — or should have known — that voters, commentators, and individuals with personal knowledge of a political candidate may challenge the accuracy of campaign statements, particularly those that are not true. That is exactly what happened here. Waters lied — and got caught. What happened in this case was not an invasion of privacy. It was an example of the political process working to uncover a candidate's deliberately misleading statements, which all too often go unnoticed. Put differently, Waters did not suffer any invasion of privacy. If anything, she is a victim of *her* strategic choice to manipulate the truth.

B. Waters Tortious Invasion Of Privacy Claim Should Be Dismissed Because The Information On Harrison'S Blog Was Not Private.

A plaintiff states a cause of action for wrongful disclosure of private information, when the plaintiff alleges: (1) public disclosure; (2) of a private fact; (3) the disclosure of which would be offensive and objectionable to a reasonable person; and (4) the fact is not of legitimate public concern. *See Shulman v. Group W Productions, Inc.*, 18 Cal. 4th 200 (1998). Waters does not satisfy the second and third prongs of this test.

1. THE STATEMENTS ON HARRISON'S BLOG CONSTITUTE PUBLIC DISCLOSURE.

Harrison concedes this element.

2. THE FACTS HARRISON DISCLOSED WERE NOT "PRIVATE."

Nothing that Harrison posted was private. Waters was a candidate for the United States Senate, and voluntarily thrust her character — and a past struggle with substance abuse — into the public arena. Waters cannot take information that she willingly disclosed before a national audience, stamp it will the label "private," and claim that it somehow violated her privacy. California law does not allow litigants to have it both ways.

To begin with, information about criminal charges and judicial proceedings is not private. *See Wasser v. San Diego Union*, 191 Cal. App. 3d 1455, 1462 (1987). Courts simply do not protect as private information that is a matter of public record. *See Green v. Uccelli*, 207 Cal. App. 3d 1112 (1st Dist. 1990); *Bradshaw v. City of Los Angeles*, 221 Cal. App. 3d 908 (2d Dist. 1990) (information disclosed at public hearing not private).

Furthermore, there can be no wrongful disclosure where the fact is known, or where the disclosure merely increases the degree of publicity of a previously public fact. *See Sipple v. Chronicle Publishing Co.*, 154 Cal. App. 3d 1040 (1st Dist. 1984) (disclosure of plaintiff's homosexuality to general public was not actionable where plaintiff was well-known member of San Francisco gay community). Generally, private facts are those that an individual *intends* to keep private by, for example, limiting the information to "one's circle of intimacy," or telling "a few people." *Moreno v. Hanford Sentinel, Inc.*, 172 Cal. App. 4th 1125, 1130 (5th Dist. 2009).

Harrison's comments did not involve private facts. First, there can be no question that Waters' arrest and plea bargain is a matter of public record. Furthermore, Waters' claim that this information is private, particularly after she discussed her criminal history during a nationally televised debate, has no support in California law.

Likewise, when considered in context, Harrison's comments regarding Waters' educational and personal history are not private. Waters represented to California voters that she was a candidate of outstanding moral fiber, who has come "to know the value of accountability, hard work, and perseverance." The statements Harrison made on his blog cast doubt upon those statements. And Harrison had every right to make them and California's voters had every right to hear them.

Furthermore, Harrison supplied readers with a letter from Waters' probation officer — the facts of which Waters has not contested — supporting the veracity of his comments about her criminal history. Regarding Waters' alleged acts of infidelity, Harrison stated that Waters' fiancé was a mutual friend, and that Waters wrote a letter acknowledging her infidelity. Waters has not contested the truthfulness of those statements either. Also, Harrison's comments regarding Waters' admission to the University of California-Berkeley are based on his personal knowledge of Waters' academic performance at Stanford, and of her father's status as one of Berkeley's biggest donors. These are hardly facts that a candidate running for political office —

in a campaign that attracted national attention — should reasonably consider private. Waters' decision to run a "values based" campaign that included inaccurate representations to California's voters, suggests that political ambition — not concerns about privacy — drove her campaign.

None of these statements are private, and Waters has adduced no facts, material or otherwise, to suggest that they were.

3. Harrison's Comments Are Not Offensive and Objectionable to the Reasonable Person.

Reasonable voters would not object to the disclosure of relevant information about a political candidate's character and forthrightness. They would welcome it.

To be actionable, the disclosure must be objectionable to a reasonable person of ordinary sensibilities. *Gill*, 40 Cal. 2d at 229. It must go beyond the normal limits of decency, such that the defendant should have known that the disclosure would be offensive to the plaintiff. *Id.*

Harrison's comments are neither objectionable nor offensive. California voters are entitled to know whether Waters' representations are consistent with her current and past behavior. This is particularly true where a candidate, such as Waters, makes character a central issue of the campaign.

While Harrison's comments inconvenienced Waters' political aspirations, they benefitted California voters and the political process. Harrison's conduct is no different from what he has done in the past when exposing a bribery scandal in Philadelphia and the use of performance enhancing substances by several high-profile athletes. Voters learned the truth about a public official, and forced Waters to acknowledge that her statements at the debate were "inaccurate." These events are not offensive to the reasonable person. They are vital to the proper functioning of a democracy.

4. Waters Is A Public Figure, and Harrison's Comments Were of Public Concern

There can be no doubt that Waters is a public figure — and that the statements Harrison made were newsworthy.

Public officials and those running for public office "have almost always been considered the paradigm case of public figures who should be subjected to the most thorough scrutiny." *Kapellas v. Kofman*, 1 Cal. 3d 20, 36 (Cal. 1969). In such cases, "the public must . . . be afforded the opportunity of learning about any facet of a candidate's life that may relate to his fitness for office." *Id.* at 36–37. As a result, the press may publish "all information that may cast light on a candidate's qualifications," and the public is "permitted to determine importance or relevance of the reported facts for itself." *Id.* at 37. In fact, "the authorized publicity is not limited to the event that itself arouses public interest, and to some reasonable extent includes publicity given to facts about the individual that would *otherwise be purely private.*" *Wasser*, 191 Cal. App. 3d at 1463 (emphasis added). The plaintiff has the burden of proving a disclosure was not newsworthy. *See Diaz v. Oakland Tribune, Inc.*, 139 Cal. App. 3d 118 (1st Dist. 1983).

Furthermore, "the revival of past events that once were news, can properly be a matter of present public interest." *Wasser*, 191 Cal. App. 3d at 1462 (quoting Prosser, *Privacy*, 48 CAL. L. REV. 383, 418 (1960)). Indeed, "[p]ublishers are permitted to satisfy the curiosity of the public as to its heroes, leaders, villains and victims, and those who are closely associated with them." *Wasser*, 191 Cal. App. 3d at 1462. In some cases, a person may attain a position "of such persuasive power and influence" that the person will be considered a public figure "for all purposes," thus precluding an invasion of privacy under any circumstances. *Kinsey v. Macur*, 107 Cal. App. 3d 265, 273 (1980).

In *Kapellas*, a newspaper urged the public not to cast votes for the plaintiff, a candidate for city council, suggesting she was a bad mother because her children had several run-ins with local police. 1 Cal. 3d at 27. The plaintiff brought suit, alleging the newspaper invaded her privacy by publicly disclosing private facts about her family. *Id.* at 26. The court rejected plaintiff's claim, holding that the information reported by the paper was newsworthy because "the candidacy of the children's mother . . . rendered [the children's] past behavior significant and newsworthy." *Id.* at 39; *see also Beruan v. French*, 56 Cal. App. 3d 825 (1976) (candidate's prior criminal convictions were newsworthy); *Alim v. Superior Court*, 185 Cal. App. 3d 144 (1986) (public official's receipt of improper VA benefits was matter of public concern).

The same is true here — only more so. Waters' express representations portrayed an image of honesty and perseverance. The truth, however, was inconsistent with those representations, and any information relevant to them was plainly newsworthy. In fact, the California Constitution — along with California law — not only permits, but encourages the types of statements Harrison made.

Accordingly, based on the relevant law and undisputed facts, summary judgment should be granted dismissing Waters' invasion of privacy claims.

CONCLUSION

For the foregoing reasons, Plaintiff Kirsten Waters' invasion of privacy claims, under the California Constitution and governing tort law, should be dismissed.

*   *   *   *   *

WATERS' RESPONSE TO HARRISON'S MOTION FOR SUMMARY JUDGMENT

Waters files this Response to Defendant Harrison's Motion for Summary Judgment, showing the Court why Waters is entitled to have a jury consider whether Harrison's statements regarding Waters' past relationship with a former fiancé, Jonathan Berman, and her educational background were defamatory and why Harrison's motion for summary judgment should be denied in part. Waters' concedes, however, that her claim for invasion of privacy regarding the disclosure of information contained in Waters' probation file is subject to summary adjudication.

SUMMARY JUDGMENT STANDARD

To survive a motion for summary judgment, the non-moving party need only show that there is a genuine dispute over a material fact — that is, the evidence is such that a reasonable jury could return a verdict in favor of the non-moving party. FED. R. CIV. P. 56(a); *Anderson v. Liberty Lobby*, 477 U.S. 242, 248 (1986).

The trial court's function with respect to a motion for summary judgment is not to do the fact-finder's job of weighing the evidence and determining the truth. *See Anderson*, 477 U.S. at 249. Instead, the court's function is to determine whether "the claimed factual dispute [is] shown to require a jury or judge to resolve the parties' differing versions of the truth at trial." *Elec. Serv., Inc. v. Pac. Elec. Contractors Ass'n*, 809 F.2d 626, 631 (9th Cir. 1987). Moreover, for purposes of summary judgment, the non-movant's version of the truth must be believed and "all justifiable inferences" must be drawn in the non-movant's favor. *Anderson*, 477 U.S. at 255.

ARGUMENT AND CITATION TO AUTHORITY

I. INVASION OF PRIVACY

The tort of invasion of privacy under both the California constitution and California tort law is distinct from the tort of defamation. An invasion of privacy claim is proper when the plaintiff "does not challenge the accuracy of the information publicized," but asserts that the publicity is "so intimate and so unwarranted as to outrage the community's notion of decency." *Diaz*, 139 Cal. App. 3d at 126.

To allege a claim for invasion of privacy under either the California constitution or California tort law, a plaintiff must prove: "(1) public disclosure; (2) of a private fact; (3) the disclosure of which would be objectionable to a reasonable person; and (4) the fact is not of legitimate public concern." *Id.*

Waters concedes that the statements Harrison made about her past criminal history and substance abuse treatment are truthful and, therefore, her claim related to those statements is properly one for invasion of privacy. After discovery, Waters also concedes that the disclosure of information contained in Waters' public probation file is not "private" and, therefore, she cannot state a cause of action for invasion of privacy in light of *Gates v. Discovery Communications, Inc.*, 34 Cal. 4th 679 (2004).

However, Harrison's statements about Waters' past relationships and his allegations about Waters' educational background are not truthful — as discovery in this matter has shown. Thus, Waters' claim related to those statements is not one for invasion of privacy but one for defamation.

II. DEFAMATION

Waters' defamation claim is not subject to summary judgment, and a jury should be allowed to consider whether and to what extent Waters was defamed by Harrison's statements about Waters' past relationship and her graduation from Berkeley Law School. A party seeking damages for defamatory statements must demonstrate the following: (1) publication; (2) of a false statement; (3) that is defamatory; (4) unprivileged; and (5) results in damages. *Ringler Assocs. Inc., v. Maryland Cas. Co.*, 96 Cal. Rptr. 2d 136, 148 (Cal. Ct. App. 2000). The level of fault required — negligence or actual malice — depends on whether the party alleging defamation is deemed an all-purpose public, limited-purpose public, or private figure. *McGarry v. Univ. of San Diego*, 64 Cal. Rptr. 3d 467, 479–480 (Cal. Ct. App. 2007).[43] Questions of fact remain about whether Harrison's statements were defamatory, and the court should deny Harrison's motion for summary judgment.

A. PUBLICATION

There can be no dispute that Harrison's statements about Waters were published — Harrison's message was posted online on his blog and intended to attract attention from a wide audience and undermine the statements Waters made during her debate with Ted. The publication element is satisfied.

B. FALSE STATEMENTS

Statements are defamatory if they are "provably false," and statements of "fact rather than opinion." *Ringler*, 96 Cal. Rptr. 2d at 149. Courts use a "totality of the circumstances" test when determining if statements are actionable fact or non-actionable opinion. *McGarry*, 64 Cal. Rptr. 3d at 479. The language of the statements and context within which they were rendered are relevant in determining whether "a reasonable fact finder could conclude that the published statements imply a provably false factual assertion." *Id.*; *see also Copp v. Paxton*, 52 Cal. Rptr. 2d 831, 838 (Cal. Ct. App. 1996).

Importantly, an opinion-based statement is actionable "if it implies the allegation of undisclosed defamatory facts as the basis for the opinion." *Id.* (*quoting Okun v. Superior Court*, 175 Cal. Rptr. 157, 162 (1981)). The implied defamatory facts "must themselves be true." *Ringler*, 96 Cal. Rptr. 2d at 149; *see also Eisenberg v. Alameda Newspapers, Inc.*, 88 Cal. Rptr. 2d 802, 821 (Cal. Ct. App. 2000). Furthermore, even if the publisher of an alleged defamatory statement sets forth specific facts forming the basis of an opinion, "if those facts are either incorrect or incomplete, or if the person's assessment of them is erroneous, the statement may still imply a false assertion of fact." *Ringler*, 96 Cal. Rptr. 2d at 149. Categorizing otherwise-defamatory statements as opinion "does not dispel these implications, and such statements may be actionable." *Id.* The dispositive question "is whether a reasonable factfinder could conclude that published statements imply an assertion of defamatory fact." *Id.* (emphasis in original); *see also Milkovich*, 497 U.S. at 18–20.

Discovery has shown that Harrison's statements about Waters' past relationship with Mr. Berman are false or — at the very least — that a question of fact remains about the truthfulness of those statements. Waters' former fiancé, Jonathan Berman, has testified that their relationship did not end as a result of infidelity. Waters herself also has testified that she did not have an affair while engaged to Berman. Harrison

---

[43] The standards governing public versus private figures are discussed in Section (F) below.

continues to claim that Waters wrote him a letter admitting to the alleged affair, but has been unable to produce any copy of that letter. Waters has produced sufficient evidence of the untruthfulness of Harrison's statements about her relationship with Berman to survive Harrison's motion for summary judgment.

Waters also has produced evidence that Harrison's attack on Waters' educational background — his statements that her admission to the University of California-Berkeley School of Law resulted from special treatment and favoritism, that she was not a good student, and that she only graduated from law school as a result of familial influence — are untrue. Waters has obtained transcripts and her admissions file from Berkeley School of Law showing that she was properly admitted to Berkeley and that she met the requirements to graduate from Berkeley School of Law. Additionally, Waters' father has testified that he never sought favorable treatment for Waters while she was a Berkeley student and is not aware that she ever received any favorable treatment because she is his daughter. At the very least, the question of whether the statements Harrison made were false is one of fact for a jury to decide.

C. DEFAMATORY STATEMENTS

"Whether a statement is reasonably susceptible to a defamatory interpretation is a question of law for the trial court." *Smith*, 85 Cal. Rptr. 2d 397, 403 (Cal. App. 1999). If the court determines that a statement can be reasonably understood as defamatory, it becomes a question for the trier of fact. *Id.* When making this determination, "courts look 'not so much [to the allegedly libelous statement's] effect when subject to the critical analysis of a mind trained in law, but [to] the natural and probable effect upon the mind of the average reader.'" *Ferlauto*, 88 Cal. Rptr. 2d at 849 (quoting *Morningstar*, 29 Cal. Rptr. 2d at 553) (brackets in original). Defamatory statements include those exposing a person "to hatred, contempt, ridicule, or obloquy, or which causes him to be shunned or avoided, or which has a tendency to injure him in his occupation." *McGarry*, 64 Cal. Rptr. 3d at 478 (quoting Cal. Civ. Code § 45).

A defamatory statement tends "directly to injure [a person] in respect to his office, profession, trade or business, either by imputing to him general disqualification in those respects which the office or other occupation peculiarly requires, or by imputing something with reference to his office, profession, trade, or business that has a natural tendency to lessen its profit." *McGarry*, 64 Cal. Rptr. 3d at 478 (quoting Cal. Civ. Code § 46).[44] Statements containing "such a charge directly, and without the need for explanatory matter, are libelous per se." *Id.* (citing Cal. Civ. Code § 45a).[45]

A statement can also be libelous per se "if it contains a charge by implication from the language employed by the speaker and a listener could understand the defamatory meaning without the necessity of knowing extrinsic explanatory matter." *Id.* (*citing*

---

[44] Although § 46 addresses slander, identical statements made through libelous means are also defamatory as a matter of law. *See Peterson v. Rasmussen*, 47 Cal. App. 694 (1920) (statements imputing that the plaintiff was unchaste are libelous as a matter of law).

[45] Section 45a states provides as follows: "A libel which is defamatory of the plaintiff without the necessity of explanatory matter, such as an inducement, innuendo or other extrinsic fact, is said to be a libel on its face."

MacLeod v. Tribune Publishing Co., 52 Cal. 2d 536, 548-550 (1959)). If a statement is libelous per se, general damages are presumed. *See Clark v. McClurg*, 215 Cal. 279 (Cal. 1932). If, however, the listener "would not recognize the defamatory meaning without 'knowledge of specific facts and circumstances, extrinsic to the publication, which are not matters of common knowledge rationally attributable to all reasonable persons,' the matter is deemed defamatory per quod and requires pleading and proof of special damages." *See McGarry*, 64 Cal. Rptr. 3d at 478–479 (*quoting Barnes-Hind v. Superior Court*, 226 Cal. Rptr. 354, 360 (1986)).

Harrison's statements about Waters' past relationship and educational background are libelous per se or, at the least, libelous per quod. These statements have seriously injured Waters' "office, profession, trade or business" because they could easily be understood to imply dishonesty, deceit, and deliberate betrayal of the public trust. They suggest Waters does not possess the high ethical standards, trustworthiness, and character expected from those who serve the public in a professional or elected capacity. As a result, Harrison's statements have the tendency, without requiring extrinsic or explanatory evidence, to prevent or disqualify Waters from pursuing future political opportunities, public-office designations, or the practice of law. At the very least, these statements have exposed Waters to "hatred, contempt, ridicule, or obloquy," establishing a cognizable claim for libel per quod. The defamatory nature of these statements has been established.

D. Privilege

Cal. Civ. Code § 47 sets forth several privileges protecting otherwise-defamatory statements, including statements: (1) made in the proper discharge of an official duty; (2) occurring in judicial, legislative, or other proceedings authorized by law (the "litigation" privilege);[46] (3) between individuals with a shared interest, provided the communications are made without malice (the "common interest" privilege);[47] (4) constituting fair and true reports to a public journal of matters discussed in judicial, legislative, or other public proceedings, including verifiable charges or complaints made against public officials (the "fair reporting" or "fair comment" privilege); or (5) concerning lawfully convened public meetings or matters beneficial to the public. *Id.* at § 47(a–e).

Importantly, California has not adopted the "neutral reportage" privilege, which protects the "accurate and disinterested reporting" of "serious charges made against public officials by a respectable, prominent organization." *Khawar v. Globe Intern, Inc.*, 79 Cal. Rptr. 2d 178, 186 (Cal. 1998) (*quoting Edwards v. National Audubon Society, Inc.*, 556 F.2d 113, 120 (2d Cir. 1977), *cert. denied* 434 U.S. 1002 (1977)). Further, although the "common interest" privilege protects "communications made in good faith on a subject in which the speaker and hearer shared an interest or duty,"

---

[46] This privilege is absolute, providing protection even if the statements were made with actual malice. *See Beroiz v. Wahl*, 100 Cal. Rptr. 2d 905, 909 (Cal. Ct. App 2000).

[47] The common interest privilege is usually described as a qualified or conditional one, meaning it can be overcome by a showing of actual malice. *See Kashian v. Harriman*, 120 Cal. Rptr. 2d 576, 594 (Cal. Ct. App. 2002).

it does not create "any broad news media privilege." *Lundquist v. Reusser*, 31 Cal. Rptr. 2d 776, 783-784 (Cal. Ct. App. 1994); *see also Brown v. Kelly Broadcasting Co.*, 257 Cal. Rptr. 708, 752 (Cal. 1989) (refusing to expand the common interest privilege into a "public interest" privilege because doing so would, as a practical matter, "mean that everything they [the news media] publish would be a matter of 'public interest' and therefore privileged.") (brackets in original).

Harrison's statements are not privileged. They were made on his personal blog and not in the performance of any official duty. The statements did not occur in a judicial or legislative proceeding, between Harrison and any individual with a shared interest, and were never communicated to a public journal. Finally, the debate was not a "lawfully convened" public meeting, and no cases exist holding that political debates involve matters beneficial to the public. Thus, no privilege protects Harrison from suit.

E. DAMAGES

Even if Harrison's statements are libelous per quod, Waters has shown that the statements were both defamatory and injurious. Harrison's comments, as evidenced by public opinion polls, caused a sharp decline in Waters' popularity, leading to her ultimate resignation only one week after she won the election. The public humiliation and reputational damage Waters has suffered at the hands of Harrison may permanently jeopardize her chance of becoming a viable candidate for public office in the future. Additionally, Waters is a lawyer, and her career hinges on her clients' belief that she is a smart, trustworthy individual whose advice should be followed. If Waters returns to the legal profession, her ability to gain the trust of prospective employers or clients may be compromised. Waters has made a sufficient claim for damages.

F. FAULT REQUIRED

Regardless of whether Waters is an all-purpose public figure or a limited public figure, she can prove that Harrison acted with actual malice and, therefore, can meet her burden of proof. An "all purpose" public figure is an individual "who has 'achiev[ed] such pervasive fame or notoriety that he becomes a public figure for all purposes and in all contexts.' " *Gertz v. Robert Welch, Inc.*, 418 U.S. 323, 351 (1974)) (brackets in original). A public figure must show that the alleged defamatory statement was made with actual malice, namely, "knowledge that it was false or with reckless disregard of whether it was false or not." *McGarry*, 64 Cal. Rptr. 3d at 480 (*quoting Reader's Digest Ass'n v. Superior Court*, 208 Cal. Rptr. 137, 149 (Cal. 1984)); *see also New York Times Co. v. Sullivan*, 376 U.S. 254, 296 (1964).

A limited-purpose figure, unlike a public figure, is someone who has inserted himself into a "public controversy, which means the issue was debated publicly and had foreseeable and substantial ramifications for nonparticipants." *Gilbert v. Sykes*, 53 Cal. Rptr. 3d 752, 762 (Cal. Ct. App. 2007). An individual "must have undertaken some voluntary act through which he or she sought to influence resolution of the public issue." *Id.* This requirement is satisfied where the plaintiff "attempts to thrust him or herself in the public eye." *Id.*

A limited-purpose figure is entitled to some greater level of protection for statements not "germane to the plaintiff's participation in the controversy." *Gilbert*, 53 Cal. Rptr. 3d at 762 (*quoting* Ampex Corp. v. Cargle, 27 Cal. Rptr. 3d 863, 871 (Cal. Ct. App. 2005)). Unlike "the 'all-purpose' public figure, the 'limited purpose' public figure loses certain protection for his [or her] reputation only to the extent that the alleged defamatory communication relates to his role [or her] in a public controversy." *McGarry*, 64 Cal. Rptr. 3d at 480 (*quoting Reader's Digest Assn.*, 208 Cal. Rptr. at 142). Like the all-purpose public figure, however, a limited-purpose public figure is required to show actual malice by clear and convincing evidence to recover for statements germane to the situation or controversy that made her a limited-purpose public figure. *Gilbert*, 53 Cal. Rptr. 3d at 763. The limited-purpose figure need only prove negligence to recover for statements not germane to the situation or controversy. *Id.*

Having "serious doubts" about the truth of a publication is generally sufficient to establish actual malice. *Copp*, 52 Cal. Rptr. 2d at 844–845 (*quoting St. Amant v. Thompson*, 390 U.S. 727, 731 (1968)). While the issue "turns on the subjective good faith of the defendant," a plaintiff may "attempt to prove reckless disregard for truth by circumstantial evidence." *Copp*, 52 Cal. Rptr. 2d at 845 (*quoting St. Amant*, 390 U.S. at 731). For example, "failure to investigate, anger and hostility toward the plaintiff, reliance upon sources known to be unreliable, or known to be biased against the plaintiff. . .may, in appropriate an appropriate case, indicate that the publisher himself had serious doubts regarding the truth of his publication." *Copp*, 52 Cal. Rptr. 2d at 845. In each case, "the evidence must 'permit the conclusion that the defendant actually had a high degree of awareness of . . . probable falsity.' " *McGarry*, 64 Cal. Rptr. 3d at 480 (*quoting Harte-Hanks Communications v. Connaughton*, 491 U.S. 657, 688 (1989)).

Regardless of whether Waters is an all-purpose public figure or a limited purpose public figure, and regardless of whether Harrison's statements are germane to the "public controversy" into which Waters inserted herself by running for public office, Waters has presented sufficient evidence that Harrison acted with actual malice in making statements about Waters on his blog.

With respect to the statements about Waters' past relationship, Harrison has alleged Waters sent Harrison a letter in which she admitted she had an affair while engaged to Berman. Harrison has been unable to produce this letter, and both he and Berman testified that Harrison did not contact Berman prior to posting the statements to verify their truthfulness. Harrison also did not contact Waters prior to posting the statements. Further, Harrison has been unable to identify the name of the man with whom Waters allegedly had this affair. This is evidence from which it may be inferred that Harrison acted with malice both because he knew or had serious doubts about the truthfulness of the allegations and failed to investigate his allegations before publishing them.

With respect to the statements about Waters' educational history, the same is true. Harrison has admitted that he did not reach out to Waters or anyone from Berkeley Law School or actually obtain Waters' transcripts, which would have shown that Waters met the requirements to graduate from Berkeley Law School. Moreover, to the extent Harrison alleges professors at Berkeley were "forced" to give Waters certain grades by administrators eager to please her father, Harrison did not contact any of Waters' former professors and has presented no evidence that allegation is true. Waters' father, conversely, has testified that his support of Berkeley Law School was the result of his status as an alumnus and that he was a substantial donor to the school before, during, and after the time Waters attended, but that he never asked or suggested that Waters be given any grades other than the ones she earned. At the very least, Waters has presented evidence sufficient to permit a jury to determine whether Harrison's statements were made with actual malice.

CONCLUSION

For the reasons outlined above, Waters stipulates to summary adjudication of the invasion of privacy claims. Waters has presented evidence, however, sufficient to survive summary judgment regarding the defamation claim, including evidence that Harrison acted with actual malice in publishing the untrue statements.

*   *   *   *   *

HARRISON'S REPLY

The Hon. Helen Montana
1000 Main Street
United States District Judge
Northern District of California
San Jose Division

Re: **Waters v. Harrison — motion for summary judgment**

Dear Judge Montana:

Please accept this short reply in lieu of a more formal brief, in response to the arguments made by Plaintiff Kirsten Waters in her brief.

First, Waters is correct that her invasion of privacy claims should be dismissed. Waters' assertions concerning the defamation claim, however, are troubling. First, Harrison did not move for dismissal of the defamation claims. If Waters' discussion of those claims is taken as an invitation to the Court to consider them for purposes of summary judgment, Defendant Simon Harrison ("Harrison") respectfully submits that they too should be dismissed.

A. THE STATEMENTS ABOUT WATERS' CRIMINAL HISTORY

The statements regarding Waters' criminal history are true. Truth is an absolute defense to defamation.

The Court need look no further than Waters' own statements during the final debate with then-Senator Larson and in her statement resigning from office. Waters admitted that the statements she made during the debate — essentially fabricating a recovery story to influence voters — were inaccurate.

Harrison showed that they were not simply inaccurate, but untrue. He posted a letter from Waters' probation officer conclusively demonstrating that Waters served a term of probation and community service. Nothing more, and certainly not, as Waters represented, jail time.

Waters has adduced no evidence in discovery to dispute this fact. As a result, the statements pertaining to Waters' criminal history cannot support a defamation claim.

B. THE STATEMENTS ABOUT WATERS' EDUCATIONAL BACKGROUND

All of the statements about Waters' educational background are opinion. While they may be distasteful, Harrison's comments are nothing more than hyperbolic — or imaginative — expressions that reflect Harrison's subjective beliefs. Under California law — and the Constitution — those beliefs are protected by the First Amendment. *See Nygard, Inc. v. Uusi-Kerttula*, 72 Cal. Rptr. 3d 210, 226 (Cal. Ct. App. 2008).

Additionally, no reasonable reader would believe that Harrison's comments implied the assertion of underlying facts. As the record shows, after graduating from Stanford, Harrison and Waters went their separate ways. Harrison is not privy to any knowledge about the circumstances surrounding Waters' admission to the University of California-Berkeley School of Law, including Waters' application, Berkeley's admissions standards, or whether Waters' father donated money to Berkeley during that time. Furthermore, Waters' has not adduced any evidence in discovery to show that her admission was based on factors such as outstanding standardized test scores, grades, or stellar recommendations. On that basis alone, the defamation claim should be dismissed.

Even if she had adduced such evidence, there is no way to conclude that her father's status as a donor influenced her admission. And even if money did play a role, so what? That fact does not imply anything defamatory. It merely suggests a reality that exists at nearly every school throughout the country. Money matters. Donors sometimes get favorable treatment. To suggest that, as Harrison did, is to state the obvious, not to defame Waters' character.

Harrison's statements about Waters' academic ability also constitute protected opinion. Harrison was friends with Waters when they were in college. Like everyone else, Harrison has a right to form an opinion about her academic ability. And it does not matter whether Waters received a perfect grade-point-average at Stanford or was ranked at the top of her class. People do not form opinions solely on the basis of objective facts. They base opinions on personal experience, which is precisely why statements calling someone the "worst lawyer" or "worst teacher" are not actionable. *See Nygard*, 72 Cal. Rptr. 3d at 226. Stated simply, Harrison's statements expressed his feelings about Waters' academic skills. Feelings, however, are not facts.

C. THE STATEMENTS ABOUT WATERS' ALLEGED INFIDELITY

Waters has not set forth any facts in her pleadings, or adduced any facts during discovery, to disprove Harrison's statements concerning alleged infidelity while in college. One must also question whether, even if these statements were false, if they would be the type of infidelity contemplated by California's defamation statute. After all, Harrison's statements did not allege that Waters engaged in *marital* infidelity. He stated, essentially, that Waters cheated on a boyfriend while in college. As unfortunate as this may be, it is not uncommon for young people who are still maturing in college — and have often not reached the age of 20 — to make questionable choices. The undergraduate years are a transformative time for young people; to say that those choices are objectively immoral, or that they would invite scorn and ridicule, is questionable. In fact, beyond the bald allegations contained in her complaint, Waters has not alleged that they did injure her reputation.

Ultimately, this case is less about what Harrison said and more about what Waters did. She lied before a sold-out crowd at the Shrine Auditorium and nationally televised audience. She got caught, and was forced to resign. Harrison may be the scapegoat, but he is certainly not the cause.

For these reasons, Harrison respectfully requests that this Court dismiss Waters' invasion of privacy and defamation claims.

*   *   *   *   *

What made the summary judgment brief and Waters' response effective?

▶ *Standards.* Notice how each party frames the summary judgment standard. Harrison's standard makes the court want to grant summary judgment, while Waters' standard reminds the court that if even a single material fact is in dispute, summary judgment isn't appropriate. This is good advocacy — every part of your brief presents an opportunity to persuade.

▶ *A strong introduction.* Both parties begin with a strong introduction and seek to "win the case at the beginning." You should do the same. Don't wait until page 7 of your brief to start making an argument. A short and punchy introduction that emphasizes the most favorable law and undisputed facts is an important aspect of effective advocacy.

▶ *Have a theme.* Harrison's brief has a good theme — *members of the public have the right to question a politician's qualifications and integrity.* Most people, when reading that statement, would say, "Of course they do!" Harrison's brief speaks to free speech and the right to hold politicians accountable for their conduct. An effective theme shows that you're thinking through the eyes of the judge.

▶ *The facts tell a powerful story.* Notice that Harrison's facts are actually facts, not legal conclusions. He cites deposition testimony to support each of his undisputed facts and doesn't try to slip legal arguments in where they don't belong. Harrison's Statement of Facts tells an effective narrative, in chronological order, that begins with Waters' misrepresentations and ends with her resignation. The focus is on what Waters did, not on what Harrison did. Harrison doesn't try to avoid or minimize his statements. Instead, he argues that those statements do not create a genuine issue of material fact.

▶ *Effective use of emphasis.* While Harrison's brief uses emphasis (bold), it is done strategically to highlight statements that Waters later acknowledged were "inaccurate." It's perfectly fine to use emphasis, provided you do so strategically and infrequently. If one-half of every page is italicized, you'll de-emphasize your strongest arguments.

► *Effective organization.* Both parties used headings and subheadings effectively to separate the elements of an invasion of privacy claim. As a result, the briefs flow well and are easy to follow. Make sure that you always remember your audience — make your writing reader-friendly.

► *Waters' response.* Notice that in her response, Waters doesn't mirror Harrison's brief. Instead, Waters makes her case first, then addresses Harrison's arguments and cases. She focuses on the evidence she has developed during discovery to support her position that the trier of fact should decide her defamation claim.

► *Size matters.* Harrison's brief (excluding the caption and conclusion), is about 3,800 words. For a single claim, that's a bit long, but the invasion of privacy claim has multiple elements that are relevant to the analysis. Make your summary judgment brief as short as possible while adequately addressing the elements or issues. We know this is hard — but don't make the judge read 20 pages when you could have made your point in 10. Remember, writing is re-writing, so if you can't write, re-write, and revise effectively, then you won't communicate persuasively.

► *Strategic concessions can be effective.* Waters makes a good strategic move by conceding the invasion of privacy claim. Sometimes, as litigation proceeds, you may realize that one or more of your claims is not as meritorious as you once believed. If your claim is sunk, admit that to the court. An honest advocate "knows when to hold them, and knows when to fold them." Strategic concessions show that a lawyer has good judgment and discretion.

What other persuasive writing techniques do you see in these briefs? Is there anything that can make the briefs more effective? If so, what — and why?

Chapter 11

PRETRIAL MOTIONS — THE MOTION IN LIMINE

THE MOTION IN LIMINE CHECKLIST

√   Focus on evidentiary issues such as the admissibility of expert witness evidence

√   Do not argue the case — this is not a motion for summary judgment

√   Check the local rules to determine timing of motions in limine

√   Include a short statement of facts relevant to the issues to be addressed through the motion in limine

√   Outline the relevant law and analyze the legal issue in light of the law

√   Even if you lose, raise the motion again at trial to preserve the issue for appeal

---

Issues may arise prior to trial that must be resolved before trial can proceed. Parties generally should try to work out minor disputes without involving the court. Sometimes, however, you may need to seek a ruling to protect your client from undue prejudice or ensure the orderly, efficient presentation of evidence at trial. If that's the case, you'll want to file a pre-trial motion, known as a motion in limine, and have the court decide the issue before the trial starts.

Motions in limine vary widely in substance — they can relate to anything from the admissibility of evidence (most common), to the conduct of parties, to the order of witnesses at trial. For example, assume you represent a client who was injured in a car accident. During discovery, the defendant learns your client has been involved in three prior accidents — all of which were minor — and has filed suit each time. That looks bad for your client — it makes the client look like an unsympathetic serial litigant. You might file a motion in limine and seek a ruling from the court that the defendant cannot introduce evidence of your client's prior accidents or lawsuits.

You could wait until trial to raise the issue, but you want to ensure the jury never gets anywhere close to hearing about the prior accidents. What if the defendant's lawyer mentions the prior accidents during opening statements? At that point, even if you object and win, the cat's out of the bag. The jury's already heard the damning fact.

"How will I know what types of motions in limine to file?" you ask. Discussions with opposing counsel, questions raised in depositions or through written discovery, arguments made at mediation, or even information put into pre-trial orders will often tip lawyers off to the types of motions in limine they will need to bring. But you may have to be creative as well and think outside the box about the types of things that could happen at trial.

Be sure to consult the federal or state and local court rules because motions in limine generally are not governed by statute. Also, know that judges have broad discretion concerning the admissibility of evidence, and the rules about when motions in limine may be filed will vary within and across jurisdictions.

I. PROVIDE A SHORT STATEMENT OF FACTS RELEVANT TO THE MOTION

Motions in limine generally are less formal than other types of motions. Unless the court is familiar with the facts, you should still provide a short statement of facts relevant to the motion in limine. For example, in the case above, where you want to keep out testimony that your client has previously filed three personal injury lawsuits, your statement of facts might look like this:

> **Plaintiff brought this lawsuit to recover for injuries sustained in a March 14, 2010 auto accident. Plaintiff was involved in three auto accidents prior to the accident at issue in this matter and brought suit against the tortfeasors in each of those prior accidents. Defendant has indicated he intends to introduce evidence of these prior accidents at the trial of this matter. Plaintiff believes Defendant intends to introduce this evidence to suggest to the jury that Plaintiff is litigious. Plaintiff believes that evidence is wholly irrelevant to the issues in this lawsuit and would be unduly prejudicial to Plaintiff's case.**

As you can see, the statement of facts needn't be long and need only relate to the issues that will be addressed through the motion in limine. There is no reason to go into detail about the March 14, 2010 accident or the injuries the Plaintiff sustained because they have no bearing on the issue to be addressed through the motion. As always, the length and content of your statement of facts will depend on the issues.

II. OUTLINE THE RELEVANT LAW AND EXPLAIN HOW IT APPLIES

Just as you would in a motion to dismiss or motion for summary judgment, you will need to lay out the law for the court and apply it to the facts of your case. Because motions in limine are often fact-specific, you may not find a case directly on point to support your position. Instead, you may have to outline the law broadly and make your argument from those broad principles. In the car accident example above, your argument against admissibility is based on relevance and undue prejudice. So, your outline of the law might start like this:

> **In order to be admissible, evidence must be relevant. Tex. R. Evid. 402. "Relevant evidence" is "evidence having any tendency to make the existence of any fact that is of consequence to the determination of the action more probable or less probable than it would be without the evidence." Tex. R. Evid. 401.**

Even if evidence is relevant, a court may still exclude it if the probative value of that evidence is "substantially outweighed by the danger of unfair prejudice . . . ." Tex. R. Evid. 403. Whether the value of evidence is substantially outweighed by the risk of unfair prejudice is within the sound discretion of the trial court. *Burke v. State*, 371 S.W.3d 252, 257 (Tex. Ct. App. 2011).

While it is true that proof of "substantially similar accidents" may be admissible, that admissibility is limited to situations where the prior accidents are "relevant to contested issues." *North American Van Lines, Inc. v. Emmons*, 50 S.W.3d 103, 125 (Tex. Ct. App. 2001). "The less similar the accidents, however, the less probative the evidence." *Id.*

III. IF YOU LOSE, OBJECT AT TRIAL, TOO

If the judge denies your motion in limine, all is not lost. Renew your motion at trial to preserve the issue for appeal. Keep a copy of your motion handy so you can remind the court of the statutes, rules, or cases that support your position. If your motion relates to the admission of evidence, object when the opposing party tenders that evidence. If the opposing party's counsel makes an improper statement or reference that you tried to keep out, object as soon as the statement is made. You'd be surprised — judges sometimes deny pre-trial motions in limine but change their minds in the midst of trial. At worst, you will be able to raise the issue on appeal.

Waters v. Harrison, Motions in Limine

Below are two motions in limine filed by Waters and Harrison on the eve of trial. As you read them, consider whether you would grant either motion, and why.

Note: As you'll see, the motions address different issues. Thus, Waters' brief does not respond to Harrison, but instead addresses a separate, hypothetical claim. We did this so that you would see examples of motions in limine that seek to include and exclude evidence.

*   *   *   *   *

HARRISON'S MOTION IN LIMINE

INTRODUCTION

Defendant Simon Harrison ("Harrison") recently became aware of a fact witness who will testify that Plaintiff Kirsten Waters ("Waters"), knowingly made false statements: (1) throughout Waters' senatorial campaign (against then-Senator Robert Larson); and (2) during the candidates' final debate at the Shrine Auditorium in Los Angeles, California. Stephanie Morris' ("Morris") testimony will show not only that Waters made material misrepresentations to California voters, but that the statements Harrison posted on his blog, www.justtellthetruth.com, were true.

Morris is a veteran campaign strategist whom Waters' employed in connection with her campaign for the United States Senate. Morris had two conversations with Waters, the first occurring before Waters' nationally televised debate with Larson, and the second coming hours before Waters released a statement resigning from the senate seat she had won just days earlier. These conversations substantiate what Harrison has been claiming since the inception of this lawsuit: Waters "intentionally lied during her debate with Senator Larson," and "exploit[ed] her past for political gain."

Concededly, Harrison did not include Morris as a potential fact witness in his initial disclosures. See Fed. R. Civ. P. 26(a)(1) (requiring parties to provide the names and addresses of all potential witnesses during discovery). Importantly, however, Harrison — who until recently had not met Morris — was neither aware nor could reasonably anticipate that this evidence would surface.

Furthermore, Morris' testimony would not unfairly surprise or prejudice Waters because Waters was a party to these conversations, and will have ample opportunity at trial to impeach Morris' testimony. Thus, the omission of Morris' name from the initial disclosures required by Fed. R. Civ. P. 26(a)(1) is "substantially justified," or "harmless." Fed. R. Civ. P. 37(c)(1).

The value of this evidence cannot be underestimated. In defamation actions, "the truth of the offensive statements or communication is a complete defense against civil liability, regardless of bad faith or malicious purpose." *Ringler Associates Inc., v. Maryland Casualty Co.*, 96 Cal. Rptr. 2d 136, 148 (Cal. Ct. App. 2000); *see also Campanelli v. Regents of University of California*, 51 Cal. Rptr. 2d 891, 897 (Cal. Ct. App. 1996). As set forth below, Morris' testimony will demonstrate that the statements Harrison made on www.justtellthetruth.com were true and therefore preclude liability as a matter of law.

LEGAL ARGUMENT

MORRIS' TESTIMONY WILL SHOW THAT HARRISON'S STATEMENTS WERE TRUE, AND WILL NOT UNFAIRLY SURPRISE WATERS OR DISRUPT THE EFFICIENT RESOLUTION OF THIS ACTION.

"A party who fails to make the required initial disclosure[s]" may still introduce undisclosed evidence is the party's failure was "substantially justified" or "harmless." *San Francisco Baykeeper v. West Bay Sanitary Dist.* 791 F. Supp. 2d 719, 733 (N.D. Cal. 2011) (*quoting* Fed. R. Civ. P. 37(c)(1)); *see also Hoffman v. Constr. Protective Serv., Inc.*, 541 F.3d 1175, 1179 (9th Cir. 2008). In determining whether the admission of undisclosed evidence is "substantially justified" or "harmless," courts consider: (1) the surprise to the party against whom the evidence would be offered; (2) the party's ability to cure the surprise; (3) whether allowing the evidence would disrupt the trial; (4) the importance of the evidence; and (5) the nondisclosing party's explanation for its failure. *San Francisco Baykeeper*, 791 F. Supp.2d at 733 (*quoting Dey, L.P. v. Ivax Pharm., Inc.*, 233 F.R.D. 567, 571 (C.D. Cal. 2005)).

In this case, any surprise to Waters is, at best, modest. Morris' testimony relates solely to statements that Waters allegedly uttered during private and highly confidential campaign strategy sessions. Given that these conversations occurred in the relatively recent past, and that they relate to matters for which Waters has intimate and personal knowledge, Waters has ample opportunity — by testifying at trial or introducing other witnesses — to challenge their veracity. Accordingly, Morris' testimony will result in minimal surprise and not prejudice Waters' ability to present materially relevant evidence.

Furthermore, Morris' testimony will not disrupt or otherwise compromise the efficient resolution of this matter. In fact, Morris' testimony will do the opposite because it relates to an issue that it potentially dispositive: whether the alleged defamatory statements are true. If the court finds Morris' testimony credible, it will substantiate Harrison's defense and could preclude a finding of liability. *See Ringler*, 96 Cal. Rptr. 2d at 149; ("[i]n all cases of defamation, whether libel or slander, the truth of the offensive statements or communication is a complete defense against civil liability, regardless of bad faith or malicious purpose"); *see also Campanelli*, 51 Cal. Rptr. 2d at 897 ("A defendant is not required, however, to prove the literal truth of every word contained in the allegedly defamatory matter . . . so long as the imputation is substantially true so as to justify the 'gist or sting' of the remark").

Finally, Harrison did not become aware of Morris' testimony until recently, and certainly not during or shortly after the time when initial disclosures were made. Based on the above, Morris' testimony is substantially justified and harmless, and should be admitted at trial.

*   *   *   *   *

WATERS' MOTION IN LIMINE

Plaintiff Kirsten Waters files this Motion in Limine under Rule 404 of the Federal Rules of Evidence ("Rule 404") to prevent Defendant Simon Harrison from attempting to introduce irrelevant, inadmissible character evidence.

FACTUAL BACKGROUND

The Court is familiar with the extensive factual history of this case, so Waters will outline only the relevant portions here. This is a defamation case in which Waters has filed suit to recover for defamatory statements made by Harrison. As a result of these defamatory statements, Waters was forced to resign her California Senate seat. The defamatory statements include allegations that Waters is unfit for office, dishonest, and committed adultery while engaged to her former fiancé, Jonathan Berman.

Waters has testified, under oath, that she did not cheat on Mr. Berman, and Mr. Berman also has testified that his engagement to Waters did not end as a result of infidelity. Harrison continues to claim that Waters wrote Berman a letter admitting to the alleged affair but has been unable to produce any copy of that letter. Now, to prove that his statements about Waters' relationship with Mr. Berman are true, Harrison seeks to introduce evidence that Waters' first marriage, to Matthew Hamilton, ended as a result of adultery. That evidence is irrelevant and inadmissible under Rule 404(b).

ARGUMENT AND AUTHORITY

A motion in limine is "essentially a preliminary opinion that falls entirely within the discretion of the district court." *United States v. Bensimon*, 172 F.3d 1121, 1127 (9th Cir. 1999). Rule 404 governs the admission of character evidence. "Evidence of a person's character or character trait is not admissible to prove that on a particular occasion the person acted in accordance with the character or trait." FED. R. EVID. 404(a)(1). Specifically, "[e]vidence of a crime, wrong, or other act is not admissible to prove a person's character in order to show that on a particular occasion the person acted in accordance with the character." FED. R. EVID. 404(b)(1).

Character evidence may be admitted for an alternate purpose, including to prove "motive, opportunity, intent, preparation, plan, knowledge, identity, absence of mistake, or lack of accident." FED. R. EVID. 404(b)(2). Evidence that is otherwise admissible for another purpose under Rule 404(b)(2) may still be excluded if the probative value of the evidence is "substantially outweighed by the danger of unfair prejudice." *United States v. Flores-Blanco*, 623 F.3d 912, 919 (9th Cir. 2010) (quoting *United States v. Bibo-Rodriguez*, 922 F.2d 1398, 1400–01 (9th Cir. 1991)). The trial court has broad discretion in weighing the probative value of evidence versus the danger of unfair prejudice. *United States v. Sims*, 617 F.2d 1371, 1378 (9th Cir. 1980).

Upon information and belief, Harrison intends to offer evidence of allegations made against Waters in her prior divorce proceedings with Matthew Hamilton. Specifically, in 2000, Mr. Hamilton filed for divorce from Waters and initially alleged adultery by Waters as a ground for the divorce but later withdrew that allegation.

Evidence that Mr. Hamilton alleged adultery as a ground for divorce in 2000 is not relevant to this litigation and is inadmissible character evidence. Harrison seeks to introduce this evidence to prove the truthfulness of his allegation that Waters cheated on Berman while the two were students at Stanford. This attempt falls squarely within the prohibition of Rule 404(b) — evidence of the adultery allegation made by Mr. Hamilton is not admissible to prove Waters' character or show that in college, Waters acted in accordance with that character.

More importantly, Mr. Hamilton's adultery allegation in the 2000 divorce proceedings was withdrawn, and Waters' divorce was granted on the ground of irreconcilable differences. Thus, even if evidence of adultery were admissible, which it is not, evidence from Waters' 2000 divorce should not be admitted because the allegation of adultery was withdrawn and the divorce was granted on other grounds. In order for evidence of a prior act to be admissible under Rule 404(b), the party seeking to offer the evidence must prove by clear and convincing evidence that the act occurred. *United States v. Simtob*, 901 F.2d 799, 807 (9th Cir. 1990). Harrison cannot present clear and convincing evidence that Waters engaged in the adultery alleged in the 2000 divorce proceedings. Therefore, Harrison should not be permitted to offer the improper character evidence stemming from Waters' prior divorce proceedings.

Harrison cannot offer a permissible alternative purpose under Rule 404(b)(2) that would allow him to introduce pleadings from Waters' 2000 divorce proceedings. Motive, intent, opportunity, and the like are wholly inapplicable to the facts of this case. The only reason Harrison seeks to introduce that evidence is to impugn Waters' character by suggesting that she committed adultery in her marriage and, therefore, must have committed adultery in college.

Even if the evidence Harrison seeks to admit were admissible, which it is not, the evidence should not be admitted. The probative value of the evidence from Waters' divorce is substantially outweighed by the prejudice Waters would suffer if that evidence were admitted. Harrison has already dragged Waters and her reputation through the mud. He should not be permitted to "pile on" by presenting evidence of allegations — not proven facts — that arose in a completely distinct proceeding more than 13 years ago and that were withdrawn and formed no basis of the outcome of that proceeding. Waters' motion in limine should be granted.

*   *   *   *   *

Why are these motions in limine effective?

▶ *They follow the rules.* Both parties filed a common type of motion in limine — one designed to prevent evidence from being presented at trial. Each outlines the facts succinctly, focusing on those facts relevant to the issue addressed in the motion in limine. The parties then discuss the concepts of relevance and prejudice under the Federal Rules of Evidence.

You might have noted that Harrison makes sure to tell the court that his proposed witness could not be discovered until recently and that she would assist the court in properly deciding Waters' defamation claim. Why include this information? Because the court likely will wonder why Harrison failed to list Morris in the pre-trial order and will question if Harrison is attempting to surprise Waters at the last minute.

Waters' motion is also effective in demonstrating that evidence about the dissolution of her marriage to Matthew Harrison would be neither relevant to nor helpful in deciding Waters' defamation claim. Waters points out that the evidence about her divorce would result in substantial prejudice to her because it would serve no purpose but to attack her character in a prior (and private) relationship.

▶ *They are narrow in scope.* Neither Harrison nor Waters tries to use motions in limine to argue the merits. Their arguments are confined to the expected testimony of witnesses and the effects of that proposed testimony. Be very careful here: making inappropriate arguments in motions in limine not only damages your credibility with the judge, but might give the adversary new ideas for new arguments (or evidence) that may be used against you.

▶ *They are short.* By the time cases are ready for trial, judges generally want to move the cases along — they don't want them to get stalled by millions of lengthy motions. Motions in limine, like other motions, should be kept as short as possible. The parties to a good job here in keeping their motions short and to the point.

After reading the motions, would you change anything? What, and why? How would you rule on both motions?

Chapter 12

THE COURT'S DECISION

The moment has arrived. The judge has made her decision.

Kirsten Waters and Simon Harrison both agreed to waive their right to a jury trial, and have this matter decided by the Hon. Helen Montana, a judge on the United States District Court for the Northern District of California.

After the parties filed their respective Motions in Limine, Judge Montana ruled that Stephanie Morris would be permitted to testify on Harrison's behalf. Judge Montana would not, however, allow evidence from Waters' first marriage, holding that the evidence would be irrelevant and overly prejudicial.

At the trial, which lasted two days, Waters and her former fiancé at Stanford, Phillip Berman, testified, along with Harrison and Stephanie Morris.

I. WATERS' TESTIMONY

Waters testified that, while she misrepresented her prior criminal history at the final debate with then-senator Larson, she did not intend to mislead California's voters.

In addition, Waters denied ever cheating on Berman and claimed that Harrison's statements to the contrary constituted a "malicious attempt to defame [her] character and destroy [her] reputation before the voters of California."

Waters testified that her admission to the University of California-Berkeley School of Law was based solely on merit. In support of this assertion, Waters' attorney, Amanda Allred, introduced evidence from Waters' law school application, showing that Waters achieved a 3.81 Grade Point Average at Stanford University, and a 167 on her Law School Admissions Test, which is at or around the 98th percentile. The current admission statistics for the University of California-Berkeley School of Law show a Median Grade Point Average of 3.71, and Median Law School Admissions Test score of 166.

On cross-examination, Waters admitted that she knew the statements about her criminal history at the final debate were "inaccurate," but stated that "the arrest was a long time ago. My response was designed to send a message of hope, not prove that I have a photographic memory."

Also on cross-examination, Waters acknowledged that "my dad is a big donor to Berkeley, and I did have two classes with Simon [Harrison] at Stanford — organic chemistry and introductory Latin. I got a C in both classes." On re-direct, Waters stated that "these were the only Cs I received at Stanford, and as my transcript shows, I was pretty much an A student."

II.   PHILLIP BERMAN'S TESTIMONY

Berman testified that his relationship with Waters "did not end as a result of infidelity. We broke up because our lives were going in different directions, and it was time to go our separate ways. I have nothing but respect and admiration for Kirsten."

On cross-examination, Berman conceded that "there were a few occasions when I suspected her of cheating, and on one occasion I mentioned to Simon [Harrison], who was a mutual friend, that she seemed to be acting differently toward me and not wanting to spend as much time together. But Harrison reacted in a strange manner and said something like, 'I wouldn't trust that woman any more than I would my worst enemy.' I got the sense that something wasn't right between Simon and Kirsten. It was almost like her was jealous of her or just didn't like her."

Harrison and Stephanie Morris ("Morris") testified for the defense.

III.   HARRISON'S TESTIMONY

During his testimony, Harrison stated: "When I saw the debate with Larson and heard her answer, I knew Kirsten was lying. Sure, she got arrested for DUI and possession of a controlled substance, but she never served a day in jail and wasn't ordered to spend time in a treatment center."

Harrison's attorney, Warren G. Bell, offered into evidence the November 10, 1994 letter from Waters' probation officer, confirming Harrison's account. On cross-examination, however, Harrison testified that, "yes, it's possible that Kirsten forgot the details of her sentence, but she was so far off that I could only come to one conclusion: she intentionally lied."

Concerning his comments about Waters' academic abilities, Harrison stated that he "had Latin and organic chemistry with her, and she's lucky she got a C in both classes. Kirsten had no clue what was going on, and I spent hours tutoring her in both classes. No matter how hard I tried, she just didn't get it. So I find it astonishing that she got into a school like Berkeley without some help from her dad. I'm telling you, she wasn't a good student and that's the way I see it."

On cross-examination, Harrison admitted that Waters "was really driven and got awesome grades in most of her other courses." Harrison also admitted that "I thought of going to law school, and we studied for the LSAT at the same time. She got really high scores on the practice tests and actually helped me improve my score by about five points."

With respect to her affair with Berman, Harrison stated that "Phil came to me and was really concerned that she was cheating on him. I saw the look in his eyes and he seemed pretty sure. Quite frankly, it didn't surprise me. I had a feeling that Kirsten was always looking out for herself and would do anything to herself look good in other peoples' eyes."

On cross-examination, Harrison testified that he could "not currently locate" the letter that Waters apparently wrote to Berman. Harrison testified that, "when I mentioned it on my website, I thought I still had it. But I must've thrown it out."

IV. STEPHANIE MORRIS' TESTIMONY

Morris testified that, before the final debate, Waters had a campaign strategy session where Waters "basically concocted the scheme to lie about her criminal history." Morris also testified that, before Waters resigned, Waters "was shocked that Simon remembered the truth and even more shocked that he would expose her."

On cross-examination, Morris stated: "I don't like Kirsten because she screwed me out of a lot of money. I was glad when Harrison exposed her, even if some of it isn't true."

At the conclusion of closing argument, Judge Montana spent one day deliberating before reaching a final decision. Below is a transcript of the decision.

WATERS v. HARRISON
United States District Court
Northern District of California
Opinion and Order

Montana, Helen, U.S.D.J.,

After carefully reviewing the parties' testimony at trial and considering the relevant law, the Court hereby makes the following findings of fact and conclusions of law.

Findings of Fact

Defendant Simon Harrison ("Harrison"), a resident of Erie, Pennsylvania, made various comments regarding Plaintiff Kirsten Waters ("Waters"), a resident of San Jose, California on his blog, www.justtellthetruth.com. See Waters' Complaint, ¶12. At the time, Waters was a candidate for the United States Senate. *Id.*, ¶7.

Harrison's comments, which are contained in Paragraph 12 of the Waters Complaint, caused Waters to resign the senate seat she had recently won in a hotly contested election. *Id.*, ¶ 16. Harrison's comments are set forth in subsections A, B, and C below.

Waters alleged that the statements constituted an invasion of privacy (under both California tort law and the California Constitution) and were false and defamatory. *Id.*, Counts One and Two, ¶¶ 17–29. In her Complaint, Waters sought five million dollars in damages. *Id.*, ¶ 43. Waters conceded that she could not state a claim for invasion of privacy after Harrison filed a motion for summary judgment as to both Waters' defamation claim and invasion of privacy claim. The court denied Harrison's motion with respect to the defamation claim, and it is the sole remaining cause of action.

At the conclusion of discovery and after pre-trial motions were filed, this Court held a two-day trial, during which the following witnesses testified:

(1) Waters;

(2) Phillip Berman, Waters' fiancé while in college;

(3) Harrison; and

(4) Stephanie Morris, a former member of Waters' campaign staff.

This Court finds that Harrison's statements broadly fall within the following three categories:

A. STATEMENTS ABOUT WATERS' CRIMINAL HISTORY

Harrison alleged that Waters lied about her criminal history during a debate with then-senator Robert Larson:

> Kirsten's statements about her past struggle with substance abuse — obviously designed to sway California voters — are fabrications. I was Kirsten's friend during college, and I unconditionally supported Kirsten while she struggled to overcome addiction. I am shocked that Kirsten would exploit her past for political gain. More specifically, while Kirsten was arrested for Driving under the Influence of Alcohol and possession of a controlled substance, **she was neither incarcerated nor ordered to spend even a single day in a residential treatment program. After pleading guilty, Kirsten was sentenced to 90 days probation and 100 hours of community service. Additionally, as part of the plea deal, the controlled substance charge was dropped. Kirsten only sought residential treatment because her parents threatened to stop paying her tuition at Stanford. Kirsten's lies show that she is not fit for public office.**

Waters Complaint, ¶ 12 (emphasis in original). At trial, Harrison's counsel, Warren G. Bell, proffered a letter dated November, 10, 1994, allegedly from Waters' probation officer at the time, stating that "the court sentenced you to a probation term of 90 days, and 100 hours of community service."

B. STATEMENTS ABOUT WATERS' ALLEGED INFIDELITY WHILE IN COLLEGE

Harrison stated that, while in college, Waters was unfaithful to her fiancé:

> In addition, because I am committed to telling the whole truth, I must disclose that, while at Stanford, Kirsten engaged in highly questionable conduct. During our last two years at Stanford, Kirsten was engaged to a mutual friend (who I will not reveal at this time). Kirsten suddenly broke off the engagement and admitted to having a lengthy affair with another man throughout the duration of the relationship. I will soon release a letter Kirsten wrote to our friend admitting the affair.

Id. At the trial, it was revealed that Phillip Berman was Waters' fiancé at the time. Berman testified that Waters was not unfaithful during their relationship, but that the couple had "grown apart" and decided to go their "separate ways."

C. Statements about Waters' Educational Background and Academic Abilities

Harrison also made statements questioning Waters' academic ability, including the circumstances surrounding her admission to the University of California — Berkeley School of Law:

> While at Stanford, Kirsten performed poorly in her studies. Kirsten was not a good student, and I doubt she has the abilities to effectively serve in any elected capacity. I don't know how she was accepted by the University of California-Berkeley School of Law. I do know this: her dad is one of Berkeley's most generous donors. Kirsten's admission to Berkeley wasn't about merit. It was about favoritism and money. I also question how Kirsten ever graduated from Berkeley. I can't imagine her passing all of those difficult law school classes without receiving significant help from her family.

Id.

Conclusions of Law

To succeed in a defamation action, Waters must prove that Harrison's comments resulted in: (1) publication; (2) of a false statement; (3) that is defamatory; (4) unprivileged; and (5) results in damages. *See Ringler Associates Inc., v. Maryland Casualty Co.*, 96 Cal. Rptr. 2d 136, 148 (Cal. Ct. App. 2000). The level of fault required — negligence or actual malice — depends on whether the party alleging defamation is deemed an all-public, limited-purpose public, or private figure. *See McGarry v. University of San Diego*, 64 Cal. Rptr. 3d, 467, 479–480 (Cal. Ct. App. 2007).

As a threshold matter, this Court finds that, for purposes of proving defamation, Waters is a public figure. As a former attorney and candidate for the United States Senate who attracted national media attention during the race against Larson, I conclude that Waters achieved such "pervasive fame or notoriety" to be deemed "a public figure for all purposes and in all contexts." *Gertz v. Robert Welch, Inc.*, 418 U.S. 323, 351 (1974). As a result, Waters must show that Harrison's statements were made with actual malice; that is, "knowledge that [the statements were] false or with reckless disregard of whether it was false or not." *McGarry*, 64 Cal. Rptr. 3d at 480 (*quoting Reader's Digest Ass'n v. Superior Court*, 208 Cal. Rptr. 137, 149 (Cal. 1984)).

A. Publication

"Publication, which may be written or oral, is defined as a communication to some third person who understands both the defamatory meaning of the statement and its application to the person to whom reference is made." *Ringler Associates*, 96 Cal. Rptr. 2d at 148.

There is no dispute regarding publication. Harrison posted his comments on www.justtellthetruth.com, a fairly well-known internet blog.

Harrison's comments were viewed by individuals who visited www.justtellthetruth-.com, and the comments received media attention throughout the country. In fact, Harrison's comments were re-published by media organizations nationwide. While

Harrison cannot be held liable for the re-publication of these statements (the relevant media sources were not acting under his authority or direction), the evidence shows that the statements were communicated to third parties and that they referred to Waters. The publication element is satisfied.

B. FALSITY

A statement can only be defamatory if it is "provably false," and a "statement of fact rather than opinion." *Ringler*, 96 Cal. Rptr. 2d at 149 (emphasis in original). The language of the statement and context within which it was rendered are relevant factors in determining whether "a reasonable fact finder could conclude that the published statements imply a provably false factual assertion." *Id.*; *see also Copp v. Paxton*, 52 Cal. Rptr. 2d 831, 838 (Cal. Ct. App. 1996).

Importantly, comments that are "broad, unfocused and wholly subjective" constitute non-actionable opinion. *Fletcher v. San Jose Mercury News*, 264 Cal. Rptr. 699, 709 (Cal. Ct. App. 1989). For example, "shady practitioner," "crook," and "creepazoid attorney" are opinions, not facts. *Copp*, 52 Cal. Rptr. 2d at 837 (*quoting Lewis v. Time, Inc.*, 710 F.2d 549, 554 (9th Cir. 1993); *Lauderback v. American Broadcasting Companies*, 741 F.2d 193, 195-198 (8th Cir. 1984); *Milkovich v. Lorain Journal Co.*, 497 U.S. 1, 20 (1990)). Put differently, "rhetorical hyperbole," "caricature," "vigorous epithet[s]," and "lusty and imaginative expression[s] of . . . contempt," are constitutionally protected and cannot form the basis for a defamation claim. *Nygard, Inc. v. Uusi-Kerttula*, 72 Cal. Rptr. 3d 210, 226 (Cal. Ct. App. 2008) (citations omitted).

An opinion-based statement can, however, be actionable "if it implies the allegation of undisclosed defamatory facts as the basis for the opinion." *Id.* (*quoting Okun v. Superior Court*, 175 Cal. Rptr 157, 162 (1981)). The Court will analyze each of Harrison's statements independently.

1. WATERS' CRIMINAL HISTORY

Harrison's statement that Waters lied about the sentence she received in connection with her August 2, 1994 arrest is provably false. At the final debate, Waters claimed that a court in that case sentenced her to 30 days in a Palo Alto jail and mandatory substance abuse treatment. At trial, as in her letter of resignation, Waters acknowledged that these statements were inaccurate but denied that she intentionally lied.

Harrison stated on www.justtellthetruth.com that the court imposed on Waters a sentence of probation and community service. Harrison corroborated this statement at trial by introducing the November 10, 1994 letter from Waters' probation officer.

From the relevant testimony and evidence, I find that, while Harrison's statements regarding Waters' criminal history are provably false, Waters has not carried her burden of demonstrating that the statements are, in fact, false. On the contrary, the November 10, 1994 letter, coupled with Waters' acknowledgement that she misrepresented the facts relating to her sentence, suggest that Harrison's statements were true. As a matter of law, truth is an absolute defense to defamation. *Ringler*, 96 Cal. Rptr. 2d at 149 ("[i]n all cases of defamation, whether libel or slander, the truth of the offensive statements or communication is a complete defense against civil liability, regardless of bad faith or malicious purpose"). The statements regarding Waters' criminal history are not actionable.

Additionally, this Court does not give much, if any, credibility to the testimony of Stephanie Morris. As a disgruntled former campaign worker, the likelihood that Morris harbored conscious or subconscious bias is high. Furthermore, Morris' willingness to share intimate details of private campaign strategy sessions raises concerns with this Court about Morris' commitment to ethical behavior.

2. INFIDELITY WHILE IN COLLEGE

Harrison stated on www.justtellthetruth.com that Waters "admitted to having a lengthy affair with another man throughout the duration of the relationship [with Berman]." In support of this claim, Harrison promised to "release a letter Kirsten wrote to our friend admitting the affair." These statements are provably false and can support a defamation claim.

At trial, Harrison failed to produce the letter he claims supports this statement, and the testimony of Waters, Berman, and even Harrison supports the conclusion that Harrison's statements are false. In addition to Waters' testimony that no infidelity occurred during the course of their relationship, Berman testified that "our relationship did not end as a result of infidelity."

Furthermore, on cross-examination, Harrison acknowledged that he could not produce the letter and seemed to base this statement about an affair on "a feeling that Kirsten was always looking out for herself, and would do anything to make herself look good in other peoples' eyes."

Based on the weight of the evidence, Waters has carried her burden of showing that the statements regarding her alleged infidelity were false.

3. WATERS' EDUCATIONAL BACKGROUND AND ACADEMIC ABILITIES

Harrison also stated on www.justtellthetruth.com that Waters was not a "good student," and that he doubted that Waters possessed the "abilities to effectively serve in any elected capacity." Harrison claimed that Waters' admission to the University of California-Berkeley School of Law "was about favoritism and money," and that Harrison could not imagine "her [Waters] passing all of those difficult law school classes without receiving significant help from her family."

At trial, Waters offered into evidence her undergraduate transcripts from Stanford University, and Law School Admission Test scores, both of which demonstrate that her qualifications were slightly above the average grades and tests scores for admitted applicants. Waters did acknowledge on cross-examination that her father was a "big donor to Berkeley."

Harrison testified that Waters received "Cs" in two classes that they took together at Stanford. On cross-examination, Harrison acknowledged that Waters "got really high scores on the practice [LSAT] tests and actually helped [him] improve [his] score by about five points."

This Court finds that the statements regarding Waters' educational background constitute "non-actionable" opinion. This is not to say that the statements, *e.g.*, Waters was not a "good student" or lacked the "abilities to effectively serve in any elected capacity," did not imply false facts. The court, however, does not believe that Waters adduced any facts showing, by a preponderance of the evidence, that she was, in fact, a "good student."

With respect to Waters' admission to the University of California, Berkeley School of Law, this Court finds that, while Harrison's statements in this regard are provably false, Waters has again failed to carry her burden of demonstrating that they were false. This is not to say that Waters' father's status as a donor played any role in her admission. Rather, the evidence is insufficient to conclude, by a preponderance of the evidence, that Harrison's statements were false.

Thus, the only statements the court will consider are those related to Waters' relationship with Mr. Berman.

C. Whether the Statements Are Defamatory

"Whether a statement is reasonably susceptible to a defamatory interpretation is a question of law for the trial court." *Smith*, 85 Cal. Rptr. 2d at 403. When making this determination, "courts look 'not so much [to the allegedly libelous statement's] effect when subject to the critical analysis of a mind trained in law, but [to] the natural and probable effect upon the mind of the average reader.' " *Ferlauto v. Hamsher*, 88 Cal. Rptr. 2d 843, 849 (Cal. Ct. App. 1999) (*quoting Morningstar, Inc. v. Superior Court*, 29 Cal. Rptr. 2d 547, 553 (Cal. Ct. App. 1994)).

Defamatory statements include those exposing a person "to hatred, contempt, ridicule, or obloquy, or which causes him to be shunned or avoided, or which has a tendency to injure him in his occupation." *McGarry*, 64 Cal. Rptr. 3d at 478 (*quoting* Cal. Civ. Code § 45). Under California law, statements that tend "directly to injure [a person] in respect to his office, profession, trade or business, either by imputing to him general disqualification in those respects which the office or other occupation peculiarly requires, or by imputing something with reference to his office, profession, trade, or business that has a natural tendency to lessen its profit," are defamatory per se. *McGarry*, 64 Cal. Rptr. 3d at 478 (*quoting* Cal. Civ. Code §§ 45(a), (46)).[48] A statement can also be libelous per se "if it contains a charge by implication from the language employed by the speaker and a listener could understand the defamatory meaning without the necessity of knowing extrinsic explanatory matter." *McGarry*, 64 Cal. Rptr. 3d at 478 (*citing MacLeod v. Tribune Publishing Co.*, 52 Cal. 2d 536, 548-550 (1959)).

The Court finds that the statements concerning Waters' infidelity are defamatory

---

[48] Although § 46 addresses slander, identical statements made through libelous means are also defamatory as a matter of law. *See Peterson v. Rasmussen*, 47 Cal. App. 694 (1920) (statements imputing that the plaintiff was unchaste are libelous as a matter of law).

per se. Claiming that someone is unchaste, regardless of whether the comments are made in the context of a marital relationship, cause incalculable injury to a person's personal and professional reputation. A person may face reprisal from family members, friends, colleagues, and the larger community. Such statements — when false — are defamatory per se and do not require explanatory extrinsic evidence.

Harrison's statement — that Waters cheated on Berman and admitted to it through a written letter — suggest to a reasonable observer that Waters engaged in deceptive, immoral, and unethical behavior. Furthermore, by claiming on www.justtellthetruth-.com that he had a letter to corroborate these statements, Harrison created the impression of certainty where, as shown at trial, none existed. While these statements, in and of themselves, did not directly cause Waters to resign, they cast Waters in a negative light before a nationwide audience. Based on these facts, Harrison's statements are defamatory *per se.*

D. FAULT

The above conclusion, however, does not end the inquiry. As stated above, Waters is a public figure and therefore must demonstrate that Harrison's statements (regarding her infidelity) were made with actual malice. This, the Court concludes, Waters cannot do, particularly where, as here, actual malice must be shown by clear and convincing evidence. *Gilbert v. Sykes*, 53 Cal. Rptr. 3d 752, 763 (Cal. Ct. App. 2007).

Actual malice requires Waters to demonstrate, at the very least, that Harrison had "serious doubts" concerning the truth of his statements about Waters' infidelity. *Copp*, 52 Cal. Rptr. 2d at 844-845 (quoting *St. Amant v. Thompson*, 390 U.S. 727, 731 (1968)). While circumstantial evidence can be used to prove actual malice, including "anger and hostility toward the plaintiff," the evidence must "permit the conclusion that the defendant actually had a high degree of awareness of . . . probable falsity." *Copp*, 52 Cal. Rptr. 2d at 845 (*quoting St. Amant*, 390 U.S. at 731); *McGarry*, 64 Cal. Rptr. 3d at 480 (*quoting Harte-Hanks Communications v. Connaughton*, 491 U.S. 657, 688 (1989)).

Here, the Court finds Berman's testimony compelling. While denying that Waters was unfaithful during their relationship, Berman did admit that he "mentioned to Simon [Harrison], who was a mutual friend, that Waters seemed to be acting differently toward me and not wanting to spend as much time together." The Court finds that Berman's testimony, and his recollection of the conversation, provided a colorable basis upon which Harrison could have believed that Waters had or was engaged in infidelity. Of course, while Harrison made no attempts to verify this information, the Court cannot conclude — by clear and convincing evidence — that Harrison entertained serious doubts about their truthfulness. Harrison's failure to provide the letter he claims was written by Kirsten admitting to the infidelity, while suspicious, does not rise to the level of actual malice.

Ultimately, Harrison's publication of statements alleging infidelity — the existence of which both parties to the relationship denied under oath — arguably supports a finding of negligence (even gross negligence). Given Waters' status as a public figure, however, negligence is not the standard. Thus, while the Court sympathizes with

Waters and finds Harrison's comments lack taste and discretion, it cannot say that such statements support a finding of liability under California defamation law.

E. DAMAGES

The foregoing discussion renders moot any discussion of damages.

CONCLUSION

Based on the foregoing, Counts Three and Four of Plaintiff Kirsten Waters' Complaint are hereby dismissed.

A copy of the Court's decision shall be sent to all counsel of record.

_____

Hon. Helen Montana
United States District Judge

United States District Court,
Northern District of California
San Jose Division

DATED: 10/28/2014

*   *   *   *   *

Do you agree with this decision? Why? If not, what are the possible grounds for an appeal?

Chapter 13

THE APPELLATE BRIEF

THE APPELLATE BRIEF CHECKLIST

- √ Check the rules
- √ File the notice of appeal
- √ Know the required sections
    - √ Keep the statement of facts as short as possible
    - √ Lean toward objectivity in the statement of facts
    - √ Use a one fact equals one paragraph approach
    - √ Support each fact with evidence from the record (deposition transcripts, documents etc.)
    - √ Don't make legal conclusions
- √ Know the appellate standards of review
- √ Draft the Statement of Jurisdiction
- √ Draft the Statement of the Issues
- √ Draft the Statement of the Case
    - √ Factual Background
    - √ Procedural Background
- √ Draft the Summary of the Argument
- √ Draft the Argument
- √ Check last-minute details
    - √ Check for overall aesthetic appearance
    - √ Double-check citations
    - √ Double-check the Table of Authorities to ensure page references remain correct
    - √ Double-check the Table of Contents to ensure page references remain correct and all required sections have been included
    - √ Perform a final spell-check
    - √ Certify that the brief complies with page or word limits

---

Judge Montana has just issued her ruling and as Waters' counsel, you're not happy. You hurry out of the courtroom and burst through the courthouse doors, where you're surrounded by cameras and microphones. The media wants to hear from you, but you're in no mood to speak. You've got to decide what to do now — should you appeal the ruling? What is your chance of prevailing on appeal? Is it worth the time, effort, and Waters' money to file an appeal? And how do you even go about filing one?

This book is mainly dedicated to trial-level documents, but here are some guidelines for drafting appellate briefs.

Some Preliminary Advice

A. <u>Check the Rules</u>

Before you even file your notice of appeal, you should consult the appellate court's rules, which will give you information on page limits, font type and size, characters per line, paper quality, the deadline for filing, and the cover color required for each brief. Generally, the rules are detailed, specific to each jurisdiction, and must be strictly followed. Don't think, "I complied with 90% of the rules, so I'll be alright." You might get the brief mailed back to you, saying, "Not in compliance with court rules."

B. <u>File the Notice of Appeal</u>

In most, if not all jurisdictions, the notice of appeal is filed in the trial court. The jurisdiction-specific rules and the local rules likely will govern what information must be included in the notice and whether any documents (such as the ruling or judgment you're appealing from) must be attached. The required information may include:

- The type of appeal (appeal as a matter of right or interlocutory);
- The statute, rule, or case that allows for the appeal;
- The ruling or judgment you're appealing and the date it was entered; and
- Authority showing the appeal is timely;

As always, follow your jurisdiction-specific and local rules. You don't want to waive your appeal because of an error in the contents or timing of the notice.

C. <u>Know the Standard of Review</u>

Sometimes the standard of review is a separate subsection. If not, you'll want to outline the standard of review at the beginning of your argument. Then why are we talking about the Standard of Review first? Even though the Standard of Review is generally a minor note in an appellate brief, it is *very* important and will impact how you frame your appellate issues and what you argue. Why? Because different standards of review apply in different situations, and the standard of review can make all the difference.

Are you alleging a factual or legal error? That's an important question because the standard of review differs substantially depending on the answer. If you allege that the lower court made a factual error (e.g., discredited the testimony of a witness), the chances of winning are slim. Appellate courts give substantial deference to the fact finders' findings of fact, and generally will reverse only when there is an "abuse of discretion" or if the factual findings were "clearly erroneous." Often, within each of these standards are multi-factor tests that clarify their meaning, and appellate judges are not afraid to apply the same standard in different cases depending on the complexity of the factual issue. Notwithstanding, the lower court will almost always receive wide latitude. Why? The lower court is better suited than the appellate court to make factual determinations. Think about it: the trial judge sat in the courtroom every day listening to the live testimony of each witness. As such, the court is in a unique position to assess the witnesses' credibility, not based solely on their words, but from their demeanor and to determine whether evidence should be admitted.

Legal issues, however, are generally reviewed under a less deferential standard, known as de novo review. The de novo standard is a much lower threshold, generally making legal issues the better option for appellants.

Sometimes, the appellate standard is multi-tiered: one standard for review of factual findings and another for review of legal questions. And sometimes the parties may dispute which appellate standard applies. If that happens, be prepared to make a strong case for the standard you believe is appropriate.

D. Know the Required Sections

Before beginning your appellate brief, you need to check the appellate court's rules for the required sections you must include in your brief. These usually include most or all of the listed sections (though sometimes these sections are called by different names):

- Cover page
  - List the style of the case, the title of the document, and the lawyer's name and contact information.
- Statement of oral argument
  - Explain why you think oral argument is necessary or why you believe the court can decide the case on the parties' briefs.
- Table of Contents
- Table of Authorities
  - The authorities are usually divided into subsections, such as federal cases, state cases, and statutes.
- Statement of Jurisdiction
  - Explain why the lower court had jurisdiction over the matter, citing statutes or cases, if appropriate.
  - Explain why the appellate court has jurisdiction to hear the appeal, citing statutes or cases, if appropriate.
  - Provide dates that show the appeal was timely.
- Statement of the Issues
  - List the issues you are asking the Court to address.
- Statement of the Case
  - Factual Background
  - Procedural Background
- Summary of the Argument

- Argument
- Conclusion
- Certifications
  - Some appellate courts require litigants to certify that their briefs meet page or work limits and formatting requirements.
- Certificate of Service

Many appellate courts have helpful appellate brief checklists that reference jurisdiction-specific rules and requirements. If your court has a specific checklist, use it!

1. Statement of Oral Argument

If you desire oral argument and believe it will help you better represent your client, tell the appellate court why it should hear argument. Generally, appellate courts hear oral argument in only a handful of cases, so you'd better make your Statement of Oral Argument persuasive. If the issue before the appellate court is one of first impression, point that out. And if the factual history, procedural history, or relevant precedent is complex or convoluted, be sure to explain that to the court.

If you don't believe oral argument is necessary and want to have the case decided without argument, you still must explain why oral argument isn't necessary. Explain, for example, that the case is not factually or legally complicated, that the case law, statute, regulation etc. is clear (from your perspective), and that oral argument won't assist the court in deciding the issues.

2. Table of Contents

The Table of Contents should contain all sections and subsections required by your jurisdiction's rules with references to the pages on which those sections and subsections begin. Unless your jurisdiction's rules require otherwise, don't capitalize, bold or underline all the sections and subsections in your Table of Contents — doing so makes them difficult to read. Your Table of Contents will probably look something like this:

STATEMENT OF ORAL ARGUMENT i
TABLE OF CONTENTS ii
TABLE OF AUTHORITIES iii
STATEMENT OF JURISDICTION iv
STATEMENT OF THE ISSUES 1

*   *   *   *   *

3. Table of Authorities

Your jurisdiction may require that the Table of Authorities be organized in a particular manner. If so, follow the jurisdictional requirements. If not, consider subdividing the Table of Authorities for ease of use. For example, if you are litigating a case in the Eleventh Circuit Court of Appeals, separate U.S. Supreme Court cases, Eleventh Circuit cases, other circuit cases, and district court cases. List statutes, regulations, and other materials under separate headings as well. This will keep your Table of Authorities organized.

Generally, authorities should be listed in alphabetical order, though some jurisdictions may require authorities to be listed in the order they appear in the brief. And a note on aesthetics: if the case cannot be written in full on a single line, consider putting the case name on one line and the case citation on the next, like this:

International Shoe Co. v. Washington,

326 U.S. 310 (1945) ....

4. Statement of Jurisdiction

In the Statement of Jurisdiction, you must explain to the court why the lower court had original jurisdiction to hear the case and why the appellate court has jurisdiction over the appeal. Be sure to reference statutes or cases that confer jurisdiction. For example:

The district court has jurisdiction over this matter under 28 U.S.C. § 1332 because Appellant and Appellee are citizens of different states and the amount in controversy exceeds the statutory minimum of $75,000. On July 13, 2014, the district court granted Appellee's motion for summary judgment. On July 24, 2014, Appellant timely filed its notice of appeal in the district court. Fed. R. App. P. 4(a)(1)(A) (civil appeals must be filed

within 30 days after entry of the order appealed from).

This Court has jurisdiction over the appeal under 28 U.S.C. § 1291 because an order granting a party's motion for summary judgment is an appealable final decision. *See Catlin v. United States*, 324 U.S. 229, 233 (1945) (For purposes of 28 U.S.C. § 1291, a final decision is one that "ends the litigation on the merits and leaves nothing for the court to do but execute the judgment.").

5. Statement of the Issues

Generally, you'll want to limit yourself to no more than three issues on appeal. If you must, you can probably get by with as many as five. But we advise against ever raising any more than five issues. "Why," you ask?

First, you don't have room. While the page and word limits vary greatly from court to court, you'll have to dedicate a substantial amount of your brief space to the factual and procedural background and other required sections. In a 30-page brief, you might have only 15–20 pages of space for substantive arguments. If you raise three issues, you're looking at just five to six double-spaced pages per issue. If you raise five issues, that's a mere three to four pages per issue.

Second, as we've said before, bad arguments dilute the strength of good ones. If an issue has very little chance of success, think twice about whether to include it. You don't want to lose credibility on your strong issues by including very weak ones.

Let's assume you've chosen three issues. As before, you should start with your strongest argument, then your next strongest, and finally the weakest. In deciding which argument is best, remember that the Standard of Review is very important. Unless you have a slam-dunk argument on an issue that will be reviewed under a clearly erroneous or similar standard, start with an issue reviewed de novo.

You may want to phrase your issues under a "Whether . . . when" format. Each Statement of the Issue should include a few facts that most support your position and ones that you hope will guide the appellate court's analysis. You can even include statutes or case names in your Statement of the Issues if the authorities are commonly known:

> **Whether Derrickson can state claim under 28 U.S.C. § 1983 when he was detained, assaulted, and battered by an off-duty police officer who identified himself to Derrickson as a police officer and was wearing a police uniform and carrying a badge and gun.**

Writing the Statement of Issues is the first thing you should do when drafting an appellate brief. The issues you choose will govern the information you'll include in the factual and procedural background and, obviously, the arguments and cases you cite in your Argument section.

6. Statement of the Case

Factual Background

For purpose of your appeal, the facts most relevant in the underlying action may not be as relevant (or may even be irrelevant). Consider the example above involving issues of personal jurisdiction and service. While you will need to discuss the contract that formed the basis of the underlying breach of contract suit, the relevant facts have nothing to do with whether the contract was breached. The relevant facts with respect to the first issue will touch on Jones' residency and in what capacity she signed the contract. The relevant facts with respect to the third issue will touch on what the process server did to attempt to perfect service, what Jones' daughter told the process server, and why the process server left the papers on Jones' porch.

Think critically about what issues you are asking the appellate court to address and what facts you'll need to include in your statement of the case. As it is at the trial court level, appellate brief space is at a premium. Don't waste space reciting irrelevant facts.

And please, whatever you do, don't cite facts not in the record. This is the first rule of appellate advocacy. If there's no transcript, can you argue a trial court's ruling on an oral motion was erroneous? No. If a key document on which you want to rely isn't part of the trial court's record, can you rely on the document? No. Testimony from a transcript that was never filed with the trial court? You guessed it — no. Appellate courts don't hear live testimony and you generally can't attach any exhibits to an appellate brief. Don't try to pull one over on an appellate court — they're used to this tactic. Any arguments based on facts not in the record will quickly be shot down, and you'll lose credibility.

Procedural Background

As with the factual background, you need only include the relevant procedural background in your Statement of the Case. For example, if you're appealing a jury award, you don't need to explain every filing, motion, and court appearance. But, if you think the appellate judges might be confused by missing information, include it, even if it isn't technically relevant. For example, if you're appealing a jury award, your Procedural Background might look something like this:

> **Appellant filed claims for breach of contract against Global Exports, Exporters of America, and Trans-Atlantic Shipping in 2007. Appellant subsequently settled its claims against Global and dismissed it from the case. In 2011, the trial court granted Trans-Atlantic's motion for summary judgment. Appellant did not appeal that ruling, leaving Exporters as the remaining defendant.**

> **This matter was tried by a jury in January 2013. During the trial, the trial court made several erroneous rulings that resulted in a verdict in favor of Exporters. The trial court entered judgment for Exporters on January 29, 2013. Appellant filed its notice of appeal on February 4, 2013.**

The author includes information about Global and Trans-Atlantic so the appellate court understands why Exporters was the only remaining defendant at trial.

The Procedural Background should generally be short and to-the-point. It's the place to explain how the case got to the appellate court. Notice that in this example, this author doesn't include information about why the trial court's rulings were erroneous — the author just says that they were. Argument about why the rulings were erroneous should be saved for the Argument section. But the author is using every opportunity to persuade by planting the seed in the reader's mind early.

7. Summary of the Argument

This section is pretty self-explanatory, so we'll just make a few short points. The Summary of the Argument is the persuasive sibling of the Short Answer section in a memo and should generally follow an IRAC, CREAC, or other appropriate structure. Explain your client's position, briefly outline the applicable law and apply it to the facts, then reiterate the position again.

If you are addressing multiple issues on appeal, separate your Summary of the Argument for each issue into a separate paragraph. The Summary of the Argument should flow seamlessly from one issue to the next. Use transitions and try to link your arguments, to the extent possible.

In the Linda Jones case, about whether Florida courts can exercise personal jurisdiction over her, you might transition from the first and second issues (personal jurisdiction) to the third issue (service) in this way:

> **Even if the Court agrees that Jones is subject to personal jurisdiction in Florida, the trial court erred in finding that Cain perfected service on Jones.**

Lawyers often wonder if they should put citations to authority in my Summary of the Argument. We think the better practice is remove citations to authority from the Summary of the Argument — after all, it's supposed to be a short, to-the-point summary. But some legal writing instructors and practitioners disagree. If you're a student, follow your instructor. If you're a practitioner, you should decide which method you prefer. But be consistent. If you choose to include citations, you need to include them for every legal rule you outline in your Summary of the Argument.

8. Argument

Your Argument section should mirror the Statement of the Issues, with the strongest issue first, followed by the next strongest and so forth. Just like the argument section in a motion to dismiss or motion for summary judgment, the argument section in your appellate brief should follow IRAC, CREAC, or a similar structure. Broadly speaking, your Argument section should follow this outline:

- The trial court or fact-finder erred by . . .
- The law is . . .
- In this case, the trial court or fact finder erred because . . .
- Therefore, the appellate court should . . .

And don't forget: It's ok to take issue with the trial judge's ruling, but don't personally attack the judge. As the appellant, you'll often argue that the trial judge erred in some way. And it's important to be clear about the reasons you believe the judge erred — the appellate court will only decide the issues presented to it and won't go on a roving mission looking for every place the judge might have made a mistake. But temper your language:

- The trial judge erred in granting Moore's motion for summary judgment.
- The district court misapplied *Stevens*.
- The judge improperly allowed Jones to present evidence of Moore's criminal history.

Avoid inflammatory language and terms such as *asinine*, *ludicrous*, *crazy*, and the like. Remember, if you win your appeal, the case may well go back to the very trial judge whose errors you just pointed out, so you don't want to alienate that judge.

9. Last Minute Details

Once your brief is substantively complete, you'll need to make your final edits. These include:

- √ Checking the overall aesthetic appearance, looking for orphan headings, inconsistent font size and style, bad use of white space and the like;
- √ Double-checking citations and making corrections, if necessary;
- √ Double-checking the Table of Authorities for page references and making corrections, if necessary;
- √ Double-checking the Table of Contents and making corrections to page references, if necessary;
- √ Performing a final spell-check; and
- √ Certifying that the brief complies with page or word limits, if applicable.

Waters v. Harrison

Below is an appellate brief filed by Waters in response to Judge Montana's decision, followed by Harrison's response. The Table of Contents, Table of Authorities and other sections have been omitted for brevity. After reading these briefs, would you affirm or reverse the decision?

*   *   *   *   *

Case No. 13-16352

IN THE UNITED STATES COURT OF APPEALS
FOR THE NINTH CIRCUIT

KIRSTEN WATERS,

Appellee,

v.

SIMON HARRISON,

Appellant.

On appeal from the United States District Court for the
Northern District of California

BRIEF OF APPELLANT KIRSTEN WATERS

Amanda Allred, Esq.
Allred, Jackson, Stevens, and Marshall LLC
1000 Hollywood Drive
San Francisco, California 94114
Telephone: (555) 768-0057
Facsimile: (555) 768-0058
Email: amanda@jacksonstevenslaw.com
State Bar Number: 12345-110
Attorneys for Plaintiff Kirsten Waters

I. FACTUAL BACKGROUND

Appellant Kirsten Waters filed this action to recover from Appellee Simon Harrison for making false, malicious statements about Waters while Waters was a Senatorial candidate. These statements — which Harrison intended readers to receive as statements of fact — suggest Waters does not possess the high ethical standards, trustworthiness, and character accepted from elected officials. Harrison's malicious attack on Waters ultimately cost her the Senate seat she won in one of the closest elections in California history and is likely to prevent Waters from pursuing future political office or maintaining her career as a lawyer.

A. Waters' educational history

Waters and Harrison were classmates and friends at Stanford University in the 1990s, though they lost contact after both graduated. R. 1455. While Waters was a college student, she struggled with alcohol and prescription drug abuse. R. 1510–21. Waters' addictions ultimately led her to seek professional treatment, and she has been drug and alcohol free for more than 20 years. R. 1589–95.

Despite her personal struggles, Waters excelled in her studies and was able to pursue her dream of attending law school at the University of California Berkeley School of Law. R. 1610, 2123-98. After graduating from Berkeley, Waters accepted a position with a prestigious law firm, Jones, Davis, Bartlett and Strom, LLP, where she was ultimately selected as the managing partner of the firm's litigation department. R. 1615.

B. Waters' run for Senate

As a lawyer, Waters witnessed first-hand the need for elected officials to exhibit strong leadership. R. 1629. In 2010, with the support of her colleagues, family, and friends, Waters decided to pursue the United States Senate seat then occupied by Ted Larson. R. 1631–37.

During her campaign for the United States Senate, Waters' personal struggles gained her substantial popularity among likely voters. R. 1645, 1847–1849. Waters was forthright about her past and discussed the consequences of substance abuse on her personal and professional life. R. 545–56, 1646. Waters' honesty during the campaign, coupled with her inspiring story of recovery, garnered support among voters across the political spectrum. R. 545–56. Ted Larson, however, was popular amongst his constituents, and the race between Waters and Larson was a statistical dead heat during much of the election season. R. 555–56.

Five days before the election, Waters and Larson participated in a final debate. R. 557–691. During the debate, the moderator asked Waters the following question: "Ms. Waters, can you talk about your personal struggles, how they have changed your life, and what impact, if any, they may have on you as a United States Senator?" R. 600. Waters discussed her struggles during her college years, calling it the "darkest period" of her life. R. 601. Waters described her arrest in 1994 for DUI and possession of a controlled substance as "rock bottom" and a "wake-up call." R. 601–02. She told the moderator that her struggles taught her accountability, hard work, and perseverance and "how to cope with adversity and life's difficult challenges." R. 601–605.

Five days later, Waters won the election. R. 610.

C. Harrison's attack on Waters

Harrison operates a well-known blog, www.justtellthetruth.com. R. 700–705, 747–63. A select few have called Harrison a champion for truth, but many consider him a bully who relies on questionable sources and stretches the truth to serve his own agenda. R. 707, 710.

After the debate between Waters and Larson, Harrison, who apparently holds some long-standing grudge against Waters, posted the following message on his website:

> [W]hile at Stanford, Kirsten engaged in highly questionable conduct. During our last two years at Stanford, Kirsten was engaged to a mutual friend (who I will not reveal at this time). Kirsten suddenly broke off the engagement and admitted to having a lengthy affair with another man throughout the duration of the relationship. I will soon release a letter Kirsten wrote to our friend admitting the affair. The whole truth is that Kirsten reluctantly sought treatment — only to save herself — while repeatedly lying to and eventually betraying a very decent man.
>
> While at Stanford, Kirsten performed poorly in her studies. Kirsten was not a good student, and I doubt she has the abilities to effectively serve in any elected capacity. I don't know how she was accepted by the University of California-Berkeley School of Law. I do know this: her dad is one of Berkeley's most generous donors. Kirsten's admission to Berkeley wasn't about merit. It was about favoritism and money.

R. 901–903.

Harrison's vicious attack on Waters severely harmed Waters' reputation, and she was forced to resign from her Senate seat. R. 559–561, 1661–69. Waters filed this complaint to recover for Harrison's false, defamatory statements. R. 1–12.

II. PROCEDURAL BACKGROUND

This matter was tried before the Honorable Helen Montana in the United States District Court for the Northern District of California. The trial court heard testimony from Waters, Harrison, Phillip Berman, Waters' former fiancé, and Stephanie Morris, a former campaign worker for Waters. Waters also presented copies of her application for admission to Berkeley Law School, her admissions file from Berkeley Law School, and transcripts from both Stanford and Berkeley, which were admitted by consent of the parties.

The trial court categorized Harrison's statements with respect to the content: statements about Waters' educational history and statements about Waters' relationship with Berman. The trial court found that the statements about Waters' educational history were not actionable because they were statements of opinion rather than fact. R. 3400–3403. The trial court found that the statements about Waters' relationship with former fiancé Berman were untrue statements of fact, but were not actionable because they were not made with actual malice. R. 3404–05.

This appeal followed. R. 3450.

III. STANDARD OF REVIEW

While a trial court's findings of fact at a bench trial are reviewed for clear error, conclusions of law are reviewed de novo. *United Steel Workers Local 12-369 v. United Steel Workers Int'l*, 728 F.3d 1107, 1114 (9th Cir. 2013). This case involves an appeal of both the trial court's findings of fact and its conclusions of law.

IV. ISSUES PRESENTED FOR REVIEW

A. Whether the trial court erred in finding that Harrison's statements about Waters' education background are non-actionable opinion when Harrison intended the statements to be interpreted as facts and the context shows the seriousness of the statements?

B. Whether the trial court erred in finding that Harrison's allegations of an affair by Waters were not made with actual malice when Harrison did not investigate the truthfulness of his allegations but relied on a letter he has been unable to produce and has not seen in 10 or 15 years?

V. SUMMARY OF THE ARGUMENT

The trial court erred in finding Harrison's allegations that Waters was not a good student, performed poorly at Stanford, and obtained admission to Berkeley Law School because of favoritism and money were opinion, not actionable statements of fact. Courts use a totality of the circumstances test in determining whether a statement is one of fact or opinion. The language of the statement and the context in which it was rendered are used to determine whether a reasonable fact finder could conclude that the published statement implies a provably false factual assertion.

When viewed in the context in which they were made, Harrison's allegations about Waters' educational background are expressions of fact, and Harrison indisputably intended that readers understand them as such. His statements are not "loose, figurative or hyperbolic" expressions of opinion, but are capable of being proved — academic records, testimony from Waters' professors and others at Stanford can prove if Waters "performed poorly" or was "not a good student." A student who receives As and Bs in her classes cannot be said to have "performed poorly," while a student who receives Ds and Fs is "not a good student." While the terms "poorly" and "good" could be interpreted subjectively, statements that could otherwise be interpreted subjectively are actionable when the context of the surrounding statements reinforces the seriousness of the allegation. That is the situation here. And Harrison's objective intent cannot be questioned. Harrison himself testified that he intended readers of his blog to believe Waters was not a good student and lacks the mental acuity to serve as a United States senator. The trial court's finding that Harrison's statements about Waters' educational background are unactionable opinions should be reversed.

The trial court also erred in finding that Harrison's allegations of an affair by Waters were not made with actual malice. The test for malice is subjective, meaning that to find malice, the fact finder must conclude that the defendant had "serious doubts" about the truthfulness of his statements or had "obvious reason" to suspect his statements are untrue. Additionally, evidence that the defendant failed to investigate the truthfulness of a statement or harbors ill will toward the plaintiff are circumstantial evidence that may be used to prove actual malice.

Harrison knew or should have known that his allegations of an affair were untrue and should have investigated before publishing such serious allegations. The sole bases for Harrison's contention that Waters engaged in an affair were a nearly 20-year-old letter from Waters that Harrison had not reviewed in 10 or 15 years, which Harrison was unable to produce at trial, and statements made to him by Mr. Berman — again, nearly 20 years ago — that Ms. Waters *might* have cheated on Mr. Berman.

The existence of the letter is in question as Harrison has been unable to produce the letter. However, even if the letter did exist, Harrison did not review the letter to ascertain its exact contents before alleging that Waters is a cheater. He did not contact Mr. Berman. He did not contact Ms. Waters. He did not attempt to contact the man with whom Waters allegedly engaged in the affair.

For reasons unknown, Harrison has an extreme dislike of Waters, which is further evidence of the actual malice with which he acted in publishing statements about Waters' relationship with Berman. Harrison has admitted that he "wouldn't trust [Waters] any more than [he would trust his] worst enemy." This anger and hostility toward Waters, coupled with the other evidence presented at trial, support the conclusion that Harrison's untrue statements about Waters' relationship with Berman were made with actual malice. The trial court's finding should be reversed.

VI. ARGUMENT AND CITATION TO AUTHORITY

A party seeking damages for defamation must prove the following: (1) publication; (2) of a false statement; (3) that is defamatory; (4) unprivileged; and (5) results in damages. *Ringler Associates Inc., v. Maryland Casualty Co.*, 96 Cal. Rptr. 2d 136, 148 (Cal. Ct. App. 2000). The level of fault required — negligence or actual malice — depends on whether the party alleging defamation is deemed an all-public, limited-purpose public, or private figure. *McGarry v. University of San Diego*, 64 Cal. Rptr. 3d 467, 479–480 (Cal. Ct. App. 2007). There is no dispute between the parties that Harrison's statements about Waters were "published" or that Harrison is not protected by any privilege that would prevent Waters from recovering from him. Further, the trial court expressly found that Waters was substantially damaged as a result of Harrison's statements and Harrison has not appealed that finding. Thus, the first, fourth, and fifth elements of a defamation claim have been established with respect to both the statements about Waters' educational background and the statements about Waters' prior relationship with Berman.

A. The trial court erred in finding that Harrison's statements about Waters' educational background are non-actionable opinion.

The trial court found that, with respect to statements about her educational background, Waters cannot prove the second element of her defamation claim because Harrison's statements were not assertions of fact, but opinions protected by the First Amendment to the United States Constitution.

Statements are defamatory if they are "provably false," and a "statement of *fact* rather than opinion." *Ringler*, 96 Cal. Rptr. 2d at 149 (emphasis in original). Courts use a "totality of the circumstances" test when determining if a statement is actionable fact or non-actionable opinion. *McGarry*, 64 Cal. Rptr. 3d at 479. The language of the statements and context within which they were rendered are relevant in determining whether "a reasonable fact finder could conclude that the published statements imply a provably false factual assertion." *Id.*; *see also Copp v. Paxton*, 52 Cal. Rptr. 2d 831, 838 (Cal. Ct. App. 1996).

"Whether published material is reasonably susceptible of an interpretation which implies a provably false assertion of fact . . . must be resolved by considering whether the reasonable or 'average' reader would so interpret the material." *Coach v. San Juan Unified School Dist.*, 33 Cal. App. 4th 1491, 1500 (Cal. Ct. App. 1995) (citations omitted). The average reader is "a reasonable member of the audience to which the material was originally addressed." *Id.*

Importantly, an opinion-based statement is actionable "if it implies the allegation of undisclosed defamatory facts as the basis for the opinion." *Id.* (*quoting Okun v. Superior Court*, 175 Cal. Rptr. 157, 162 (Cal. Ct. App. 1981)). The implied defamatory facts "must themselves be true." *Ringler*, 96 Cal. Rptr. 2d at 149; *see also Eisenberg v. Alameda Newspapers, Inc.*, 88 Cal. Rptr. 2d 802, 821 (Cal. Ct. App. 1999) Furthermore, even if the publisher of an alleged defamatory statement sets forth specific facts forming the basis of an opinion, "if those facts are either incorrect or incomplete, or if the person's assessment of them is erroneous, the statement may still imply a false assertion of fact." *Ringler*, 96 Cal.Rptr.2d at 149. Categorizing otherwise-defamatory statements as opinion "does not dispel these implications, and such statements may be actionable." *Id.* The dispositive question "is whether a reasonable factfinder could conclude that published statements *imply* an assertion of defamatory fact." *Id.* (emphasis in original); *see also Milkovich* 497 U.S. at 18–20.

The dispositive question before the trial court is "whether a reasonable factfinder could conclude that the published statements imply a provably false factual assertion. *Moyer v. Amador Valley Joint Union High School Dist.*, 225 Cal. App. 3d 720 (1990). That question is not "whether the statements were *actually* true or false" which is a question for the fact finder but, rather, "whether the statements contain *provably* false factual assertions and thus fall outside the protection of the First Amendment." *Id.* at 725 n.2 (emphasis in original).[49]

The court should consider three questions in reaching its conclusion: (1) whether the statement is "the sort of loose, figurative or hyperbolic language which would negate the impression that the writer was [seriously maintaining the truth of the statement]"; (2) whether the "general tenor" of the statement negates the impression that the writer is serious about the truth of the statement; and (3) whether the statement is "sufficiently factual to be susceptible of being proved true or false." *Edwards v. Hall*, 234 Cal. App. 3d 886, 903 (1992) (citation omitted). Thus, if a statement cannot "reasonably be interpreted as stating actual facts," it is not actionable. *Id.* at 902.

The court should apply a "totality of the circumstances" test and consider "the nature and meaning of the language used, including the verifiability of the statements, and the context in which the statements appeared." *Moyer*, 225 Cal. App. 3d at 725. A statement "phrased" as an opinion may still be understood as a factual assertion. *Id.* at 723 n.1.

In *Edwards*, the California Court of Appeals held that a television host's statement

---

[49] The trial court did not even reach the second question — that is, whether the statements are actually false — because it found that Harrison's statements about Waters's education history did not contain provably false factual assertions.

that the head of the NAACP in Hollywood was an "extortionist" was actionable and not merely an opinion. 234 Cal. App. 3d at 903. The court noted that while the accusation alone might be hyperbolic, the statement, "[t]aken in the context of [the defendant's] surrounding statements" "reinforced" the seriousness of the allegation that the plaintiff was an extortionist. *Id.*

Similarly, in *Widener v. Pacific Gas & Electric Co.*, 75 Cal. App. 3d 415 (1978) (overruled on other grounds), the defendant's allegation that the plaintiff produced a documentary full of "halftruths" and "innuendos" and that the plaintiff surreptitiously taped the defendant and dubbed the tape was deemed actionable. More recently, the California Court of Appeals upheld the actionability of an allegation that priest became involved in parishioner's life only "to help himself," finding that the statement was a provable factual assertion. *Gallagher v. Connell*, 123 Cal. App. 4th 1260, 1270 (2005).

Cases from other jurisdictions involving political figures also show why Harrison's statements about Waters are actionable. *See Newman v. Delahunty*, 293 N.J. Super 491 (1994) (allegations that politician was corrupt, used office for personal gain by awarding township contracts to his business, used township funds for personal investments, and funneled funds to friends and family members were actionable factual assertions, not opinions); *Nevada Indep. Broadcasting Corp. v. Allen*, 99 Nev. 404 (1983) (statements that gubernatorial candidate's election campaign bounced a check, coupled with insinuation that candidate was not honorable and would not be able to properly handle state funds were found to be actionable factual assertions).

With respect to Waters' educational history, Harrison said Waters "performed poorly in her studies," and was "not a good student." He alleged Waters' "admission to Berkeley wasn't about merit. It was about favoritism and money."

Harrison himself testified that he intended readers of his blog to believe Waters was not a good student and lacks the mental acuity to serve as a United States senator. Harrison also testified that he wanted his readers to believe Waters, though a woman, is part of the "good old boys" political network and could not effectively represent average citizens because she comes from a background of — in Harrison's words — "power and privilege." At trial, Harrison testified as follows:

Q: Now Mr. Harrison, you intended visitors to your website who read your posts about Ms. Waters to believe that she's not very bright, didn't you?

A: Yes, of course I did.

Q: And why did you want people to think that?

A: Because I don't think Kirsten is smart enough to be a senator.

Q: And you wanted your readers to believe Ms. Waters isn't smart enough to be a senator, didn't you?

A: Yes.

Q: And you wanted them to think that so they wouldn't vote for her, didn't you?

A: Yes.

Q: And why did you say that Ms. Waters was admitted to Berkeley Law
            School because of favoritism and money?

A: Because she was.

Q: But why did you want to convey that information to your readers?

A: Because Kirsten's never worked for anything. She's gotten where she's
            gotten in life because of her family's power and influence. Average
            citizens can't relate to that, and someone who comes from that type of
            background can't fairly represent average people. Through the cam-
            paign, Kirsten made it seem like she had a "rags to riches" type of
            story. Like she'd worked so hard to overcome her past, and studied so
            hard to get into law school, and risen to become this great person and
            leader. Americans respond to those types of stories because we'd all
            like to think that America is a place where you can come from nothing
            and make something of yourself through hard work. But that's not
            Kirsten's real story. She came from a world of privilege — and the
            public had a right to know that. And that's what I told them. The truth.

R. 2953–54, 57.

The context in which Harrison's statements were made also shows that the
statements were not asserted as Harrison's opinions but, rather, Harrison intended
them to be understood as facts. These statements are not "loose, figurative or
hyperbolic" and are capable of being proved — academic records, testimony from
Waters' professors and others at Stanford can prove if Waters "performed poorly" or
was "not a good student." While the terms "poorly" and "good" could be interpreted
subjectively, this case is akin to *Edwards*, where the court concluded that an otherwise
hyperbolic statement was actionable when the context of the surrounding statements
"reinforced" the seriousness of the allegation. The "general tenor" of Harrison's
statements and the context in which they were made does not negate but rather
reinforces the impression that Harrison intended the statements to be understood as
factual assertions. And, the statements are capable of being proved true or false. A
student who receives As and Bs in her classes cannot be said to have "performed
poorly," while a student who receives Ds and Fs is "not a good student."

And Harrison's statement that Waters' admission was "not about merit" is certainly
provable as true or false. Either Waters was qualified for admission to Berkeley (i.e.
she met the academic standards) or she was not. An examination of Waters' application
to Berkeley and her Berkeley admissions file will show whether she was properly
admitted or whether, as Harrison has told the world, her admission was based on some
factor other than academic merit.

Moreover, Harrison should not be able to hide behind his "opinion" when he knew
or had "serious doubts" that the statements he made were untruthful and he failed to
investigate to determine their truthfulness before making them. Harrison himself
admitted that he intended his readers to accept his statements as those of fact. R.
2953–54. And, even worse, while contending Waters was "not a good student," Harrison
admitted that Waters was "really driven and got awesome grades in most of her other
courses." R. 689. Incredibly, while contending Waters was not a good student who

could not have obtained admission to law school without political influence, Harrison admitted he knew Waters "got really high scores on the [LSAT] practice tests." R. 692. And, in perhaps his most damaging admission, Harrison actually benefitted from Waters' intelligence and drive — he admitted that he studied for the LSAT with Waters and she "actually helped [Harrison] improve [his LSAT] score by about five points." R. 694.

When asked about the discrepancy between his statement that Waters was not a good student and his admission that she was "really driven," "got awesome grades" in many of her courses, and achieved "really high scores" on the LSAT, Harrison could offer no explanation:

Q: So if you knew Ms. Waters was a very bright student who did very well in many courses, but had gotten a C is a very difficult chemistry course that many students struggle with, why did you falsely tell the world that Ms. Waters wasn't a good student?

A: Because I don't think she's very smart or "very bright" as you said.

Q: But you just told me she did very well in many of her classes at Stanford, did you not.

A: Yes.

Q: And you knew she had done well in many classes when you told the world that she wasn't a good student.

A: I knew that overall, her grades at Stanford were good.

R. 2989–90.

While the Court did not consider this evidence because it found the statements about Waters' education background were non-actionable opinion, the context in which the statements were made is evidence that Harrison intended the statements to be received as factual assertions, not his opinions. The trial court's finding that Harrison's statements about Waters' educational background are non-actionable opinions is erroneous and should be reversed.

B. The trial court erred in finding that Harrison's allegations of an affair by Waters were not made with actual malice.

The trial court found that, with respect to statements about her relationship with Berman, Waters failed to prove that Harrison made those statements with the requisite level of intent — actual malice.

Waters does not challenge the district court's ruling that she is an all-purpose public figure. Because she is deemed to be an all-purpose public figure, Waters concedes that she must prove Harrison's statements were made with actual malice, which means that the statements must have been made with either actual knowledge they were false or with "reckless disregard of whether [they were] false or not." *McGarry v. University of San Diego*, 64 Cal. Rptr. 3d 467, 480 (Cal. Ct. App. 2007) (*quoting Reader's Digest Ass'n v. Superior Court*, 208 Cal. Rptr. 137, 149 (Cal. 1984)). Waters does, however, challenge the trial court's factual finding that Harrison did not act with actual malice in claiming that Waters had an affair when she was engaged to former fiancé Berman.

The test for malice is subjective, meaning that to find malice, the fact finder must conclude that the "defendant in fact entertained serious doubts about the truth of his publication." *Reader's Digest Ass'n, Inc. v. Superior Court*, 37 Cal. 3d 244, 256 (1984). A defendant, cannot escape liability, however, simply by testifying that the publication was made in good faith. *Id.* at 257. Where a defendant's statements are based on a fabrication or where the defendant has obvious reasons to doubt the accuracy of a source, malice may be proven. *Id.* Similarly, a failure to investigate the truthfulness of statements and anger toward the plaintiff are circumstantial evidence that a publisher had "serious doubts regarding the truth of his publication." *Id.* at 258.

Actual malice may be shown where the maker of the statements had "serious doubts" about their truthfulness. *Copp*, 52 Cal. Rptr. 2d at 844–845 (*quoting St. Amant v. Thompson*, 390 U.S. 727, 731 (1968)). While circumstantial evidence can be used to prove actual malice, including "anger and hostility toward the plaintiff," the evidence must "permit the conclusion that the defendant actually had a high degree of awareness of . . . probable falsity." *Copp*, 52 Cal. Rptr. 2d at 845 (*quoting St. Amant*, 390 U.S. at 731); *McGarry*, 64 Cal. Rptr. 3d at 480 (*quoting Harte-Hanks Communications v. Connaughton*, 491 U.S. 657, 688 (1989)).

Having "serious doubts" about the truth of a publication is generally sufficient to establish actual malice, which may be proven by circumstantial evidence. *Copp*, 52 Cal. Rptr. 2d at 844–845 (*quoting St. Amant v. Thompson*, 390 U.S. 727, 731 (1968)). For example, "failure to investigate, anger and hostility toward the plaintiff, reliance upon sources known to be unreliable, or known to be biased against the plaintiff" may all establish that the publisher acted with actual malice. *Id.* Where the evidence " 'permit[s] the conclusion that the defendant actually had a high degree of awareness of . . . probable falsity,' " actual malice is proven. *McGarry*, 64 Cal. Rptr. 3d at 480 (*quoting Harte-Hanks Communications v. Connaughton*, 491 U.S. 657, 688 (1989)).

In cases similar to this one, courts have frequently found evidence of actual malice. For example, in *Young v. Gannett Satellite Information Network, Inc.*, 734 F.3d 544 (6th Cir. 2013), a newspaper published a story alleging that a police officer had sex with a woman while the officer was on duty. *Id.* at 546. The newspaper failed to ask the officer for comment or attempt to ascertain the truth of the woman's allegation that she engaged in sex with the officer, an allegation that an arbitrator had previous determined was not supported by evidence. *Id.* The Sixth Circuit Court of Appeals upheld a jury's finding of malice in the publication of a story about a police officer. *Id.* at 547.

With respect to the statements about Waters' past relationship, Harrison has alleged Waters sent Harrison a letter in which she admitted she had an affair while engaged to Berman. Harrison has been unable to produce this letter and failed to confirm that he still had the letter, or confirm the exact language in the letter, before he published defamatory statements accusing Waters of engaging in an affair. At trial, Harrison testified:

Q: So you say Ms. Waters sent you a letter or wrote you a letter when you were at Stanford where she told you she did cheat on Mr. Berman, she was very sorry, and she needed your advice on what she should do?

A: Yes.

Q: When do you claim she sent you this letter?

A: Sometime our junior year.

Q: Do you remember when during that year?

A: No.

Q: Do you know if it was in the fall, or winter, or spring?

A: No, I don't remember.

Q: So this very important piece of evidence that supports your claim that my client cheated on her ex-fiancé and is a very bad person, you don't have any idea when you received that, other than that you got it sometime your junior year? And did you tell Mr. Berman about this letter?

A: I don't know. I don't remember.

Q: Now this letter you claim you got from Ms. Waters, you got that letter nearly 20 years ago, didn't you?

A: Yes.

Q: And do you remember any specifics about the contents of the letter?

A: Just that Kirsten admitted she had cheated on Phil.

Q: And you thought you still had the letter when you told the world that my client was a cheater?

A: Yes.

Q: Did you go look at that letter, to make sure you knew exactly what it said, before you posted the statement that my client is a cheater on your website?

A: No.

Q: And how many times in the last 20 years have you looked at that letter?

A: Once, maybe.

Q: Approximately when did that happen? Recently, or was that a while ago?

A: Maybe 10 or 15 years ago.

Q: So you accused my client of cheating on her ex-fiancé based on statements she allegedly made in a letter you hadn't look at in 10 or 15 years.

A: And based on what Phil had told me — that he suspected that she was cheating on him.

Q: But Phil never told you he was certain Ms. Waters was cheating on him, did he?

A: He said that he thought she was.

Q: And did Ms. Waters tell you the name of the man she allegedly cheated with?

A: I think the guy's first name, and maybe his last name, were in the letter.

Q: But you didn't look at the letter again before you made your blog post, did you?

A: No, I didn't.

Q: And since you didn't look at the letter again, you didn't attempt to contact the guy Ms. Waters had allegedly cheated with to determine if that was true?

A: No, I didn't.

Q: And you didn't call up Mr. Berman and try to confirm that Ms. Waters had cheated on him before you posted statements about my client on your website?

A: No.

Q: And you didn't call Ms. Waters about that either, did you?

A: No.

Q: Now did you ever have a conversation with Ms. Waters about the contents of this letter that you claim you received from her?

A: Maybe, but not that I remember.

Q: So the sum total of evidence you have that Ms. Waters cheated on Mr. Berman was a letter and Mr. Berman telling you he thought Ms. Waters might have cheated on him?

A: Yes.

R. 3125–29.

Harrison did not contact Waters or Berman prior to posting the statements to verify their truthfulness. Further, Harrison apparently failed to even attempt to identify the man with whom Waters allegedly had this affair, much less contact that man to confirm the truthfulness of the allegation. This is evidence from which it may be inferred that Harrison acted with malice both because he knew or had serious doubts about the truthfulness of the allegations and because he failed to investigate his allegations before publishing them.

For unknown reasons, Harrison also harbors anger and hostility against Waters that is circumstantial evidence of malice. Harrison testified about his belief that Waters "was always looking out for herself" and would "do anything to . . . look good in other people's eyes." R. 801. Berman also testified about Harrison's extreme dislike of Waters. Harrison has stated he "wouldn't trust [Waters] any more than I would my worst enemy." R. 874. And Harrison confirmed at trial that he still does not trust Waters and "[does not] believe she is a good or trustworthy person." R. 3063. This anger and hostility toward Waters, coupled with the other evidence presented at trial, support the conclusion that Harrison's untrue statements about Waters' relationship with Berman were made with actual malice. The trial court's finding otherwise is an abuse of discretion and should be reversed.

VII. CONCLUSION

The trial court erred in finding that Harrison's allegations that Waters was not a good student, performed poorly at Stanford, and obtained admission to Berkeley Law School because of favoritism and money were not actionable statements of fact. The context in which Harrison's statements were made shows that they were expressions of fact, and Harrison unquestionably intended that readers understand them as such. Academic records and testimony from Waters' professors at Stanford can prove if Waters "performed poorly" or was "not a good student." Similarly, Waters' admissions file from Stanford and testimony from admissions officers will show whether Waters met admissions standards at Berkeley Law School. And Harrison himself testified that he intended readers of his blog to believe Waters was not a good student, lacks the mental acuity to serve as a United States senator, comes from a powerful family, and cannot relate to the average California citizen. Therefore, Harrison's statements were actionable factual assertions. The trial court's finding that Harrison's statements about Waters' educational background are unactionable opinions should be reversed.

The trial court also erred in finding that Harrison's allegations of an affair by Waters were not made with actual malice. Circumstantial evidence offered by Waters shows that Harrison knew or should have known that his statements were not true and should have investigated before publishing such serious allegations. Harrison failed to review a letter her claims was sent by Waters admitting to an affair to ascertain its exact contents before alleging that Waters is a cheater. He did not contact Mr. Berman. He did not contact Ms. Waters. He did not attempt to contact the man with whom Waters allegedly engaged in the affair. Harrison harbors anger toward Waters, further evidence of the actual malice with which he acted in publishing statements about Waters' relationship with Berman. The overwhelming evidence presented at trial proves that the trial court abused its discretion in finding that Harrison's statements were not made with actual malice. The trial court's finding should be reversed.

(HARRISON'S RESPONSE)

Case No. 13-16352

IN THE UNITED STATES COURT OF APPEALS
FOR THE NINTH CIRCUIT

KIRSTEN WATERS,

Petitioner,

v.

SIMON HARRISON,

Respondent.

On appeal from the United States District Court for the
Northern District of California

BRIEF OF RESPONDENT SIMON HARRISON

STATEMENT OF FACTS

A. BACKGROUND

Plaintiff Kirsten Waters ("Waters"), who attended Standard University and the
University of California-Berkeley School of Law, is an attorney and former candidate
for the United States Senate. During her campaign against then-incumbent senator
Robert Larson ("Larson"), Waters acknowledged that she battled alcohol and prescription drug abuse while in college. In fact, Waters openly discussed these struggles
throughout the election, and her story of recovery inspired voters across the political
spectrum.

Unfortunately, Waters lied about her past. During her final debate with Larson,
Waters claimed that, while in college, she was arrested for Driving under the Influence
of Alcohol and Possession of a Controlled Substance. Waters also stated that, as part
of her plea bargain, she was ordered to serve thirty (30) days in the Palo Alto County
Jail, and spend ninety (90) days in a residential treatment facility. Before a sold-out
crowd at the Shrine Auditorium in Los Angeles — and a nationally-televised audience
— Waters stated as follows:

> As you know, I've been very forthcoming about my struggle — many years ago
> — with alcohol and prescription medication. It was the darkest period of my
> life. Perhaps the worst moment came on August 2, 1994, the summer of my
> junior year at Stanford when, due to a regrettable mistake in judgment, I was
> responsible for Driving under the Influence of Alcohol and possessing an
> unauthorized controlled substance. For me, this was rock bottom and a
> wake-up call that I had to made immediate changes in my life. My first step
> was to accept responsibility for my actions, which I did. After being ordered
> to serve 30 days in the Palo Alto, County Jail, followed by a 90-day stay at a

residential treatment facility, I continued the life-changing process of taking my life back. Looking back, I don't know if I would be here tonight without having faced the consequences of my actions. From this experience, I learned what it means to truly struggle in life. I learned how to cope with adversity and life's difficult challenges. I came to know the value of accountability, hard work, and perseverance. These are values, in my opinion, to which all of California's voters, regardless of background or political party, can relate.

Five days later, Waters defeated Larson by 314 votes, one of the closest elections in California history. One week later Waters resigned, admitting that these statements were "inaccurate."

Defendant Simon Harrison ("Harrison") operates www.justtellthetruth.com, a blog dedicated to exposing corruption and dishonesty in all areas of public life. Harrison met Waters while they were both undergraduates at Stanford, and they shared a friendship throughout their undergraduate career.

Harrison played a substantial role in exposing the truth about Waters' criminal history. Shortly after watching the final debate, Harrison posted the following statement on www.justtellthetruth.com:

> [Kirsten] was neither incarcerated nor ordered to spend even a single day in a residential treatment program. After pleading guilty, Kirsten was sentenced to 90 days probation and 100 hours of community service. Additionally, as part of the plea deal, the controlled substance charge was dropped. Kirsten only sought residential treatment because her parents threatened to stop paying her tuition at Stanford.

Harrison also provided a letter from Waters' former probation officer, dated November 10, 1994, which he posted on www.justtellthetruth.com, and which corroborated his statement.

In addition, Harrison claimed, while a student with Waters at Standard, that Waters had substandard academic abilities and was unfaithful to her former fiancée, Phillip Berman. Waters resigned shortly after Harrison's statements were made public.

B. The Trial Testimony

1. The statements about Waters' criminal history.

At trial, Harrison testified that he "knew Kirsten was lying" about the details of her criminal history. Harrison testified that "she never served a day in jail and wasn't ordered to spend time in a treatment center." On cross examination, Harrison did admit that Waters may have "forgot[ten] the details of her sentence," but Waters offered no evidence at trial to support that assertion, or that Harrison's claims were untrue. As Harrison's testified, "she was so far off that I could only come to one conclusion: she intentionally lied."

Waters' former campaign strategist, Stephanie Morris, also testified that Waters "basically concocted the scheme to lie about her criminal history." Morris stated that Waters was "shocked that Simon remembered the truth, and even more shocked that he would expose her."

2. The statements about Waters' educational history.

Harrison stated on his blog that Waters "performed poorly in her studies" at Stanford and "was not a good student." At trial, Harrison testified that he had taken organic chemistry and Latin with Waters. Despite spending "hours tutoring her in both classes," Harrison testified that "she got a C in both classes," and "had no clue what was going on." Harrison did acknowledge that Waters "was really driven and got awesome grades in most of her other courses."

Ultimately, though, based on his personal experience with Waters, Harrison formed the opinion that Waters did not possess the qualifications for admission to the University of California-Berkeley School of Law, and likely received special consideration because her father is a well-known donor to the law school. As Harrison testified at trial, "she wasn't a good student and that's the way I see it."

3. The statements about Waters' alleged infidelity.

Harrison also stated on www.justtellthetruth.com that, while in college, Waters was unfaithful to her former fiancée, Phillip Berman, who was a mutual friend at the time. Harrison testified at trial that "Phil came to me and was really concerned that she was cheating on him," and that "he seemed pretty sure." He also testified that "it didn't surprise me," because "Kirsten was always looking out for herself and would do anything to make herself look good in other peoples' eyes."

C. The Trial Court's Decision

1. The statements regarding Waters's criminal history.

The trial court held that the statements regarding Waters' criminal history were not actionable. Specifically, Harrison's testimony, the November 10, 1994 letter, and Waters' acknowledgement that her statements were inaccurate "suggest[ed] that Harrison's statements were true." Because truth is an absolute defense to defamation, the trial court held that the statements could not support a defamation claim.

2. The statements regarding Waters' educational history.

With respect to the statements regarding Waters' educational history, the trial court found that they were constitutionally-protected opinion and therefore not actionable. The statement that Waters was not a "good student," or without the "abilities to serve in any elected capacity," reflected Harrison's opinion of her qualifications, not a demonstrably false assertion of fact.

The court also found that, even if the statements did imply the assertion of defamatory facts, Waters had not adduced sufficient evidence to demonstrate by a preponderance of the evidence that the statements were false. While Waters did produce her undergraduate transcripts and standardized test scores, which showed that her qualifications "were slightly above the average grades and test scores for admitted applicant," she did admit that her father was a "big donor at Berkeley." Waters' transcripts also confirmed Harrison's claim that she received a grade of "C" in both organic chemistry and Latin. Furthermore, Waters did not introduce testimony or other evidence from admissions officials at the University of California-Berkeley stating that her admission was solely merit-based. Based on these facts, the trial court held that Waters had not satisfied her burden of proving that the statements about her educational history were false.

3. The statements regarding infidelity.

The trial court held that the allegations of infidelity were provably false and constituted defamation *per se*. Importantly, however, Waters — a public figure — could not demonstrate that the statements were made with actual malice. The court relied on the testimony of Phillip Berman, who stated that he "mentioned to Simon . . . that she seemed to be acting differently toward me and not wanting to spend as much time together." The Court found that these statements "provided at least a colorable basis upon which Harrison could believe that Waters had or was engaged in infidelity." Because Waters could not demonstrate — by clear and convincing evidence — that Harrison knew the statements were false, she could not prevail.

PROCEDURAL HISTORY

This matter was tried before the Hon. Helen Montana, United States District Judge for the Northern District of California. After a trial on the merits, Judge Montana concluded that the statements regarding Waters' criminal history were probably true, and therefore not actionable. Judge Montana also held that Waters had failed to demonstrate that the statements regarding her educational history were false. With respect to the statements alleging infidelity, Judge Montana held that Waters failed to demonstrate that Harrison acted with malice. This appeal follows.

STANDARD OF REVIEW

This appeal involves mixed questions of law and fact, although the factual issues predominate. The trial court's findings of fact are subject to review for clear error, while the legal conclusions are reviewed *de novo*. *See United Steel Workers Local 12-369 v. United Steel Workers Int'l*, 728 F.3d 1107, 1114 (9th Cir. 2013).

SUMMARY OF THE ARGUMENT

Harrison does not — as Appellant's counsel would have this court believe — harbor "anger and hostility" toward Waters. Instead, he believes that politicians should be truthful, and that individuals should be entitled to express their subjective, albeit hyperbolic, opinions on matters of public concern. That is precisely what Harrison did here. And the trial court correctly held that the statements posted on www.justtellthetruth.com were protected by the First Amendment, and corroborated by Waters' own admission that her statements at the final debate were "inaccurate." In other words, Waters was not the victim of false, injurious, and defamatory statements. She misrepresented her criminal history in front of sold-out crowd and a nationally televised audience, and got caught. Exposing the truth about Waters is not grounds for a defamation action. It is the essence of what the First Amendment was designed to protect.

Those protections also encompass an individual's opinion. Harrison's statements that Waters was "not a good student," "performed poorly," and benefitted from her father's status as a big donor at Berkeley, at Stanford are precisely the type of statements that this Court held are constitutionally-protected opinion. *See, e.g., Lewis v. Time, Inc.*, 710 F.2d 549, 554 (9th Cir. 1993) (statements that someone is a "shady practitioner," "crook," "crooked politician," "creepazoid attorney" and "loser wannabe lawyer" are not actionable). And Harrison had a factual basis to make this assertion — the evidence at trial demonstrated that Waters received a grade of "C" in two courses that she took with Harrison. This does not mean, of course, that Waters is "not a good student." It shows, as Appellant admits, that these words "could be interpreted subjectively," making them opinions, not provably false facts.

To be sure, the trial court gave Appellant the benefit of every doubt and, contrary to Appellant's assertions, held that these statements could conceivably imply the false assertion of facts. Appellant, however, could not satisfy her burden of proving falsity. As the trial court noted, even if these statements were provably false, Appellant failed to adduce "any facts showing, by a preponderance of the evidence, that she was, in fact, a "good student." Appellant confirms, rather than refutes, this finding in her brief, focusing on what Waters *could* prove or *will* show in demonstrate falsity, such as testimony from Appellant's professors at Stanford. But Waters did not introduce *any* of this evidence at trial. And the trial court correctly concluded that what she *did* introduce — a standardized test score and overall grade point average — was "insufficient to conclude, by a preponderance of the evidence, that Harrison's statements were false."

In addition, Appellant did not satisfy her burden of demonstrating that Harrison published these statements with actual malice, particularly concerning the statements about Appellant's alleged infidelity while in college. Harrison based these statements on a conversation with Appellant's former fiancée, Phillip Berman, who approached Harrison at the time and expressed concerns that Appellant had, in fact, been unfaithful. Thus, Harrison did not make these statements knowing that they were false, nor did Appellant demonstrate — by clear and convincing evidence — that Harrison entertained serious doubts about their truth. As the trial court found, Harrison had a "colorable basis upon which . . . [to] believe that Waters had or was engaged in infidelity."

Ultimately, it is Appellant, not Harrison, who harbors "anger and hostility." Those feelings do not justify a claim for defamation, and certainly do not warrant reversal of the trial court's well-reasoned decision. Harrison respectfully requests that this Court affirm the trial court's ruling.

ARGUMENT

POINT I

APPELLANT FAILED TO DEMONSTRATE THAT THE STATEMENTS REGARDING HER EDUCATIONAL HISTORY WERE FALSE.

The statements about Appellant's educational history are constitutionally-protected opinion, and therefore not actionable.[50] To the extent, however, that the statements

---

[50] Appellant concedes that the statements regarding her criminal history are not actionable. As stated

implied the false assertion of facts, Appellant did not prove by a preponderance of the evidence that they were false.

A. The Statements Are Constitutionally Protected Opinion

Statements are not actionable if, based on the totality of the circumstances, a reasonable fact-finder would not interpret these statements as conveying a "false factual imputation." *Manufactured Home Communities, Inc. v. County of San Diego*, 544 F.3d 959, 964 (9th Cir. 2008). It is well-settled that, "[a]lthough statements of fact may be actionable as [defamation], statements of opinion are constitutionally protected." *McGarry v. University of San Diego*, 154 Cal.App.4th 97, 112 (2007).

Importantly, California courts have held that statements consisting of "rhetorical hyperbole," or "imaginative expression[s] of . . . contempt," are protected by the First Amendment. *Nygard, Inc. v. Uusi-Kerttula*, 72 Cal.Rptr.3d 210, 226 (Cal. Ct. App. 2008) (citations omitted). For example, in *Moyer v. Amador Valley Joint Union High School Dist.*, the California Court of Appeals held that statements calling the appellant "the worst teacher at FHS" and a "babbler" are not actionable because they can be "reasonably understood only 'as a form of exaggerated expression conveying the student-speaker's disapproval of plaintiff's teaching or speaking style.'" 275 Cal.Rptr 494, 498 (Cal. Ct. App. 1990).

Likewise, statements calling an individual a "whore," and claiming that the individual was "worthless, not a good employee and did not deserve to be working as an EMT," are considered opinion." *Rangel v. American Medical Response West*, 2013 U.S. Dist. LEXIS 59579, . . . (E.D.Cal. April 25, 2013). Also, statements describing a party's lawsuit "as 'stupid,' 'a joke,' 'spurious,' and 'frivolous,' are common characterizations which are nothing more than "the predictable opinion" of one side to the lawsuit." *Ferlauto v. Hamsher*, 74 Cal.App.4th 1394, 1403 (Cal. App. 1999) (*quoting Information Control v. Genesis One Computer Corp.* 611 F.2d 781, 784 (9th Cir.1980)).

Furthermore, where statements are made in an adversarial context, they are more likely to be construed as opinion. *See Ferlauto v. Hamsher*, 74 Cal.App.4th 1394, 1401–02 (Cal. App. 1999). In *Ferlauto*, the California Court of Appeals held as follows:

> Part of the totality of the circumstances used in evaluating the language in question is whether the statements[were made by participants in an adversarial setting. "[W]here potentially defamatory statements are published in a . . . setting in which *the audience may anticipate efforts by the parties to persuade others to their positions by use of epithets, fiery rhetoric or hyperbole, language which generally might be considered as statements of fact may well assume the character of statements of opinion.*"

Id. (*quoting Gregory v. McDonnell Douglas Corp.* 17 Cal.3d 596, 601(Cal. 1976)) (emphasis added). This is particularly true where "a necessarily broad area of discussion without civil responsibility in damages is an indispensable concomitant of the controversy." *Ferlauto*, 74 Cal.App.4th at 1402 (*quoting Gregory*, 17 Cal.3d at 602).

---

above, one week after her victory over Larson, Appellant resigned and admitted the statement she made at the final debate were "inaccurate."

Here, Harrison's statements, claiming that Appellant "performed poorly in her studies," was "not a good student," does not have "the abilities to effectively serve in any elected capacity," and benefitted from "favoritism and money," when admitted to Berkeley, are not actionable. To begin with, the statements are entirely subjective, and the words used are inherently undefinable. For example, opinions as to whether someone is a "good student," or can "effectively serve in an elected capacity," will vary considerably depending on the reader's perception and prior experience. And that will spark a debate among readers or, as in this case, voters. That is precisely the point — these statements are opinions, not actionable facts.

To be sure, Harrison's statements are equivalent to arguments that a movie was "good," that a professional baseball team was "the best ever," or, that an individual "did not deserve to be working as an EMT." 2013 U.S. Dist. LEXIS 59579 . . . at *23. In each of these instances, the speaker is offering a point of view, which readers may disagree with depending on how they define the word "good," of what it means to "effectively serve" as an elected official. This is particularly here considering that Harrison's statements were made in "an adversarial context," where readers could certainly "anticipate efforts by the parties to persuade others to their positions by use of epithets, fiery rhetoric or hyperbole." *Ferlauto* 74 Cal.App.4th at 1401–02 (*quoting Gregory*, 17 Cal.3d 596, 601(Cal. 1976)) (emphasis added).

B. Even if the Statements Implied False Assertions of Fact, Appellant Did Not Demonstrate By a Preponderance of the Evidence that they Were False.

While acknowledging that these statements were non-actionable opinion, the trial court found that they could *conceivably* imply the false assertion of underlying facts. Appellant, however, could not satisfy her burden of demonstrating falsity, which underscores opinion-based nature of these statements. Appellant goes to great lengths in her brief to quote from Harrison's testimony, apparently attempting to unearth the factual underpinning of his statements. What Appellant received, however, was more opinion, not more facts.

For example, under cross examination, Harrison testified that "I don't *think* Kirsten is smart enough to be a senator." Harrison also testified that Appellant had "never worked for anything," and came from a "world of privilege." Furthermore, while acknowledging that Appellant was "really driven," received "awesome grades" in many courses, and a high LSAT score, Harrison maintained that "I don't *think* she's *very* smart or '*very* bright' as you said." On direct examination, however, the evidence revealed that Appellant received a grade of "C" in two courses that she took with Harrison, even though Harrison spent "hours tutoring her in both classes."

Based on these facts, a reasonable reader would not conclude that Harrison was expressing anything other than an opinion. Achieving strong grades in college coursework, and a high standardized test score, does not means that a persons is a "good" student or has the ability to "effectively serve" in an elected capacity. Likewise, receiving a "C" in Latin and organic chemistry does not mean that Appellant was a substandard student or incapable of succeeding at a senator. And Harrison never claimed — to readers or at trial — that he had an objectively verifiable answer. As he stated at trial, "I don't *think* she's *very* smart." That is exactly what a reasonable reader is likely to infer from Harrison's statements on www.justtellthetruth.com: that Harrison is expressing his thoughts sand beliefs, not presenting as fact something that will almost certainly be the subject of reasonable disagreement.

Finally, and perhaps most tellingly, Appellant did not offer sufficient evidence to refute that claim that she benefitted from favoritism and money when gaining admission to Berkeley. Instead, she offered nothing more than her transcripts and LSAT score, which were slightly above the mean for admitted students. Surely, though, applicants to highly competitive schools like Berkeley are routinely denied admission, even with scores that may be significantly above the median. The admission process extends far beyond numbers, and it is not inconceivable that Appellant could have benefitted, even slightly, from her father's status as a large donor. Appellant did little to dispel this claim, failing to offer even a single official from the admissions department at Berkeley to testify that Appellant's admission was merit-based. Without more, the trial court correctly held that the evidence was "insufficient to conclude, by a preponderance of the evidence, that Harrison's statements were false." The court's decision should be affirmed.

POINT II

APPELLANT CANNOT SHOW THAT HARRISON MADE THE STATEMENTS CONCERNING APPELLANT'S ALLEGED INFIDELITY WITH ACTUAL MALICE

The lower court correctly concluded that Appellant could not demonstrate that the statements — even if provable false — were made with actual malice.

A. Appellant is a Public Figure

Individuals are classified as public figures, limited purpose public figures, or private figures. Based on the relevant facts, Appellant is a public or, at the very least, limited purpose public figure. *McGarry*, 64 Cal.Rptr.3d at 479–480. Importantly, however, this is a distinction without a difference, because either designation requires Appellant to demonstrate actual malice.

An "all purpose" public figure, in contrast to a limited purpose public figure, is an individual "who has 'achiev[ed] such pervasive fame or notoriety that he becomes a public figure for all purposes and in all contexts.' " *Id.* at 479 (*quoting Gertz v. Robert Welch, Inc.*, 418 U.S. 323, 351 (1974)) (brackets in original).

On the other hand, to be classified as a limited purpose public figure, an individual "must have undertaken some voluntary act through which he or she sought to influence resolution of the public issue." *Gilbert v. Sykes*, 53 Cal.Rptr.3d 752, 762 (Cal. Ct. App. 2007). Professional and collegiate athletes, for example, are limited-public figures. *See McGarry*, 64 Cal.Rptr.3d at 481. In the limited-purpose public figure context, the alleged defamation "must be germane to the plaintiff's participation in the controversy." *Gilbert*, 53 Cal.Rptr.3d at 762 (*quoting Ampex Corp. v. Cargle*, 27 Cal.Rptr.3d 863, 871 (Cal. Ct. App. 2005)).

Here, Appellant should be classified as a public figure. Appellant was a senatorial candidate, and involved in a campaign that attracted attention from voters nationwide.

The final debate occurred before a sold-out crowd at the Shrine Auditorium in Los Angeles, and a nationally televised audience. Furthermore, Appellant defeated Larson by only 314 votes, one of the closest margins in California history. Based on these facts, Appellant should be classified as a public or, at the very least, a limited purpose public figure. In either case, however, Appellant will be required to show that Harrison's statements were made with actual malice, because the statements relate to the public controversy within which Appellant was directly and voluntarily involved.

B. Harrison Did Not Make the Statements with Actual Malice

As the lower court held Harrison had at least a colorable basis for believing that Appellant has engaged in infidelity while an undergraduate at Stanford.

To show actual malice, Appellant must demonstrate by clear and convincing evidence that "the defendant published the report with knowledge of its falsity or in reckless disregard of the truth." *Flowers v. Carville*, 310 F.3d 1118, 1129 (9th Cir. 2002); *U.S. v. Alvarez* 617 F.3d 1198, 1224 (9th Cir. 2010) (*quoting Time, Inc. v. Hill*, 385 U.S. 374, 388 (1967)). More specifically, appellant must show that "the defendant knew his statements were probably false, or that he disregarded obvious warning signs of falsity." *Flowers*, 310 F.3d at 1129. Thus, "failure to investigate before publishing, even when a reasonably prudent person would have done so, is not sufficient." *McGarry*, 64 Cal.Rptr.3d at 480. Ultimately, Appellant must demonstrate that Harrison entertained "serious doubts regarding the truth of his publication," and "high degree of awareness of . . . probable falsity." *McGarry*, 64 Cal.Rptr.3d at 480 (*quoting Harte-Hanks Communications v. Connaughton*, 491 U.S. 657, 688 (1989)). evidence must "be of such a character 'as to command the unhesitating assent of every reasonable mind.'" *McGarry*, 64 Cal.Rptr.3d at 480 (*quoting Rosenaur v. Scherer*, 105 Cal.Rptr.2d 674, 684 (Cal Ct. App. 2001)). Without such a high standard, "sanctions against either innocent or negligent misstatement would present a grave hazard of discouraging the press from exercising constitutional guarantees." *Id.*

Appellant cannot make the requisite showing here. On cross-examination, Harrison testified at Appellant's then-fiancée, Phillip Berman, approached him to express concerns that Appellant was having an affair. Berman was a mutual friend, and Harrison had no reason to suspect that Berman was lying or otherwise exaggerating his concerns. Harrison also testified he received a letter from Appellant admitting that "she had cheated on Phil" prior to the termination of their relationship. Thus, Harrison's knowledge was based on information received directly from Appellant and Berman, with both sources indicating that Appellant had, in fact, cheated on Mr. Berman. Harrison did not receive this information from third parties or unreliable sources, nor was it the product of speculation.

And Appellant introduced no evidence at trial, circumstantial or otherwise, to show that Harrison had 'serious doubts" about the truthfulness of this claim, or a "high degree of awareness" that the information from Berman and Appellant was false. Indeed, it would not be logical for Harrison to have such doubts, considering that his knowledge came from the two individuals who were in the best position to state the truth accurately. Nor should Harrison be faulted for failing to investigate, because there was no reason to doubt that the information Harrison received twenty years ago was false. His belief regarding the infidelity — and decision to post this information on justtellthetruth.com — does not even remotely approach the type of calculated misconduct that is required to show actual malice. Instead, as the trial court held, Harrison had a "colorable basis" upon which to believe that the Appellant engaged in infidelity.

CONCLUSION

Based on the foregoing, the trial court's decision should be affirmed.

*   *   *   *   *

What made Waters' appellate brief, and Harrison's response, persuasive?

What would you change, and why?

INDEX

[References are to sections.]

A

AFFIRMATIVE DEFENSES
Generally . . . 8[I][C]

ALLEGATIONS IN COMPLAINT
Generally . . . 8[I][D]

ANSWER
Affirmative defenses . . . 8[I][C]
Allegations in complaint, responding to . . . 8[I][D]
Causes of action, responding to . . . 8[I][E]
Complaint, responding to allegations in . . . 8[I][D]
Counterclaims . . . 8[I][H]
Crossclaims . . . 8[I][H]
Denials, general . . . 8[I][F]
Filing special appearance answer . . . 8[I][G]
General denials . . . 8[I][F]
Introductory sentence . . . 8[I][B]
Legal memorandum . . . 4[III][B]
Local rules
    Generally . . . 8[I]
    Affirmative defenses . . . 8[I][C]
    Allegations in complaint, responding to . . . 8[I][D]
    Causes of action, responding to . . . 8[I][E]
    Complaint, responding to allegations in . . . 8[I][D]
    Counterclaims . . . 8[I][H]
    Crossclaims . . . 8[I][H]
    Denials, general . . . 8[I][F]
    Filing special appearance answer . . . 8[I][G]
    General denials . . . 8[I][F]
    Introductory sentence . . . 8[I][B]
    Plead affirmative defenses . . . 8[I][C]
    Research before filing answer . . . 8[I][A]
    Special appearance answer, filing . . . 8[I][G]
    Third-party claims . . . 8[I][H]
Plead affirmative defenses . . . 8[I][C]
Research before filing answer . . . 8[I][A]
Special appearance answer, filing . . . 8[I][G]
Third-party claims . . . 8[I][H]

APPELLATE BRIEF
Generally . . . Ch.13

C

CLIENT LETTERS
Generally . . . Ch.5

COMPLAINT
Causes of action for punitive damages . . . 6[III]
Local rules . . . 6[I][A]
Punitive damages, causes of action for . . . 6[III]
Relief, request for . . . 6[IV]
Research before drafting complaint . . . 6[I][B]

COMPLAINT—Cont.
Writing of complaint
    Affidavits and support, expert . . . 6[II][J]
    Allegations
        Defendant, factual allegations about . . . 6[II][B]
        Factual allegations . . . 6[II][D]
        Jurisdiction and venue . . . 6[II][C]
        Venue, jurisdiction and . . . 6[II][C]
    Causes of action
        Assertion . . . 6[II][G]
        Drafting separate count for . . . 6[II][H]
    Defendant, factual allegations about . . . 6[II][B]
    Documents attachment and incorporation . . . 6[II][F]
    Expert affidavits and support . . . 6[II][J]
    Factual allegations
        Generally . . . 6[II][D]
        Defendant, about . . . 6[II][B]
    Pleading standards, heightened . . . 6[II][I]
    Statements, short and plain . . . 6[II][A]
    Subheadings for lengthy, complicated facts . . . 6[II][E]

COUNTERCLAIMS
Generally . . . 8[I][H]

COURT'S DECISION
Harrison's testimony . . . 12[III]
Phillip Berman's testimony . . . 12[II]
Stephanie Morris' testimony . . . 12[IV]
Waters' testimony . . . 12[I]

CROSSCLAIMS
Generally . . . 8[I][H]

CROSS-MOTIONS FOR SUMMARY JUDG-MENT
Generally . . . 10[X]

D

DAMAGES
Punitive damages, causes of action for . . . 6[III]

DISCOVERY
Disputes, avoid . . . 9[II][F]
Interrogatories, responding to . . . 9[II][D]
Non-responses, avoid . . . 9[II][A]
Objections, avoid . . . 9[II][A]
Questions to be avoided
    Broad questions . . . 9[II][B]
    Narrow questions . . . 9[II][C]
Requests for production of documents (RPDs), responding to . . . 9[II][E]
Responding to interrogatories . . . 9[II][D]
Rules
    Definitions . . . 9[I][B]
    Instructions and definitions . . . 9[I][B]

I-1

[References are to sections.]

[References are to sections.]